At

THE ADVENTURE
OF
PAUL OF TARSUS

THE ADVENTURE OF
PAUL OF TARSUS

BY THE REV.

H. F. B. MACKAY

Second Impression

PHILIP ALLAN

MDCCCCXXXI

First Impression, October 1930
Second Impression January 1931

PRINTED IN GREAT BRITAIN BY THE CAMELOT PRESS, LIMITED,
LONDON AND SOUTHAMPTON, AND PUBLISHED BY
PHILIP ALLAN AND CO., LTD., OF
QUALITY HOUSE, GREAT
RUSSELL STREET
LONDON

Without leave, I venture to place upon
the first page of this book the names of
three of my friends who have embarked
upon the adventure of Paul of Tarsus ;
Roscow, Bishop of Nassau, Mark, Bishop
of Colombo, and Basil, Bishop in Kobe.

H. F. B. M.

CHAPTER I

I TRANSPORT you to Tarsus in Cilicia in the spring
of a year early in the First Century. North of
Palestine the coast makes a great curve westward. Cilicia consists of the long strip of plain which
runs along the coast of this curve, at right-angles to
Palestine. At the back of the narrow plain stand
the Taurus Mountains.

We will take our stand on the flat roof of a spacious
house in the well-to-do quarter and look round us.
The house is part of a really beautiful residential suburb
built on the edge of low rolling hills – a suburb of
villas and gardens. Looking north, we are almost at
once in open country, a country of hills gradually
growing more rugged and broken, until twenty-five
miles away they roll up against the mighty flanks of the
Taurus range, a great semi-circular sweep of snow-
covered mountains filling the whole horizon on that
side. A gash in the mountain range at the point
nearest us is the famous pass of the Cilician Gates,
through which the heroic ancestors of the Tarsians had
cut and built a carriage road. Looking south, there
lies below us an illimitable plain fading away on the
horizon to the sea. A great city, through which a
dark green river runs, covers the plain two miles
away ; it is joined to our hill city by straggling suburbs.
This is Tarsus proper – too hot and enervating to be a
pleasant residence, and so the well-to-do people are all

here in the city on the hills, and go down to their business as the citizens of Bristol go down from Clifton.

The plain around the city is one vast cornfield, and the pride which the Tarsians took in their city and its surroundings is justified by the fact that their ancestors had conquered nature and created the whole scene. Once it had been as unattractive, unproductive and unhealthy as it is again to-day. Then a colony of Ionian Greeks had come, the emigrants had been guided to the spot by the Oracle of the Clarian Apollo, and so to Apollo the foundation of the city was assigned. From an Ionian colony it grew into a great Oriental city. Its earlier inhabitants drained the marshes, irrigated the plain, cut the road through the Cilician Gates, made their river navigable, gave it a new course through the heart of the city and built a harbour.

The white city is studded with temples, for Tarsus is very religious. Its life centres in the markets and on the wharves, the great marble wharves, past which the clear green river runs a rapid, glassy stream, soon to become muddy like the Tiber from its assimilation of the light soil of the plain, but here still beautiful. A great crowd of every nationality winds its way in and out among the bales of merchandise, stamped with their owners' names, which fringe the River Cydnus. The wharves are the Exchange, the Wall Street, the Rialto of Tarsus. We can easily recall the babel which is heard in such places, and here the babel is mingled with the sharp cry of the river-men as they steer the great rafts of hewn logs through the shipping with their long poles and glide onward down the swell of the stream towards the sea, bending half-naked to their work like animated bronze antiques.

Let us return to the house-top. A little boy and an older girl, his sister (there is no doubt, I suppose, that the mother of the nephew who intervened at Jerusalem, when St. Paul's life was in danger there, was older than St. Paul), have come out on to the roof and are sitting on the parapet looking at the marvellous stretch of city and plain below them. They are Jews, that we can see at a glance, and the boy, although small and slight of stature, seems, from his manner, to be about ten years of age. He is a proud boy to-day, for, being now ten years of age, he has made a fresh step in his education. And this is the reason I have selected this particular day for our first look at him. He has had his first lesson in the oral law at the school of the synagogue, and his father has told him of his prospects. If he makes good progress at the school of the synagogue and also works hard at the rhetoric classes in the State schools which he is soon to join, after some further training at Tarsus University, he is to go to the University at Jerusalem, and be numbered among the pupils of the great Gamaliel.

There is so clear and consistent a tradition about his appearance, that we seem able to picture the little Saul, his pale face framed by dark hair, his thin, aquiline features, his piercing black eyes, his bent, shrunken, delicate figure. Let us keep this childish figure before us while we gather what we may of his history and parentage. St. Jerome says that the family of Saul had migrated not very long before this to Tarsus from Gischala in Galilee. It is very difficult to recon‑ cile that tradition with the position its members occupied when Saul was born. They were both burgesses of Tarsus and Roman citizens. This means that they were members of the innermost circle there, Tarsian aristocrats. And the inner circle of an Oriental Greek city was so jealously exclusive that it is very difficult to believe that newcomers, especially Jewish newcomers, could have gained entry to it. If it really was so, then they must have performed some extraordinary services to the Tarsian State of which we know nothing, and services so great as to merit the gratitude not only of Tarsus but of the Imperial power. It is useless to speculate as to what such a service can have been; we had better try to understand what it meant to be a Tarsian burgess and a Roman citizen in the usual way. Tarsus, as I have said, was originally a Greek colony which grew into a great Oriental city and continued to receive reinforcements all through its history from East and West. It is said to have kept a harmonious balance between Europeans and Asiatics better than any other city, and so, you see, it was providentially designed to be the training-ground of the man whose mission required him to be a citizen of the world.

You must understand that to the ancient Greek citizen his city absorbed all his patriotism. Its past history was a great part of his religion, its present welfare was the first and chief interest of his life.

It is extremely difficult for us to understand how largely Greek religion was co-extensive with patriotism; what a great power the legendary history of the city had over the religious mind. Shinto – politico-religious legend – was a vital force in the ancient world. This formed the supreme difficulty of Jews and Christians; they both refused to take part in the religious ceremonies of Gentile citizenship. And, as it was impossible to perform civic duties without taking part in civic religious ceremonies, this withdrew them from any active part in what was considered the most sacred responsibility of a man's life, so they fell into disrepute, and really did appear to be bad citizens.

Now Tarsus was apparently one of the few cities where this difficulty did not exist for the Jews. It is evident that the Jews of Tarsus were not resident strangers, as they would have continued generation after generation to be, if they could not participate in civic duties; they were citizens with full burgess rights. There appears to have been a money qualification for citizenship, and the general desire was not to enlarge the burgess roll but to keep it small and select. For the Jews to have become burgesses of Tarsus they must have been really very important people. The citizens were divided into tribes like larger editions of our London city companies, and these tribes had their religious ceremonies just as in good old days the city companies had their chapels and their services. The Jews could only be burgesses and at the same time adhere to their religion by having a tribe of their own, and this, no doubt, was the case at Tarsus, as it was at Alexandria. This would not mean that all Jews in Tarsus were Tarsian citizens, it would mean that the most important were. There was a company or tribe of Jewish burgesses who performed the religious ceremonies of burgesses according to the religion of the Jews.

So the Jews of Tarsus did not think of their religion as of something which had nothing to do with Tarsus, they practised it not only as Jews but as citizens of

Tarsus, praying God for the welfare of their city and its people. Judaism, as a religion, had civic relations with Tarsus. That fact, again, peculiarly fitted St. Paul to have religious dealings with Gentiles and to look on them with sympathy. There was not, you see, the complete severance between Jew and Gentile in Tarsus that there was in most places; they were united in the bond of common prayer, each under his own religious forms, for their common citizenship.

Sir William Ramsay thinks that the Jews got this strong position in Tarsus under the Syrian King, whom the Jews of Palestine hated above every other character in history, Antiochus Epiphanes. Antiochus Epiphanes, who reigned about 170 years before our Lord, wished to Grecise the Jews, and his policy took several forms. He planted strong Jewish colonies in Syrian cities, giving them great privileges, thereby hoping to break down their exclusiveness, and he tried to Grecise Jerusalem. He built great gymnasia and tried to train the Jewish youths like Greeks. This last was considered an inconceivable outrage, and it would, no doubt, had it continued, been the Devil's and not God's way of breaking down the middle wall of partition. St. Paul, it has been remarked, had learnt to look much more leniently than any Palestinian Jew on the Greek games or he would never have used metaphors taken from them.

On the other hand, St. Paul's family were strict Pharisaic Jews, and there is no doubt that, in a Jewish outpost with which communication from Jerusalem was so direct, the restoration of nationalism under the Maccabees must have had a great effect.

So the strict Jews of Tarsus apparently gained their

privileges under Antiochus Epiphanes, and their spirit from the splendid heroes who opposed him, the Maccabees.

So much for the Tarsian citizenship of St. Paul. Now for his Roman citizenship. Tarsus, originally an Ionian Greek colony, had been successively in the domain of the Assyrians, the Medes, the Persians and the Greek Syrian Kings. Then, a hundred years before our Lord, when the Roman influence was everywhere spreading, there arose a contest between Roman and Oriental forces over Cilicia and Tarsus. The upshot of it all was that Cilicia became a province of the Empire, with Tarsus as its capital, through Pompey's successes about sixty years before our Lord. Pompey, Julius Cæsar, Mark Antony and Augustus all developed Tarsus, and all, probably, conferred the Roman citizenship on distinguished Tarsians. The Roman citizen was the aristocrat of the Roman Empire, and he always assumed the prænomen and the nomen of the official to whom he owed his citizenship, so that any Roman Tarsian, like St. Paul, born about the time of our Lord, would be either Gnæus Pompeius or Caius Julius or Marcus Antonius.

It is interesting to reflect that St. Paul must have had one of these pairs of names, or such a pair of names before the name we know so well. It suggests the first-hand character of the New Testament narrative that neither of these names is ever mentioned. In the Greek cities, townsmen who had become Roman citizens were never called by their Roman names, but were always spoken of as if they were men of one name. Paul was always Paul to his fellow townsmen, and Saul at home. The Jews in the Greek cities had each a Hebrew name which was always used in the home circle.

As a Roman citizen, St. Paul was enrolled in a Roman tribe in addition to his Tarsian tribe, but this enrolment was a matter of mere name and law and involved no religious duties. He was able, therefore, to be united with Gentiles in this tribe, though his citizen tribe at Tarsus was exclusively Jewish.

It is plain, you see, that we are standing on the roof of a well-to-do and dignified house. Saul's father was evidently a prosperous man of business. If we ask Saul what that business is, he will tell us with a comical twist of disgust about the corners of his sensitive little mouth. His father was evidently a cloth merchant. During the last year or two, poor Saul had been obeying the Rabbinic injunction that every boy should learn a trade. If the injunction stopped there, Saul could have chosen any trade to which his boyish fancy turned; he was a well-to-do boy, he would never need his trade, was he not to be a Rabbi some day himself? But the venerable Rabbis further said that a man must have the trade of his father. And already Saul had spent hours in the workshops learning to prepare and weave into tent-cloth the goats' hair of the Taurus.

Pah ! that horrible goats' hair ! All the waters of the Cydnus were not enough to wash his hands when the lesson was over. The rich little Saul could not foresee the day when he was to depend on this poor, unskilled labour for daily bread, he could not foresee those wonderful nights when his hands would move mechanically at his trade while he held high converse with Apollos, or helped Luke to marshal the facts of his notebooks into the order of his Gospel. How shocked little Saul's father would have been if he could have foreseen that his boy would one day work like one of his many factory hands.

Up to the age of ten, Saul had led a quiet, guarded, probably very happy, child life. The Jews had a wonderful system of home education in which religious influences were impressed on their children. Saul began his lessons when he was five. They taught him the summary of the law in the sixth chapter of Deuteronomy and Psalm cxiii. to Psalm cxviii., the Psalms sung at the great Festivals which are called the great Hallel or ' Song of Praise,' while they gradually gave him a childish version of what was meant by the principal commemorations of the Jewish year. When he was six, Saul was no doubt sent to the vineyard, as it was called, the school for Jewish boys attached to the synagogue, and forming part of the building. Hither in the morning a trusty slave would pilot the little boy through the dangerous streets, and here, sitting on the floor with his little writing-desk on his knees, Saul, among other noisy and restless hopes of Israel, was taught the history of the nation. The earlier years of a Jewish boy's education were entirely devoted to history. He was taught the glory of his position among the nations of the world. His imagination was fired by a recital of the nation's triumphs and touched by the story of her woes. Every day Saul had some new, beautiful or stirring story of the past to think of. And the singing of Zion and the wailing of Babylon rang their antiphons in his childish ears. His teachers taught him about the past, and they also taught him about the future. One
Bт

day, so he learnt, King Messias would come, he would
pass through the world whirling aloft his sword,
a brighter and a stronger sword than that lance of
Apollo, which was the greatest treasure, the most
deeply venerated relic, of the city of Tarsus, and then
all the world would worship towards Jerusalem, and
King Messias would sit on his throne in Jerusalem;
and the Emperor himself would go from Rome to pay
him homage, and the Jews would be the greatest
people in the world, and perhaps Saul himself one of
the greatest men among the Jews.   Jerusalem ! ah,
how he longed to see Jerusalem, where the great God
lived in the Most Holy Place.   When the Jewish
caravans, returning from the great Feasts to the interior of Asia, passed through Tarsus, Saul heard
descriptions of its glories; its great doctors, its great
colleges, its countless priests and ministrants – above
all, that great house of God which crowned it, so
splendid with its gleaming marble walls and cloisters
and its golden roofs, that when little Saul heard the
description his eyes must have turned to the snowfields
of Taurus, and he must have whispered to himself,
"God's House must be something like the mountain-
tops when the sunrise has turned them into gold."

And now the sun is setting, and the boy and the girl
who have been talking gravely and eagerly, perched on
the parapet, descend into the house; but as the little
boy scampers down the staircase do not let us forget
that at this same moment another and somewhat older
boy, far away in a little village to the south, is putting
away His carpenter's tools and coming to His Mother
for His good-night kiss.   The boy of Tarsus knows
nothing of the Boy of Nazareth.   And yet, perhaps, as

the strange Boy of Nazareth stretches Himself on His hard bed that night He may have said a prayer for little Saul of Tarsus.

It cannot be said that the second chapter of Saul's religious studies, which opened that day, was as helpful as the first. After he had been trained in the oral law for some years, the time came when he was sufficiently far advanced to become what was called a son of the Commandment, and a ceremony took place in the synagogue like the first part of our Anglican Con- firmation service. Saul and some of his fellows had stood forward in the congregation, and their respective fathers had declared that their sons knew the elements of the law and were responsible for their own sins. It is probable that sensitive Saul felt the ceremony to be superfluous; he had always thought himself responsible for his sins. Meanwhile, under the tutelage of the Rabbis, he was discovering bushels of new sins every day. The Rabbis had collected round and built upon the Old Testament an extraordinary collection of oral com- ments and fine-spun distinctions, the whole of which they declared to be morally binding on the Jewish conscience. The oral law was a vast system of prece- dents, and its study was exceedingly attractive to a certain kind of mind. Clever men flung themselves upon it with the enthusiasm with which the lawyers in *Bleak House* engaged on that monument of Chancery practice, Jarndyce and Jarndyce. That Saul worked hard at the oral law we have every reason to believe. We shall examine his attitude towards it more closely when we reach his life at the school of Gamaliel. Meanwhile, as the years went on, during which he was alternately working at the oral law, and among his

Gentile fellow townsmen at the University of Tarsus, the oral law must have raised difficulties as to the solution of the Problem of Life. The Messianic dream of the childish days must have grown very faint and thin. As Saul reflected on the nobility of the teaching of the great Tarsian philosophers, Athenodorus and Nestor, as he reflected on the passion for culture which distinguished his city, on its religiousness, and on the extraordinary depravity which coexisted in its religion with much that was excellent – for the Tarsian religion in this respect was, I suppose, much like the Hinduism of to-day—and then as he reverted in thought to the working system of his own religion as expounded by the Rabbis, it must have seemed as if no Messiah could ever bring the one to bear upon the other.

When the boy tried to picture Tarsus accepting this narrow, rigid faith and extraordinary code of rules, his thin shoulders must have involuntarily gone up and the corners of his sensitive mouth involuntarily gone down. And then his sense of God's power and the memories of His dealings with Israel would sweep back upon him, and with a quick flush of shame the fire of an enthusiastic obedience would glow through his veins.

CHAPTER II

IT is impossible, even approximately, to fix the date at which Saul left Tarsus and went to the University at Jerusalem. He was a lad at the time, but how young a lad we do not know. In his speech to the crowd during the Jerusalem riot and in his subsequent speech before Agrippa, he naturally emphasised the Jerusalem period of his education. To the crowd he said : "I am a Jew, born in Tarsus of Cilicia, but brought up in this city at the feet of Gamaliel, instructed according to the strict manner of the law of our fathers." And to Agrippa and Festus : "My manner of life from my youth up, which was from the beginning among mine own nation and at Jerusalem, know all the Jews; having knowledge of me from the first, if they are willing to testify, how that after the straitest sect of our religion I lived a Pharisee."

Those sentences were formerly taken to mean that practically the whole of St. Paul's education was given to him at Jerusalem. But at the present day, it is generally recognised that Gentile life and ideas had also made a considerable impression on him and that he must have lived as a youth in Tarsus sufficiently long to have made an intelligent study of Gentile thought and ways. St. Paul's words do not necessarily imply a very long course at Jerusalem. In the same way, a man in giving an account of his religious

13

experiences twenty years later might have spoken of his life at Oxford under Newman or Pusey or Green or Jowett as if it had been the beginning of all things with him, although it began when he was nineteen, and lasted only four or five years. We can only roughly say, then, that St. Paul's earlier youth was passed in Tarsus, and that in addition to his Jewish studies he went through a course at the University, and that his later youth was spent under Gamaliel at Jerusalem. This later education made such a mark on him that, for a time, it swallowed up all his earlier impressions. It was after his conversion to Christ, when he was thinking out the application of our Lord's message to the Gentile world, that his earlier experiences again became of use to him.

The Tarsian religion had no influence whatever on St. Paul, but the Tarsian philosophy had. Sir William Ramsay goes so far as to say that in the philosophy of Paul the Eastern mind and the Greek have been intermingled in the closest union, like a chemical mixture, and that he was profoundly influenced by Asiatic Hellenism. A Greek city such as Tarsus differed from a Roman in giving far more scope and play to the development of individuality ; it always emphasised the freedom of the individual ; in fact, it compared with a Roman city in this respect as an English city compares with a German. But it cared much more for the education of its citizens than an English city does, it had an unequalled system of education – national, public, intellectual, physical. In this education St. Paul had a share, and it helped to fit him for his tremendous task. It brought him, first of all, not into direct contact with the religion of Tarsus – that was impossible for a Jew — but into contact and into relations of friendship with people who practised that religion. It is very difficult to get any clear view of the religious ideals of such a city as Tarsus, because the more mixed a city was and the more complicated its history the more complex became its religion. This arose from the fact that the fresh religious ideas brought in by fresh settlers were never allowed to be lost, they were all worked up into the city scheme of religion. The presiding religious idea was the conception of the Divine Power as male, and it was called the Baal-Tarz, the Lord of Tarsus, but a kind of working deputy, a kind of agent of the Lord of Tarsus, was greatly worshipped, the rural god dressed in his pictures like a peasant, the genius of the Tarsian agriculturist, of that heroic ancestry which had made of the wilderness a fruitful field.

This distinction between the supreme Deity and the working god lay deep in the Oriental mind. To the Oriental, inaction and dignity are inseparable, and this fact explains what must have puzzled many readers of the Acts. When the people of Lystra mistook Paul and Barnabas for gods, they thought Barnabas was Jupiter, the greater god, and Paul, Mercurius, the inferior, because Paul was the chief speaker. They associated activity, you see, with inferiority. Then, again, Apollo was venerated as the founder of the city because the first Greek settlers had been directed by his oracle to seek the spot. He was, as it were, the patron saint of Tarsus. Tarsus also had its heroes. I suppose the heroes were a recognition of the divine character of the noblest human efforts godward. Hercules and Perseus were the heroes of Tarsus, and

one of the great festivals of the year took the form of
a solemn procession in which the hero, who was both
Perseus and Hercules, was carried through the streets
in a wonderful pyramidal car (its pattern is preserved
on coins), and afterwards burned to signify his translation to heaven.

You will have noticed that in such conceptions there
are certain elements of truth, and in after-life Paul
came to see that this was the case, as passages in his
letters show.   But as a youth he would be too much
disgusted by the obvious evils which attended worship
in the temples to have patience to discover behind
them fundamentally right ideas.   As in Hinduism
to-day, vast accretions of evil custom had collected
round these ideas, partly due to religious degeneration,
partly to imperfection in the holding of the ideas
themselves.

But the ethical teaching of Tarsus was not in the
hands of the priests, it was in the hands of the University authorities, and there was a real passion among
them for education and high thinking in St. Paul's
early days owing to the influence of two noble men,
Athenodorus and Nestor.   Athenodorus died when
Paul was four years old, and his successor, Nestor,
was the educational genius of Tarsus in Paul's
youth.   But Paul studied in Tarsus just at the time
when there would be a romantic and grateful devotion
to the teaching of Athenodorus, who entirely deserved
the gratitude of the Tarsians.   Athenodorus was
a noble moral philosopher who was commended by
Cicero and studied and quoted by Seneca.   He had
travelled far and read widely.   When, in the autumn
of 45 B.C., Augustus came to finish his education at

Apollonia, Athenodorus was lecturing there, and six months' study under Athenodorus made a lifelong impression on Augustus' mind. He brought him to Rome ultimately, and Athenodorus lived for years at the Court. There is a striking story, a noble story, too painful in detail to quote, of how Athenodorus once saved Augustus from falling into David's great sin.

Athenodorus returned to Tarsus in the year 15 B.C., with a commission from the Emperor to perform an extraordinary task. Tarsus had fallen into the hands of a gang like Tammany Hall in New York. The leader of Tammany at Tarsus was a man named Boethus. Athenodorus from his chair in the University was expected to reform the civic morals of the place. He soon found that the ring was too strong to be dissolved by indirect measures, but he had an order up his sleeve from the Emperor giving him plenary power to do what he thought needed. At the right moment he asserted himself and cleared the gang out, and ultimately succeeded in reforming the constitution and putting the citizenship on a sound basis again. At the same time he created an ardent passion for education. The young University, for it was not of old standing, got a very honourable name for zeal under this great teacher and his successor, Nestor. And St. Paul was studying in Tarsus as a young lad just in this golden time.

It is probable that the impression which the sayings of Athenodorus made on Paul partly accounts for the resemblance between some of St. Paul's thoughts and the thoughts of Seneca, the great philosopher at Rome, who was strictly St. Paul's contemporary. Bishop

Lightfoot's essay on St. Paul and Seneca, in his commentary on the Epistle to the Philippians, deals exhaustively with this interesting subject, but knowledge of life in Tarsus was not sufficiently recovered in Bishop Lightfoot's day to enable him to give this suggestion much consideration. It is known that Seneca greatly admired Athenodorus, and the probability is that the unquestionable resemblances between sentences of St. Paul and sentences of Seneca arose out of their having both absorbed the teaching of the Tarsian philosopher.

Here are two striking sayings of his quoted by Seneca, the second being rather Seneca's own summary of Athenodorus :

' Know that you are free from all passions only when you have reached the point that you ask God for nothing except what you can ask openly.'

' So live with men as if God saw you ; so speak with God as if men were listening ! '

It was, you observe, a youth already extraordinarily well prepared to break down the middle wall of partition between Jew and Gentile who stood on the house-top at Tarsus on his last evening at home and said farewell to the wonderful view of the city, the river, the sea, and the snows of Taurus flushed in sunset. It was a Saul already grave and meditative who went down to his ship next day, the lumbering Phœnician trading vessel with her little propitiatory shrine in the bows to the gods of the sea and of commerce, and set sail for Cæsarea.

We do not know, of course, whether Saul's journey to Jerusalem to complete his education was the occasion of his first visit there ; that depends upon the age at which he went. But I like to dwell on the experiences of that first visit whenever it took place. There was the evening when the well-known mountains of the Taurus sank into the sea, the morning when the range of the Lebanon rose into sight. Then began the enchanting voyage down the coast. Between Berytus and Ptolemais, Saul would gaze and gaze at the great blue-green, precipitous, rounded hills, rising apparently straight out of the sea, with Tyre and Sidon sitting on the edge of the water at their feet, like huge, white-plumaged water-birds, the general effect like the North Welsh coast between Conway and Bangor, but backed by the noble, snowy summits of Lebanon and Hermon. Then, between Ptolemais and Carmel, the beginning of the great memories. The narrow entrance to the plain of Esdraelon. Saul would picture Sisera's army marching inwards from the coast to its destruction. And Carmel itself, thrusting what Father Hugh Benson so well called its long bull head out into the sea — as the ship ran out to round the point where the heavy surf of lapis lazuli and snow rolls and roars below the cave where, tradition says, Obadiah hid the prophets — his friends would show the lad the bare knoll on the loftier landward peak as the scene of the sacrifice of Elijah. South of Carmel the big rolling hills grow lower and draw back from the flat sea strip until the strip widens into the plain of Sharon. Nowadays, the plain of Sharon keeps up the general resemblance of Palestine to Wales, and the rough pastures might be rough pastures of Pembrokeshire, the low hills with the great patches of broom, the gorse-covered hills of Radnorshire. But when St. Paul saw it, it was, I suppose,

splendidly cultivated and covered with cornlands and
groves of palm. Soon Cæsarea would gleam on the
horizon, and Saul would land in a magnificent city,
which, plainly enough, displayed the security and extent of the Roman occupation. Cæsarea, as Saul saw
it, was magnificent in the rather coarse Oriental
classical fashion. You can see the style of architecture
to-day in the façades of some of the tombs at Jerusalem. It is a coarse, debased style, but it was all big
and sumptuous. There was a great temple on an
immense artificial mound, a theatre, an amphitheatre,
with a lovely view of the sea, great palaces, and a really
magnificent artificial harbour, with an enormous breakwater broad enough to carry houses and towers, with
a great curved quay in front of them, running right
round the whole haven, and forming, as Josephus
says, ' a most pleasant walk for such as had a mind for
that exercise.' High above the temple, two shining
statues dominated the scene, the statue of Augustus
and the statue of Rome. It was a heart-breaking sight
to young Saul, and the Jews called the place the
Daughter of Edom. It was, says Professor Sir George
Adam Smith, heathendom in all its glory at the very
door of the true religion. Yes, but the contrast might
be reversed. It was justice and freedom in the most
fanatical and turbulent province in the world.

Saul little dreamed when he groaned over the
heathenesse of Cæsarea, that the day would come when
they would give him no fair hearing in the Holy City,
when to escape the assassin's knife he must be
smuggled privately to this place where his all-powerful
Roman citizenship would protect him. Cæsarea was
virtually Rome. We follow him in thought as he

crosses the richly cultivated green and smiling plain ;
at length the cornland and the blue-green orchards
run up into the bays at the foot of the hills, and the
traveller enters one of the curiously narrow winding
gorges of the central range, with sides sharply inter-
laced at the bottom.   The hills are nowadays desolate,
stony, sparsely sprinkled with stunted olive and larch ;
then they were terraced into vineyards watered by
artificial irrigation, as the Lebanon is to-day.   As Saul
climbed and climbed, the air blew fresh and cold, and
the mountain forms grew finer ;   at last he came out
upon the high plateau of Judæa, desolate, barren, stone-
strewn.   At no time can it have been fertile ; to-day it is
like a stonier edition of the Peak country in Derbyshire.
It is very beautiful and pathetic that the Jews love this
high, bleak plateau so passionately : to young Saul it
was the holiest of holy ground, for he entered it by the
great road of those days, near Bethel, in the portion of
Benjamin, his own tribe.   Then he turned south and
soon Jerusalem lay before him.   I can easily imagine
how it must have looked in those days as one approached it from the north.   There would be a great,
straggling, unimpressive suburb to the right, as there
is to-day ; on the left would rise the high ridge of the
Mount of Olives seen in profile, and between the suburb and the Mount, the oval, compact space of the city
proper and the Temple of Herod, rising out of the
deep ravine of the Kedron, between the city and the
Mount, a gleaming expanse of marble cloister, surrounding the golden splendours of the Holy House.
Behind, on what is now called Mount Zion, a hill of
palaces crowned by the new palace of Herod, for what
is now a desolate waste to the south of the present

city was then a pyramid of palaces, with densely populated quarters lying below them in the now obliterated Tyropean valley.

Soon the parent or guardian who had brought the lad up to Jerusalem, having made the necessary arrangements, would return, and Saul would begin to face life as a student of the University enrolled among the pupils of the great Gamaliel. These great Rabbinical schools were a feature of the age. Jerusalem was full of students, and bore a strong resemblance to a mediæval Christian University at the zenith of the power of the Schoolmen. You remember how in the centuries before the Reformation, the theologians were hard at work systematising theology. These Schoolmen, as you further remember, fell ultimately into two groups, which, although agreeing in fundamentals, differed on many important points. The one group followed the teaching of that profound Dominican, the greatest of the Schoolmen, and one of the greatest glories of the Church, St. Thomas Aquinas, and the other group followed the brilliant and subtle Franciscan, Duns Scotus. The first were called the Thomists, and the second the Scotists. The students of Jerusalem were divided in similar fashion in Saul's day, between the school of Hillel and the school of Shammai. These great doctors had flourished about fifty years before this time, and it was Hillel's grandson, Gamaliel, who now taught his disciples. Hillel had been a man of extraordinary power and nobility of character ; he was descended from Babylonian Jews, and had come as a poor youth to Jerusalem, attracted by his passion for learning. He earned half a denarius a day, and this he divided between his boarding house and the porter of the school where Shemaiah and Abtalion taught (they were the great doctors of the time), and the porter gave him entrance and permitted him to hear the lecturer. One Sabbath eve, when it was bitterly cold, young Hillel came to the school with no money — he had failed to earn any that day — and the brutal door-keeper refused him entrance. It was dark and there were no lights outside the college buildings, so Hillel climbed up on a window sill and listened to the learned talk within. Far on into the night Shemaiah and Abtalion held high converse. Meanwhile, the snow fell, and gradually the listening Hillel was buried under a coverlid of snow. As the day dawned, Shemaiah said to Abtalion : " Dear brother, why is our school so dark this morning ? " They went to the window, and against it lay the figure of a young man, benumbed and buried in the snow. They bore him in, chafed his limbs, and rubbed them with oil, and gradually restored him to life, saying as they did so : " We break the Sabbath, but for his sake it is worth while." The differences between Hillel and Shammai would seem to us minute, but there was a great difference between them in spirit. Shammai was the hard literalist, Hillel was the man of tender, reasonable spirit, and this difference continued to distinguish the one school from the other. ' Be gentle as Hillel, not as harsh as Shammai,' became a proverb which enshrined the judgment of posterity on the two men.

Gamaliel, Hillel's grandson, was worthy of his ancestry, a noble-hearted, liberal Pharisee of the best type, and Saul would soon learn to love him. ' He is one of the Seven Doctors in Jewish history to whom

the title ' Rabban,' ' My Master,' was given. It was
said that the glory of the law perished when Gamaliel
died.

Let us close this chapter by looking at the Jerusalem
into which the young Saul entered. Judæa had become
a Roman province some years before, and was no
longer under the titular rule of the Herods. The
Roman supremacy under the Procurators was now
thoroughly established. The Procurator lived at
Cæsarea, and Jerusalem was heavily garrisoned with
Roman soldiers. The Procurator of the moment was
one of the four predecessors of Pontius Pilatus, either
Coponius or Marcus Ambivius or Annius Rufus or
Valerius Gratus. Jerusalem society was divided into
two camps, the Foreign party and the National party.
The two parties were completely severed from one
another ; it was like the state of things in Venice under
the Austrian occupation, when the two parties prom-
enaded on opposite sides of the Piazza, and had their
separate cafés. Saul belonged, of course, to the
Temple party, and found himself obliged to talk only
Aramaic, Greek being forbidden by party feeling. The
old noblesse of Jerusalem is said to have been very
charming, like the people in France in the reign of
Louis XV and XVI. They were a curious mixture of
piety and frivolity. They talked a light and graceful
Aramaic, superior in accent and turn of expression to
other Aramaic, just as the language of Boston and of
Vienna is superior to other American and German. Jeru-
salemites were witty and polished and enthusiastically
hospitable. The ladies of Jerusalem had naturally got
into the way of exhibiting the latest fashions in dress
and jewellery to the country cousins who came up for

the great Feasts. They had beautiful houses, and
what amazed the country people most of all — mirrors.
Mirrors ! their use had been discussed in the Rabbinical schools. Was it lawful to look at oneself in
a mirror on the Sabbath ? The decision was Yes, provided the mirror was nailed to the wall, but it was not
lawful to carry on the Sabbath one of the ingenious
little hand mirrors which were so popular, the hand
mirrors with tweezers attached for pulling out grey
hairs. It was a civilised, luxurious world into which
young Saul had come, with a good postal system, and
even a parcels post. A world of newspapers, and even,
in times of excitement, of Sabbath newspapers.

For some years, I suppose, the absorbing interest
of his studies took complete possession of Saul's mind,
and wider interests were laid aside ; here in Jerusalem, where the religious influence was so over-
whelming, they would not seem so pressing. To
a certain extent, no doubt, he pursued his study of
Greek literature — Gamaliel encouraged the study, and,
probably quite early in his time, Saul was marked off
as a remarkable young man, and, perhaps, specially
trained to be what he ultimately became, an agent between the Sanhedrin and the outlying posts of Judaism.
But the great bulk of his studies would be purely
Scriptural. It was all very much like Mohammedan
education to-day — El Azhar at Cairo is a modern
parallel to the schools at Jerusalem, and the influence
of those years during which he studied the Old Testament under the Rabbis is deeply marked on all Paul's
life and writings. The scene and method of instruction
we know. Literally, Saul sat at Gamaliel's feet — the
students were arranged on very low benches in a series

Cт

of semi-circles, and in the midst, on an imposing-looking elevated chair, sat the lecturer. A passage of the Old Testament was taken for discussion. It was first read in Hebrew, then in the vernacular Aramaic, then everything that ever had been or ever could be said about it was said by the lecturer. The students were then invited to interrogate him, a permission of which they took full advantage, so that every lecture ended in a more or less clever contest of wits.

CHAPTER III

SAUL is sitting on one of the low semi-circular benches beneath the throne-like chair of the great Gamaliel. Gamaliel has expounded a passage of Scripture – the students are vying with one another in proposing to him sharply pointed questions. We must think now for a few minutes upon the sort of way in which Saul was taught the Old Testament. It can be summed up in a sentence – the Rabbis treated the legal part of the Old Testament in a strictly legal way, weighing each word as lawyers weigh the words of an Act of Parliament, while the historical part, on the contrary, they handled very freely.

The great mass of legal traditions and legal determinations was called the Halacha ; the teaching, derived from the history of the Old Testament, together with the less authoritative legends which surrounded it, was called the Haggada. The students fell into two groups – those who studied the Halacha, and those who studied the Haggada. The first were canonists – ecclesiastical lawyers, moral theologians. The second were not historians in our modern sense – the modern scientific study of history had no existence then – but religious and practical teachers who drew their material from the history of the nation.

It does not seem to me that we have sufficient evidence from his writings to be able to conjecture to which group Paul belonged. There are examples

27

of Haggada in his letters — but that there would be anyhow, for all Jews read the history of the Old Testament in this way, they all looked at it from a symbolic and didactic point of view. And it is certainly difficult to imagine St. Paul having ever cared passionately for the discussions on the minutiæ of the law ; debating, for example, at great length whether an egg might be eaten which the hen had been so profane as to lay on the Sabbath day. But great and restless minds have sometimes given themselves to strange mental exercises ; we cannot tell. This, however, is clear : while the Halacha has no concern for us — the whole of the Halacha was left behind on the threshold of the Christian Church — the Haggada has great importance, for it largely governed the way in which the early Jewish Christians handled the Old Testament Scriptures.

I suppose it would be true to say that the whole Old Testament narrative was regarded by the Jews rather as the history of man than as the history of men ; it was regarded as a history of the relation of human nature, embodied in certain historical figures and scenes, to God. While taught as actual history it was valued for its symbolic character, and the history was freely handled so as to put the lesson, whatever it happened to be, in the clearest light. Round the text had collected a great mass of historical amplification, some of it no doubt good tradition, but which, from a historical point of view, needed much sifting ; and this was mingled with legends in which, as in the *Fioretti* of St. Francis, spiritual histories had become translated into external incidents of a more or less marvellous kind.

This accounts for the free way in which New Testament writers handle the details of Old Testament narrative.   Anything less like good modern students armed with reference Bibles cannot be imagined.   They will quote it quite loosely from memory.   They will add to it without saying they are adding to it, or probably being conscious that they have run off the text on to the marginal fringe.   For example, the allusion to Moses' culture and his great works as an Egyptian potentate in St. Stephen's speech is not to the Old Testament, but to a vast quantity of Jewish tradition about Moses' life in Egypt.   So again the references to the law having been given through the mediation of Angels – by St. Stephen, St. Paul, and the writer to the Hebrews ; the reference in 2 Timothy to Jannes and Jambres ; and the legend quoted in the Epistle of Jude about St. Michael contending with the Devil for the body of Moses are not drawn from our Old Testament.

They had not our conscience about it exactly.   For example, in Samuel and Kings we have a compilation of historical documents.   In Chronicles we have the same history idealised and amplified with a certain didactic intention – the two versions stand side by side.   We collect in the same way the various versions of the Arthurian legend – realising that each has a valuable spiritual history, and conveys its own aspect of truth.

As the editors of Chronicles treat the narrative of Kings, so Jewish teachers generally handled the whole history of the people – they realised that it is inspired to be a history of human nature, and not an infallibly accurate report of the occurrence of certain external events.

In fact they taught the historical part of the Old Testament as we tell a child a true story with a moral in it, handling the detail as will best help the child to learn the essential lesson.

Further, while the Halacha was binding in every jot and tittle on the conscience, and constituted the burden grievous to be borne which the Rabbis had laid upon the people, the Haggada was not binding, except on a few cardinal points, the creation and government of the world by God, the Divine origin of the law, the resurrection of the dead.

In his method of arguing from the Old Testament, again we notice a difference between St. Paul's education and ours. He has a way of marshalling a row of passages to illustrate an argument, which is itself independent of them ; he will weave passages together from memory to illustrate a point. He is deeply mystical, he finds predictions and types of the history of the Church in the Old Testament scenes and incidents ; the form of his argument in all this is Jewish, but the underlying argument is Catholic – that is, for all ages. It is of course the moral consistency of God, which demands that, if under a certain set of circumstances God acts in a certain way, given a parallel set of circumstances He will act in the same way. But you have very often to look behind the form of St. Paul's argument, its Rabbinic form, in order to see what is of universal validity in it. And you must always remember that he did not deduce his Gospel from the Old Testament. His Gospel came to him in another way, through personal experience, but having once reached it he knows it must be in the Old Testament and he searches for it there, and searches of course like

a Jew, but, let us add, not merely as a concession to
orthodoxy, but, because the facts really require us to
say it, like a Jew who is guided in his search by the
torch of the Holy Spirit.

We return to our story.

The years passed by in the school of Gamaliel and the
pale little boy of Tarsus became one of the marked
men of the new generation. We have no means of
filling the gap between his college days and the day
when he first faced St. Stephen in the Cilician synagogue. He was then something like thirty-one or
thirty-two – and a trusted and prominent agent of the
Sanhedrin. It is possible – probable – that some years
were spent at home in Tarsus, domestic concerns having called him back. They were the sort of years a young
man has to spend nowadays very often between his
degree and his ordination – years of great importance
to him but about which there is nothing to tell the
world. So St. Augustine spent some time at home
between his degree at Carthage and his return there
as a tutor. Saul seems to have accepted a post ultimately which kept him going to and fro between
Jerusalem and outlying Jewish colonies. We have no
other way of accounting for his not having been in
Jerusalem with sufficient frequency to have come into
personal contact with the movement raised by the
preaching of Jesus, while so soon after he is found in
close and confidential relations with the Sanhedrin.
The only history of these years we possess is the bit of
autobiography in the seventh chapter of the Romans,
where St. Paul describes so vividly the struggles of
a young man after strict conformity to the will of God
and the failure of the Rabbinical teaching to help him.

The history of Israel inspired him, but the pre-
occupations of the Scribes seemed to have no more to
do with the remedy for sinfulness and the means of
sanctity than has a volume on Constitutional History
or Contracts.

And so we seem to see him in these last years of his
pre-Christian life, torn by inward struggles, and yet
perfectly loyal to his creed, testing his faith in it by
hard fiery proselytising, a young man of whom the
Sanhedrin was, perhaps, a little afraid and whom, perhaps, it kept moving about as much as possible.
During some of Saul's visits to headquarters he must
have heard a good deal of talk about Galilæan disturbances and the Galilæan hero. The Galilæans,
always difficult to manage, had at the time, it appeared,
a local hero, a carpenter of Nazareth, a certain Jesus,
about whom they were saying many wild and foolish
things. Saul would not concern himself very much
over Galilæan aberrations, such information would not
draw his eyes or his attention from the book he was
reading ; he would smile grimly and forget it. These
disturbances were always happening.

But Saul was not able to forget the Galilæan disturbances for long : they increased, they infected
Jerusalem, ultimately the Galilæan hero was dealt with
by the Romans and hanged under circumstances of
considerable disorder. But the execution of the leader,
instead of giving a quietus to the annoyance, became
a fresh starting point for it. His followers insisted
that he had returned from the grave – and the
authorities had failed to produce the body in contra-
diction of the story. There must have been some
collusion, they whispered, between the Guard and

the disciples, because the body had entirely disappeared. The whole episode with the Guard had
been most annoying – disquieting – humiliating. They
had had the indescribable effrontery to bring the news
of the disappearance of the body themselves to the
authorities, simulating the most violent excitement and
terror, and announcing that there had been a manifestation of force of an inexplicable kind, that the
stone had been rolled back and that the tomb had been
found to be empty. The natural thing, of course,
would have been to have handed the men over for
punishment, but frankly the authorities had been
afraid to do so. The men told their story with
such incredible assurance and consistency that undoubtedly had they been put on their defence they
would have found people to believe them. The religious authorities had been obliged to have recourse
to the deplorable expedient of buying the men's silence
with a sum – a very large sum – of money, undertaking to square matters with the Roman authorities.
This placed them more or less at the mercy of a group
of subordinates, but it was the best that could be done.

For a time matters subsided. The followers of
Jesus came constantly into collision with authority, but
no doubt the thing would gradually die down. But,
on some return of Saul to Jerusalem, he found the
whole place in a ferment. The followers of the
Galilæan had begun an organised attack, he was told,
on the religious institutions of the nation, in particular
the synagogues of the Freedmen and of the Cilicians
were convulsed by the outrageous speeches of a young
Hellenistic Jew, one Stephanas or Stephen.

Let us try to understand Saul's view of the Christian

Church when the Jewish authorities sent for him and asked him to assist them in suppressing it. It had hitherto been regarded as a new and heretical synagogue. There are said to have been 480 synagogues in Jerusalem at this time, places of exhortation, prayer and instruction, which formed rallying points for the various sections of the community. There would be some divergence of opinion between these synagogues on such points as orthodoxy permitted to be disputed. One such point was the doctrine of Messiah, different groups of Jews holding different theories about the Deliverer. The Church then first appeared before the world as a new Nazarene synagogue, which held the extraordinary and horrible theory that a notorious disturber of the public peace, lately crucified by the Romans, was Messiah. This in itself would merely rouse the contemptuous disgust of the leading Pharisees and Sadducees. Transient crazes of this sort, they would remark, were not uncommon, although it is true they had never taken so bizarre a shape before. But the persistent proselytising of these Nazarenes, the spread of their organisation (a public building, of course, they had not), the constant disturbances they caused in the Temple, forced the authorities to take them seriously. They proceeded to deal with the matter of their sermons – and now their opposition to the Church split on the rock of the doctrine of the Resurrection. The Hierarchy in our Lord's day, the latitudinarians who wished to stand well with the Imperial authorities, denied the resurrection of the body and future retribution, and are said not to have believed in any survival after death. The Resurrection was the great matter of controversy between Pharisees and

Sadducees.   Consequently, when it was found that the Nazarenes were preaching the doctrine of the Resurrection earnestly and effectively, half at least of their persecutors became disinclined to intervene actively, and when the great Gamaliel had himself risen in his place in the Council, and had argued that it would be unwise for human agents to attempt to unravel the strange web of truth and fiction which constituted the Nazarene heresy, and that, therefore, the solution of the problem should be left to God, it was felt that to a certain extent the Pharisees had extended to the Nazarenes a cool protection.

But now all was changed.   Pharisee and Sadducee alike demanded the extirpation of the sect.   What had occurred ?   Simply this.   The second chapter of the Christian doctrine had been unfolded by Stephen. How glorious our glimpse of the Proto-Martyr is ! His position in the Church was a humble one, and yet during his brief career his figure fills the whole landscape ;   the Apostles themselves sat at the Deacon's feet.   To describe him is to utter a string of superlatives.   He had a magnetic personality which, transfigured by grace, performed great miracles, apparently great personal beauty, great oratorical power, great learning, great administrative capacity.   He was the first very great man in the natural order whom the Church captured, and his submission to truth was rewarded by his being the first to proclaim quite clearly a vital truth on which in their public teaching the Apostles had hitherto maintained some reserve – the transience of Judaism, and the finality and universality of the Christian Church.   Here then was the point at which Saul was required to enter the lists ;

he was put forward by both Pharisees and Sadducees to champion orthodoxy against the brilliant heretic whose sermons were crowding the various synagogues in which he preached and doing serious harm to the people. We wish we had detailed reports of the controversies in the Cilician synagogue, and yet we know a good deal about them – for when Saul became a Christian he annexed his opponent's theology in one swoop. It was Stephen's Gospel, Stephen's sermons, the memory of Stephen's face, which Saul took away with him into his Arabian retreat, and on which he fashioned the lines of his own teaching.

We have probably all seen the arrangements of a synagogue. What they are to-day they were then in Jerusalem – oblong stone buildings divided by several rows of pillars, with a deep gallery for women over what we should call the west door. Opposite is a recess containing the chest in which the sacred books are kept ; a curtain hangs before the recess, a lamp before the curtain ; in the middle of the building there is a raised platform on which stands the desk from which the Scriptures are read, and the large chair in which the Preacher sits to deliver his sermon. Nowadays comfortable benches placed lengthways down the building flank the platform ; then, I suppose, men stood or squatted round it. Imagine such a building packed to excess. The sermon is ended, the disputants have crowded round the rostrum, a controversy is raging. In the chequered light, the seething maddened crowd sways like a cornfield in a breeze – gradually one figure after another emerges before us. Above them all Stephen, king of men, his eloquence at the service of his theology, under the control of his perfect nerve.

Perhaps, down by his side, Simon Peter watching the
scene with keen anxiety ; and surely somewhere near,
in his customary attitude of service, the steadfast figure
of the Judgment Hall and of Calvary, the figure of the
Beloved Disciple.   And then, confronting Stephen
somewhere in the front row, that thin restless figure
we are beginning to know, his delicate face drawn and
set, his eyes burning like coals of fire, darting out his
brilliant sword thrusts.   The battle would rage over
two propositions.   First, the crucifixion of Messiah.
Secondly, the transience of the Temple.   The first
proposition was horrible and grotesque to the Jews –
that their Messiah could be crucified by the Romans
at the instance of their own authorities was a monstrous
thought.   What conception had they of their Messiah ?
It is very difficult to answer that shortly.   All through
the history of prophecy the three elements in Messiah's
character, the Priest, the Prophet and the King, had,
as it were, been striving for the mastery.   In popular
thought the idea of King Messiah was now supreme.
The Book of Enoch describes Him as a man seated
beside the Ancient of Days and possessed of the grace
of the Angels.   His attributes are majesty, tenderness,
dominion and righteousness.   At His coming sinners
will be yielded up for punishment to the righteous.
In the Fourth Book of Esdras, He rises from the
fathomless sea and utterly destroys all the heathen.   In
the Apocalypse of Baruch, written thirty years later
than the events we are now recalling, all the kingdoms
of the earth are destroyed before His appearing, except Palestine.

And yet there was a strong school in that day who
denied the coming of Messiah.   Hillel said that

Hezekiah had fulfilled the prophecies, and the Gordian knot of any early difficulties Saul may have had as to Messiah's conquest of Tarsus would be cut in the school of Gamaliel by a frank repudiation of the hope. Now it had all to be fought out again with Stephen. Our Lord, the fulfilment of prophecy, that was Stephen's first theme.   Would we had the sermon in which he illustrated the 53rd chapter of Isaiah from the story of our Lord.   In those days the Jews understood that great prophecy to apply to their Deliverer, they regarded the Suffering Servant as an aspect of Him.   Now, under pressure of the Christian facts they deny the reference, but then St. Stephen could use it. In answer, his opponents had only the bare dictum of the law to bring forward, ' He that is hanged is accursed of God.'   And it was thus that Stephen was brought to criticise the whole Jewish interpretation of the law.   He taught his congregation that the Law and the Temple marked a stage in the process of God's dealings with men – a process which stretched back far behind them and would stretch far beyond them.   The huge Jewish error had been blocking up the whole perspective of history with the Law and the Temple, trying to fix for ever what was destined to pass.   The Temple – here he roused the deepest feelings of his hearers.   Their love for their Temple was a beautiful thing, a band of young Tarsians, fellow townsmen of St. Paul, devoted themselves to its defence when the great siege came, and perished in the flames.

How did all this affect Saul at the time ?   I can only offer you my own conjectures.   I imagine that he was shocked to find himself attracted to the person of the heretic.   Saul was not a devil who became a demi-god, he was a noble Jew who became a Christian saint. And I imagine him stirred by the appeals away from the minutiæ of the law to the glorious outlines of Jewish history. Listening to Stephen I picture Saul occasionally losing himself in memories and finding himself once more a child at the feet of the old Rabbi at Tarsus, dreaming of universal righteousness. I imagine Stephen ministering to any doubts Saul had ever had. So gradually Stephen, as I picture it all, seemed to him to be Satan in the garb of an Angel of light. This triumphant wresting of the Scriptures to the prediction of a crucified Messiah, this thought of the law as a stage to a less trammelled future, this Jesus whose life and death had so bewitched His followers. Ah, it was all either God or the Devil. Which? And so Saul would raise his weary eyes and, lo, the sunshine flashed into them from the golden roof of the most holy house, dearest spot on earth, whose destruction Saul saw was involved in the New Teaching. And so with heart and soul and will he cried, " This thing is of Satan," and henceforth every new touch of power and beauty hardened his heart the more.

He gave his consent to a plan to rid the world of Stephen. There was no Procurator in Jerusalem at the time ; it was an opportunity for showing a little national independence. So they arrested Stephen one day when they knew the Sanhedrin was sitting in the Hall of Squares, and placed him in the great semi-circle of the Fathers of Israel. Witnesses appeared and twisted his words, no difficult task. Stephen listened. His magnificent oratory might still deliver him. Should he use it ? As he listened and pondered, he

was deciding his fate and the fate of another man in
the Hall of Squares. It was the Mount of his Temp-
tation. Satan is whispering to him of his importance
to the Church, how he sees her Catholicity more clearly
than any, and is sketching to him his triumphant
career as the great Apostle of the Gentiles, and the
Angels are whispering that God means him to declare
the greatness of His designs for the world here in
Jerusalem, and that the supreme moment is come.
Somebody watched him as he took his holy resolve,
and that somebody (and can you doubt who that somebody was ?) afterwards told St. Luke that his face then
was, as it were, the face of an Angel. " Guilty or not
guilty ? " said the High Priest. And then Stephen
gave his life away in the speech which was not a defence but a confession.

.   .   .   .

When the echo of his awful denunciation had died
away, they sat awhile paralysed to silence by their
fury, while he, unconscious of their rage, stood rapt in
the ecstasy of his vision and called them to look with
him on the glory. Then with a yell they rushed upon
him and dragged him without the walls and murdered
him. Saul, the agent of the Sanhedrin, presided over
the work. He saw the Martyr drag himself up upon
his knees, no longer angel-faced, now a spectacle of
horror, and pray for his murderers, and then he saw
the thing which had once been Stephen compose its
limbs in death, but as he went back to his lodgings
one strange thing struck a vague terror to the agent's
heart. " Notwithstanding all, " he muttered, " he
fell asleep, yes, actually – he fell asleep."

CHAPTER IV

EVOUT men carried Stephen to his burial and
made great lamentation over him. Evidently
there was a great demonstration of indignation and sorrow among the Hellenistic Jews and Jewish
Christians. After the murder, many who had secretly
sympathised, or partly sympathised, were moved to
come out into the open and show their feeling.
Jerusalem, in fact, was found to be more seriously
divided on the subject of these new heretics than had
been supposed.

Saul had suffered a good deal in the contests with
Stephen, and he suffered more when the death of
Stephen was first added to his memories. But he
gloried in his sufferings ; they were in the cause of
truth. And now he must finish his work, this
dæmoniacal heresy must be blotted off the earth. It is
generally supposed that the New Testament greatly
underrates the persecution through tenderness to the
great Apostle. And yet he is spoken of as uprooting
the Church as a wild boar uproots a vineyard, as
devastating it like an invading army. Those were
exciting months when Saul commanded the secret
police, the regulation of the spies, the midnight raids,
the application of the torture. The doubts which had
stabbed his heart under the bewitchment of Stephen
were no longer felt. Nero may have been more cruel,
but Saul beat him in thoroughness. It was a reign of

terror. The Christians were imprisoned, tortured, put
to death. St. Paul tells us he assisted in these trials and
gave his vote for the death penalty. That, I think, may
be a strong figure of speech, and that his vote was given
behind the scenes, not as a member of the Sanhedrin.
If he was a member of the Sanhedrin, he must have
been a married man at the time, with children, since
no one without a wife and family could belong to it.
Consequently, many students of St. Paul suppose him
to have had a brief marriage episode in his life. Somehow, I cannot think St. Paul was ever married ; it
seems improbable that no sort of trace of his marriage
should have survived. My impression is that he got
into the habit of using very strong self-accusing
language about the persecution, and that the word
' vote ' is an illustration of it.

    There is one point of great interest connected with
the persecutions. How was it that when the Christians
were scattered in all directions from Jerusalem the
Apostles were able to remain there ? Did any line of
division exist at this time between Palestinian Jewish
Christians and Hellenistic Jewish Christians ? Were
the first more conservative, and so less suspected than
the second ? Was this persecution mainly against
Hellenistic Jewish Christians such as Stephen was ?
In the present state of our knowledge we cannot
answer the question.

    At last the work seemed done in Jerusalem. Saul
felt it would be unwise to pursue his searches further.
He had read the heretics a lesson and written it in
blood. No doubt he was greatly congratulated, but
his mind was not at rest, the accursed thing was appearing in other places. Damascus was very deeply

affected.   Saul got leave to open an inquisitorial court
there.   Theophilus, the High Priest, gave him letters
to the local synagogue and his paternal benediction,
and one fine day the legate of the Sanhedrin rode out
through the Damascus gate at the head of his well-
armed retinue, and turned his horse's head towards
the north, the observed, the admired, the envied of all
beholders.   The journey to Damascus generally took
a week.   It is about 150 miles, and there are three
possible routes.   Almost certainly Saul took the most
direct.   Over the stony, bleak plateau of Judæa, past
Bethel, down into the charming glens of Samaria, on
to Shiloh and the big broad plain below Ebal and
Gerizim, then, as now, a vast, unbroken cornfield.
Thence through the narrow vale of Shechem to the
hill city of Samaria, on across the plain of Dothan into
the burning limestone defiles of Jenin, from which the
traveller emerges with such infinite relief into the great
plain of Esdraelon, swept by the breeze between the
Jordan valley and the sea.   Here Saul turned east,
and passing under Gilboa, rode down the vale of
Bethshan to the Jordan.   Thence he struck north-
eastward, passing up the east side of the Lake of Galilee,
through the wilds of Gadara, and so across the desolate,
volcanic plains which lie east of Hermon and form so
amazing a contrast to the luxuriance of the oasis in
which Damascus lies.   His method of progress I have
experienced – leisurely, as all Eastern progresses are,
he himself on horseback, his retinue, some mounted,
some on foot.   I remember the cold of the tent at
night, the watch fires, the glittering stars, the long hot
rides in the early morning and the late afternoon, the
breathless heat of the noontide and the long hot siesta.

During the whole week Saul was alone, his attendants were no companions for the legate of Theophilus, and for the first time since the murder of Stephen he was forced to think. The dæmoniacal influence which Stephen had gained over him was not destroyed ; it was intensified by Stephen's death. It began to be hard for Saul to kick against this goad. Surely, Stephen's spirit was haunting his path ! To the allurement of the picture of the untrammelled religion of the Nazarene with its world-wide hope was now added that awful exhibition of heroism outside the city gate. And yet Stephen and the crucified carpenter could not be right, and Saul and the Jewish Church wrong. The Jewish Church — Saul would begin involuntarily to review the condition of Jerusalem, and the character of his patron, Theophilus. It was not unlike Rome under the Renaissance Popes, Sixtus IV, Alexander VI, Julius II, Leo X. Certainly the picture was not inspiring. So he rode on across those interminable stretches of desert plain east of Hermon, towards the crisis of his fate, the moment which revolutionised his life and views, the moment he afterwards regarded as the greatest honour and privilege of his life. One of a series of such moments, but differing from the others in the appeal it made to his external senses, and the first and most momentous of all. A moment, the awful reality of which was going to reduce all else to shadow and semblance, a moment in which he came into direct personal contact with the truth of the world, with the Divine Reality, with God. During all the last morning they had pressed on, forfeiting their siesta in order to get to their journey's end in the early afternoon. Gradually on the gentle crests of the undulating desert

road, far away could be descried a blue-green sea lying
among the distant mountains, the wonderful luxuriance
of the oasis which the Abana and the Pharpar watered.
At last – I well remember how gradually the city, when
approached from this side, comes into sight – at last
all lay clear in the near distance. Damascus sleeping
in the high noon, just as I first saw her riding in on the
same side, engirdled by her walnuts, her pomegranates
and her palms, the pearl-grey city rising out of the sea
of blue-green foliage among the pink desert mountains. All was silent as the grave, no human life was
visible under the searching rays of the quivering white
light. Saul pressed on at the head of his party, his set
white face half hidden under the protecting head veil.
They were close to the gate ; how hard the clatter of
their horses' hoofs sounded on the Roman pavement !
Then suddenly – suddenly with a fearsome, terrified
swerve, they were trying to escape a blinding white
glare, there was a crash of metal, the riders were un-
horsed, there was a stampede, a babel of voices, and
then silence, and the leader lay stretched upon the
ground. Gradually he gathered himself together, and
rose to his feet. They heard a hoarse, broken question : " Who art thou, Lord ? " And then he stood
and appeared to listen, but they heard no voice, no
reply. After a moment's pause, they mastered themselves and rushed round him. He turned a white,
blank face from side to side ; he was blind, stone
blind ! They cried aloud with anguish. Ah, the
pity of it ! Apparently this explosion out of the
clear sky had destroyed the sight of the agent of the
Sanhedrin, the most promising career of the rising
generation was nipped in the bud. They brought

him in, those rough men, so tenderly, into the city,
touched to the heart at the proud strength struck down
into a helpless dependence.   They led him through the
triple gate and down the glorious street called Straight,
of which, here and there, a trace still remains amid the
ramshackle modern houses, then a vast avenue between
a double row of Corinthian columns.   They lodged him
in the house of one Judas, and left him in loneliness,
blindness and pain.

What had really happened ?   Saul had seen Jesus of
Nazareth and had heard His voice.   There could be
no mistake, the figure which stood in the heart of the
unbearable light did not say, " I am King Messiah ! "   It
said, " I am Jesus of Nazareth, whom thou persecutest ! "
And now, all of a moment, that under-current of tendency which had been making towards Christianity in
him came to the surface, the long misgivings had been
brought to a head and decisively confirmed.   All the
kickings against the goad were over for ever.   He had
seen the risen Jesus !   This vision convinced him for
ever of the truth of the Christian story.   Jesus *was*
risen : therefore, no matter what the manner of His death,
Jesus was Messiah and enthroned at God's right hand.

Some words of Dr. Liddon sum up what remains to
be said :

' Remember, this vision of Saul's did not operate
irresistibly on his will.   He was free to disobey it still.
He might have persuaded himself that it was an
hallucination, that his brain had formulated the words
of Jesus, that the blindness was due solely to physical
causes.   If he did not do this, it was because he was
looking out for Truth.   Many a man in his circumstances would have acted otherwise ! '

We cannot attempt to analyse the agony of those three days of darkness, those days during which, like his new-found Master, Saul lay in the tomb. One moment in them only is chronicled for us, that moment when the winter of Saul's life was past, and, with the suddenness of the northern spring, the proud remorse broke down into the broken-hearted sorrow of the little child, and the Angels said, "Behold he prayeth." And then, at last, the agent of the Sanhedrin slept, and in his sleep he stood before an ambassador of the new religion, and, lo, they had forgiven and forgotten all and had received him as a brother.

Meanwhile, a simple-hearted old peasant was rousing himself from his sleep with a strange look of determination in his eyes, and was preparing to seek the lodging of the agent. The misfortune of Saul was, of course, the talk of Damascus, and there must have been some amongst the Christians who recognised the stroke of God's judgment in that bolt from heaven, but it had been impressed upon Ananias in his dream — (and we must remember that it is we materialised modern Westerns who are in an abnormal state as to dreams. Dreams in other ages and states of civilisation have been much more valuable as a link with the unseen than they are with us to-day) — it had been impressed upon Ananias in his dream that God had smitten in mercy and not in judgment, and, with the simple courage of a child with his hand in his father's hand, Ananias obeyed a mysterious impulse to seek out this terrifying inquisitor in his blindness. The narrative in the Acts describes the dream so bluntly as a message from God that we are led by it to forget that it was a dream after all, and that it needed

extraordinary courage to take it as a practical direction
and obey it.   There is not a more heroic figure in history
than this gentle old man, seeking for Saul's lodgings in
the street called Straight.   And so he enters the
darkened sick room, and fulfils the old prophecy,
'And the sucking child shall play on the hole of the
asp, and the weaned child shall put his hand on the
cockatrice' den, and they shall not hurt nor destroy in
all my holy mountain.'   I do not think anyone has
ever painted the great legate sitting at the feet of the
poor old man, his eyes, restored although perhaps
never thoroughly restored, turned wistfully towards
the gentle face.

There are several indications that St. Paul was partly
blind.   His stake in the flesh may possibly have
been attacks of recurrent ophthalmia.   Apparently
he did not write his own letters.   It may be that
he did not recognise the High Priest when he
was before the Sanhedrin in after years at Jerusalem.   I think when Saul wrote in after years,
'God hath chosen the foolish things of the world to
confound the wise, and God hath chosen the weak
things of the world to confound the things which are
mighty,' he must have thought of those simple lessons
in the house of Judas.   They did not last long.   Saul's
position was extremely critical.   He put himself un-
reservedly in the hands of the disciples of Jesus, and
they prescribed a long rest and a long retreat ; and
so, ere many days were past, Saul had fled into the
desert of Arabia, taking with him his knowledge of
the risen Jesus, the instructions of Ananias and what
other disciples he had seen, the recollection of St.
Stephen's sermons, and the Scriptures of the Old

Testament. With these materials he worked out the main lines of his faith and teaching.

Where did he go ? How long did he stay ? It is impossible to answer the last question. He tells us that his first visit to Jerusalem as a Christian took place three years after his conversion. There he is speaking according to the ancient reckoning ; according to our reckoning that means two years after. The years were spent in Arabia and in Damascus, but how long in each we do not know. I imagine almost the whole time was spent in Arabia. The Arabic translator of this passage in Galatians renders the passage : ' Immediately I went to El Belka,' and the later passage in Galatians he translates : ' This Hagar is Mount Sinai in El Belka and is contiguous to Jerusalem.'' El Belka was apparently a region north-east of the Dead Sea, and it is conceivably possible that a wandering Arab tribe may have named a portion of it Mount Sinai in memory of the great peninsula. The origin of this tradition cannot be traced, and the translation is too late for it to be considered of any historic value. Arabia is a wide word and might apply to the desert near Damascus itself, but to the majority of people in those days the word had a less wide significance. The Arabia of popular speech was the peninsula of Sinai and the country above and around it. Certainly in Galatians, where St. Paul alludes to this retreat, he later on in chapter iv. associates Arabia with Sinai, so it seems very probable that he deliberately sought the mountain which had burned with fire, and fashioned his Gospel in the traditional birthplace of the law. It seems probable therefore that where Elijah, the typical prophet, listened to the voice of God and

then sped forth refreshed on his mission of righteousness, Paul was strengthened and sanctified for his still
greater work. Whether on Sinai or no, St. Paul was
the first Christian religious. He worked out his
Gospel in an anchorage, in the cell of a recluse.

When he felt himself ready, he returned to Damascus. Of course, his only Christian friends were in
Damascus, and no doubt he wished to begin his labours
in the scene of his conversion. The command to
Elijah must have rung in his ears as a most delightful
coincidence. Go ! return on thy way to the wilderness
of Damascus. He returned possessed of the root
ideas of his future Gospel.

What are they ? First : Jesus is Messiah, and
Messiah is the Son of God. This knowledge was
a gift to him, a Divine gift, and it was the knowledge
of a Person whom to know was to adore. To the
Divine gift and to the adoring devotion which was its
result, Paul gave a name, the word which has changed
the character of European civilisation, ' *Faith.*' That
first. And secondly : To be fixed in this relation of
personal adoration and service towards the Son of God
is to find oneself in the ideal relation to God which is
called Righteousness. Already Saul had found this
true. Already his personal communion with the risen
Jesus had lifted him out of the sphere of his temptations. It had become easy to be and do right where
it had been hard before. Saul had not yet met the
Apostles and they had much to tell him, but he already
had enough material for his first sermons in Damascus.
The evolution of St. Paul's theology is a very interesting study. When the letters are arranged in
chronological order one can watch, first the grain, then

the ear, then the full corn in the ear. But evolution does not mean addition. The whole Catholic Faith is contained in those fundamental conceptions of Faith and Righteousness. In holding these, Saul held it all, but its extension into the full detail of the Catholic system was the work of time.

Those first sermons of St. Paul ! There is a freshness about a preacher's early sermons for which the greater finish and freedom of later years does not compensate. Without, I suppose, any of Stephen's beauty, dignity or eloquence, his assassin tried to do in Damascus what Stephen had done in Jerusalem. Those scenes in the Damascus synagogue, when Paul stood up to testify to the truth of the religion he had persecuted to the death, must have been dramatic beyond description. But they did not last long ; the preacher was a doomed man ; there was not a nook, corner or alley in Damascus but held an assassin's knife for Saul, and we want an Alexander Dumas or a Victor Hugo to sketch for us the episode of that dark night when his friends swung the ex-legate of Theophilus from the window in the wall and lowered him into the city moat. Such a writer is needed to trace the incidents of that journey on foot, in disguise, and by unfrequented ways, to the capital which he had left two years before at the head of his retinue.

It was nearing the feast of Tabernacles when Saul entered the Holy City. Jerusalem was crowded. He would meet old friends at every street corner. His was, certainly, an unenviable position ; his old associates had become his undying enemies. And how would his new world, this handful of obscure men whom he had first persecuted and then sought to join,

how would they receive him ? His worst fears were
realised. They refused to have anything to do with
him. News in those days travelled slowly and im-
perfectly. There had been the startling story of his
illness and supposed conversion two years before.
Since then, he had disappeared, no one knew where.
How were they to know that all this was not the feint
of a wolf in sheep's clothing ? And then Barnabas the
Cypriote, who had evidently known Saul in early days,
since tradition says they were fellow students both in
Tarsus and in Jerusalem, and who had early memories
of him very unlike the record of the chief detective
of Theophilus, went surety for his sincerity.

It was a providential circumstance that there were
only two Apostles in Jerusalem at the time. It would
have been very difficult to have persuaded the whole
college. It was St. Peter, the Primate, and St. James
the Apostle of the local church, who received St. Paul.
And, of course, it was dear St. Peter, always generous,
loving and delightful, who invited him to come and
stay with him. And now Saul began a wonderful set
of fresh experiences. He received the Blessed Sacra-
ment, almost certainly in the room of Its institution,
and he was the first great Pilgrim to the Holy Places.
I picture those pathetic, silent walks of the two men,
almost certainly at night. I see them coming under
the flickering light of the moon through the glades of
Gethsemane, and I see the gesture with which St.
Peter points to a certain spot beneath a certain tree.
I see them on the ugly, rough knoll in the angle of the
walls. Peter is stooping in the dim light and searching
for something. Presently he whispers : " Here it
is ! " and Saul puts a trembling hand into the rocky

socket of the Cross. I see them enter a shadowy door-
way close by and grope in total darkness through the
cavity, for they dare not show a light, until they find
the cold, flat slab of stone they are searching for, and
the hand of Peter guides the hand of Saul, and he
whispers : " There, just there, we found the head veil
all collapsed together and still untied, like a ball out
of which the air has escaped."

By day, Saul was otherwise occupied. He did
exactly what we should have expected of him ; he
went to the synagogue where Stephen had preached,
and preached in the Martyr's place. Of course, this
could not be allowed, and the authorities took steps to
have him assassinated. I feel quite sure that at this
moment Saul was expecting and longing for martyrdom. It seems to me that his great desire now was to
re-enact the tragedy of Stephen in his own person and
so make what reparation he could for his crime. The
peremptory and direct command he received from our
Lord to depart from Jerusalem was probably given
owing to Saul's great longing for martyrdom.

However this may be, the Church evidently received
the news of his departure with a deep sigh of relief.
He was evidently sincere, but utterly impossible, his
very zeal did harm. So he was smuggled out of the
country, a man marked out for assassination, dangerous to the welfare of any Christian Church in which
he might shelter. He went back to Tarsus, and it
must surely have been a loving home which sheltered
him now for seven years. They were seven years of
peace, for he was with Jesus always, seven years during
which he reviewed again the religious conditions of the
Gentiles, and pondered long and sadly on the awful

fact that there beyond the Taurus lay a world un-
conquered for Christ, and that the man obviously
designed by God to conquer it was lying in the tomb
at Jerusalem to which his own blood-stained hands
had consigned him.

CHAPTER V

I OUGHT to begin this chapter by saying a word about the chronology of the life of St. Paul. The dates are arrived at by regarding the two years' captivity at Cæsarea as the central point, and working backwards and forwards from that. The captivity began shortly after Pentecost, in June, two years before the end of the administration of Felix, and it ended when Festus arrived to take Felix' place as Roman Governor of Palestine, that is, this captivity dates from June, 57, to June, 59. Before that St. Paul had spent a year in Macedonia and Corinth. Romans was written early in 57 ; 2 Corinthians in the summer of 56. He had come to Macedonia from Ephesus, which he left shortly before Pentecost, 56. He had been there two years and three months, which means that he must have reached it in December, 53 ; he had been at Jerusalem for the Passover of 53, and had spent the time in between in Antioch and South Galatia. Before that Passover he had been eighteen months in Corinth, from August, 51, to February, 53. Then the dates get less clear ; he probably began his second missionary journey, the first in Europe, in the early summer of 50, the summer and autumn of 50 being given to the Asia Minor part ; from that time, till the summer of 51, he was in Philippi, Thessalonica, Beræa and Athens, and this brings the third visit to Jerusalem, Acts xv., to the beginning of 50. It is impossible to estimate the length of the earlier sojourns in Antioch, but Sir William Ramsay conjectures that the first missionary journey began in the spring of 46, and that the second visit to Jerusalem took place in 45.

To get the intervening dates between 45 and his conversion it is necessary to start with the latter. A very early tradition says that St. Paul served God thirty-five years and was martyred at the age of sixty-eight. The political situation at Rome in the year 68 makes it clear that no executions of Christians could have taken place then. The Neronian persecution ceased in 67, and that was probably the year of St. Paul's martyrdom ; he was therefore born in I B.C., and converted in A.D. 32, the Crucifixion being assumed in this system to have taken place in 29, and the whole Christian era to be post-dated four years. You see his time in Arabia and at Damascus, the first visit to Jerusalem, the long retreat at home in Tarsus, and the early labours at Antioch have to be distributed over the space of years between 32 and 45. I do not think we can arrive at these dates at all exactly. Most people put the visit to Jerusalem earlier, in 44, which would mean that St. Barnabas went to Tarsus to fetch St. Paul perhaps in the winter of 42, and that 43 was the year of the first work in Antioch ; at any rate, you see there was a considerable period at Tarsus about which we know nothing, between perhaps 34 or 35 and 42, and in that period we left Paul.

Let us now return to the consideration of the mental and spiritual growth of St. Paul during those difficult years of inaction at home. There was, as you remember, a corresponding period, though not so long a period, in the life of St. Francis, and there was such a

period too in the life of St. Theresa. It is very useful
to us to reflect on such periods of discipline and growth
in saintly lives ; they take saintly lives out of the region
of fairy tale to which the world is always ready to rele-
gate them. They deliver us from the view that there
was once a bad man called Saul, whom God turned all
of a minute into a practically sinless man called Paul,
and that this nearly immaculate being knew the whole
Catholic Faith at the moment of his conversion and
began to preach the morning after he had regained the
use of his eyes ; and whenever he preached and
whenever he wrote, he was possessed by Divinity to
the extinction of his own personality. Such are the
fairies' methods ; they are not the methods of God,
either in the physical or in the spiritual world. That
flashing sword of Messiah of which the baby Saul had
dreamt was no fairy fancy, it was a great and glorious
fact. But baby Saul himself was to be the sword, and
the hermit life in the desert and the failures to preach
at Damascus and Jerusalem, and the years at Tarsus
with no outlook beyond them of usefulness, these were
the successive furnaces in which the blade was being
tempered.

There is nothing so hard in life as the feeling that
one is not being used to the full by God, no discipline
is sterner than the discipline of holding powers and
gifts in trust for God for the exercise of which God
seems to refuse an opening. When Saul re-entered his
father's house at Tarsus he had given up everything
this world has to offer for the sake of Truth – he had
given up all hope of glory here ; but before he could
be used for his gigantic task he must also have given
up all hope of glory hereafter ; and so when the thin

Eт

pale son of the house returned to the tent-cloth works and settled down to his task of supervision, while he tested new hands and superintended the men and checked the accounts, interviewed the travellers and examined the quality of the evil-smelling cloth, he was secretly in the power of his Master destroying the last stronghold of self within him, and there came a moment when in complete submission – submission which had no touch of constraint about it – Saul took the lowest place in the Christian Church. Then, and not till then, came the command ' Go up higher.'

But side by side with the discipline of the Saint's character proceeded the growth of the Saint's theology. You remember that we considered in the last chapter those root ideas of his Gospel which he brought back from Arabia – *Jesus is Messiah, Messiah is the Son of God. The knowledge of this is God's gift to me, and it is the knowledge of a Being whom to know is to adore and serve.* To this gift and this adoring service St. Paul gave a name, the word which has changed the character of the dominant portion of the human race, *Faith.* Secondly, *To be fixed in this attitude of loving service to the Son of God is to find oneself in the ideal relation to God which is called Righteousness.* This had been St. Paul's experience. He found that personal communion with the living Jesus lifted him out of the sphere of his temptations, so that it became easy to do right where before it had been hard. And this tremendous experience which had transformed Paul was quite evidently God's intention for all men, and nobody was to be arbitrarily excluded from it. From the first it was clear to him that the message was alike for Gentile and Jew, and his time at Tarsus allowed him to review again and with a more sympathetic eye the condition of the Gentiles ; and, what was all important for his preaching, to get a clear line of thought about the religion of the Jews. Let us follow for a moment the line of his thought about the Jewish law. The goal of the old religion had been what he now saw his way to reach, righteousness ; he now felt himself to be already ' justified ' by his faith, that is to say, in a right relation with God, perfection being the end of a process already begun in him which must be completed unless he himself intervened and stopped it. His whole struggle up to his conversion had been a struggle to get into this right relation with God, this condition of satisfaction and peace, and it was now quite clear to him that it was unattainable by the methods prescribed by the Rabbis—indeed, unattainable by any method of human procedure. No amount of law would do it : it really required a new communication from God to man such as Paul had received. What was unattainable through adherence to even the finest programme of morality Saul found was to be attained through this personal union with the Son of God. Indeed, the law as he had experienced it, so he saw from his new standpoint, was producing two sets of results. In people like his former self it produced a sense of misery and hopelessness, while in the bulk of the people the imposition of this strong external law was producing an obscuration of the moral conception of righteousness ; they could not carry out or even recognise its spirit, and the idea of righteousness had become degraded among them into the observance of external rules. And yet the law had been God's gift to men. Why had He given it ? Saul could see several reasons.

It had regulated society in a lawless period of history.
It had disciplined men by hard precepts into the power
of yielding obedience to authority.   It had educated
men in a sense of sin by educating them in the idea of
God's holiness.   In fact, the law had been given to
produce the very misery he himself had felt, to draw
out the disease of sin into an acute stage.   The law
then had been an earlier stage in God's dealings with
men, a slave to compel God's unwilling children to the
school of Christ, even as his faithful slave long ago had
compelled the wayward feet of little Saul towards the
school of the synagogue.   At that moment one group
of men was being tempted by the law to say, 'Lord,
I thank Thee that I am not as other men are'; while
another was being inspired by the law to cry, 'Who
shall deliver me from the body of this death?'

Saul passed back in thought to the gift of deliverance
and new life he had received from Jesus Christ.   How
did He acquire the gift He had to bestow?   All
Saul's Jewish training now brought him to see that it
was through His perfect submission, even to death.
The death of the Sinless and Exalted Son of God!

At first Saul had said to himself, 'Never mind about
His death, that is an enigma.   I have seen the living
Jesus, He is the Christ of God.'   But his second
thought was, 'Stop, stop.   I must consider His
death.   The death of the Sinless and Exalted Son of
God cannot have been an accident, it must have the
gravest significance, it must have a Divine meaning.'
His Jewish training had taught him that death, as we
know it, is connected with sin.   The death of the
Anointed One, then, had to do with sin, and since He
was sinless, with the sins of other people.   At once it

took in Saul's eyes the proportions of Sacrifice, and
he saw that it explained his new experiences : the
efficacious sacrifice had been offered, with the result
that the damaged relations between God and man had
been repaired.

Saul began to work away at this thought, and by
gathering together the various aspects of the Jewish
sacrifices he arrived at his great conception of the All-
Sufficient Sacrifice, the sacrifice towards which the
Jewish ritual had looked, and the sacrifice by which
the Jewish law was abrogated. The whole of St.
Paul's theology, remember, is simply his account of
his experiences and the similar experiences of those
among whom he lived and worked.

Men may criticise the explanations the early Church
gave of her experiences as much as they please, the
fact of the experience remains.

Mankind, St. Paul felt, mankind as represented by
the Jew, had been like a drowning sailor trying to lift
himself out of the sea by tugging at his waistbelt, but
now a rope had been thrown from above to the drowning sailor ; he was being raised by a power not his
own, and this succour was being offered to all the
world.

While Saul was working out the details of his creed
at Tarsus, two events of the first importance were
taking place elsewhere. First, the hierarchy, in the
person of its primate St. Peter, had admitted Gentiles
to the Church of Jesus. She had ceased to be
entirely identified with Judaism. This had happened
at Cæsarea, and the action had been endorsed by the
Church at Jerusalem.

About the same time startling news came from

Antioch. During Saul's persecution a vigorous group of preachers had gone to Antioch where the division between Jew and Gentile was perhaps less strongly marked than anywhere else. Antioch, was an extraordinarily evil-living city, and the naturally moral among the Gentiles appear to have turned in a sort of despair to Judaism ; the wall of partition was weaker there than in most places, and this led to the dissemination of the teaching of the disciples among the heathen. Large numbers were touched by the story of Jesus and prayed to be admitted to the Church. The preachers sent to Jerusalem for instructions, and the Apostles sent Barnabas down to watch events and organise the growing community. You must understand that the moment the Apostles left Jerusalem itself and made journeys of organisation, this question about the Gentiles arose. It arose owing to the great number of Gentile proselytes ; Gentiles who conformed to the law and were Jews in so far as anybody could be a Jew who was not born a Hebrew. That distinction, the bar of race, prevented the proselytes from leavening the Jewish Church ; they remained an annexe to it. When the Gospel was preached in the synagogue it reached the proselytes, and the question at once arose : Shall they be admitted to the Church ? To refuse them was to make the Church narrower than the Synagogue, but then, could there be an outer and an inner circle of Christians, like the proselytes and the Jews in the Synagogue ? Plainly the idea was utterly contrary to the religion of Jesus ; to admit them at all was to admit them to complete fellowship. All education and prejudice was against such a thing, but the Holy Spirit triumphed and the barrier fell. At first,

all Gentiles were expected to approach the Church by
way of the Synagogue, they were expected to become
at least what were called God-fearing proselytes of the
Synagogue.   There   were   two   sets   of   proselytes.
There were the full proselytes who came under the full
law, and it was very soon decided that these should be
admitted to the Church, one of the seven deacons,
Nicholas, being a proselyte of Antioch.   These people
were strict Jews in all but birth ; but there were also
the semi-proselytes who only wished to enter into
partial relations with the Jews.   It is widely held that
the four rules of Acts xv. 28 to abstain from flesh
sacrificed to idols, and from blood, and from animals
strangled, and from fornication, which in this connection means marriage within degrees prohibited to Jews,
were the rules given to people who wished to stand in
this sort of relation to the Jewish Church, and who
are called in the Acts ' men who fear God,' and later on
in Jewish history Proselytes of the Gate, as distinguished from Proselytes of the Sanctuary.   It had at
first been thought by the Church, apparently, that all
Gentiles who sought to become Christians must first
become full proselytes and keep the whole law ; the
episode of Cornelius made it clear to the Apostles that
semi-proselytes were to be admitted, but when large
numbers of people standing in this loose relation to
Judaism wanted to come in at Antioch they sent down
Barnabas to be quite sure that the Holy Spirit was
working in the matter, as He plainly was in the case
of Cornelius.

    Soon, as you remember, a strict Jewish party was
organised inside the Church which required the converts to become full proselytes and keep the whole

law.   They were St. Paul's keenest opponents in after years.

We have not yet, you see, arrived at the moment when the Church, turning from the Jews, preached straight to Gentiles unaffected by Judaism.   That was at a later stage.   At present, everyone touched has been in some sort of relation to Judaism.

We must go rather carefully here, for this is an important moment.   The news which reached Jerusalem was that there had been great signs and wonders at Antioch – that is the meaning of the phrase, ' the hand of the Lord,' in Acts xi. 21 – that there had been great success, a great many who had believed turned to the Lord.   This means that numbers of Greeks in loose relation to Judaism had accepted the good news about our Lord and had turned to Him : they were all ready for action.

It is not stated whether they had been baptized. They probably had been, but the Apostles did not know whether the Holy Ghost had imparted Himself to them by a special manifestation as in the case of Cornelius, or whether, like the Samaritans who had been baptized by Philip the Deacon, they were waiting to receive His outpouring in Apostolic Confirmation.

The relation of these converts to the Jewish believers in a large and important Jewish colony was very delicate and critical.   They were all uncircumcised ; were they still then unclean ?   Would their Jewish fellow Christians enter their homes and eat with them ? Must they be circumcised as well as baptised ?   Or were the Jewish Christians to receive them as they were ?

St. Barnabas evidently was sent down as Apostolic

delegate with plenary powers.   When he arrived and
saw the situation he thanked God.   The manifestation
of the Holy Spirit's intention was as clear at Antioch
as it had been at Cæsarea.   He advised the Church to
accept the situation ; and his decision is described by
St. Luke in some carefully chosen words.   St. Barnabas
promised that perfect unity would be found in Jesus
Christ.   By cleaving to the Lord, they were all united
at the centre of all things.   Let them stand fast in their
new-found position.   Let the Greeks receive the
Sacraments and the Jewish Christians unite with them.
The result of this decision was a great advance and quite
a new situation, an enormous crowd of semi-heathen
converts.

Before we proceed, I must make you see Antioch.
Antioch, holding half a million people and the third
city of the Empire, was the second capital of Christianity – the order is Jerusalem, Antioch, Rome.   It lay
sixteen miles from the sea on the south bank of the
Orontes, north of the Lebanon, south of the Taurus
Mountains.   It was on the high road to Mesopotamia
and Arabia from the sea, and bore the same relation
to these that Tarsus bore to Asia Minor.   At this point
the broad Orontes flows about two miles north of
Mount Silpius, a noble craggy ridge, and on the plain
between Mount Silpius and the river the bulk of the
city lay.   But to this older town two additional quarters
had been added before this time.   One, containing the
palace of the kings of Syria, covered the island which
here divides the stream of the Orontes, the other
climbed up the rocky approaches to Mount Silpius,
terraced to receive their burden of marble villas.   A
succession of æsthetic kings had striven to make

Antioch a wonder of the world. Throughout the length of the city ran a great Corso, colonnaded, banked with flowers, lined with trees, decked with statuary, and paved throughout ; paved indeed for the $2\frac{1}{2}$ miles of its greatest splendour with white marble. The north bank of the Orontes, beyond the palace-covered island, was strewn with the country houses of the nobility, embowered in their acacias, ilexes and myrtles ; and the whole enchanted city was enclosed in embattled walls, which swept upwards to the south, and with inconceivable audacity of design extended along the summits of Mount Silpius. But the crowning marvel of all was the colossal head of Charon, the ferryman of the River of Death, fashioned out of one of the loftiest crags of the mountain by Antiochus Epiphanes during a great plague, and which frowned its perpetual menace on the meeting place of the Christians.

Antioch exhibited the characteristics of a great Oriental Greek city in an exaggerated way. Five miles down the river lay the groves of Daphne, containing the colossal statue of Apollo and his shrine of gold and gems. It was a great sanctuary, and had come to harbour not outraged virtue but triumphant vice. To charge a person with ' Daphne habits ' was to utter a gross insult, and when Juvenal wished to say his bitterest about Rome, he said that the waters of the Orontes had flowed into the Tiber.

Renan has summed up in his own picturesque way what we know of Antioch. ' It was,' he says, ' an unheard of collection of jugglers, charlatans, pantomimists, magicians, sorcerers, and priestly impostors ; a city of races, games, dances, processions, festivals,

unchecked luxury. The great Corso was like a theatre,
and in it there rolled from morning to night the waves
of a population, empty, frivolous, fickle, riotous, sometimes witty, delighting in ballads and parodies, and
witty sayings and audacious impertinences of every
description.   It was like an opium-eater's dream, a
stream of wild pleasure, delicately conceived, daintily
dressed.'   It was in an opium-eater's dream that the
Church began her triumphal march.

The simple, quiet, generous, noble Barnabas faced
a scene full of dramatic pathos : the city, day and night,
parading her painted mirth, and the steadily growing
crowd of people with wistful eager faces who had
turned with loathing from the diet of swines' food
which the city offered, and yearned for the Bread of
Life.   ' A master mind and a master hand are needed
here,' thought Barnabas, and his mind flashed towards
Saul far away across the Amanus range in Tarsus.
Here, surely, was the God-ordained opening for the
powers of Saul. His past history would be scarcely
known in Antioch, it would be difficult to rouse
Jewish feeling against him here ; and to this great
multitude of Greeks attracted to the Faith it was not
known at all.   Barnabas reflected long and deeply ; he
was perhaps not quite sure whether Peter or John
would work altogether happily with Saul ; certainly
James, the local Apostle of Jerusalem, could not, but
as for himself he had no doubts, and happily he was in
command at Antioch. I like to think of the simple and
natural way in which it all happened – of the tact and
delicacy with which Barnabas opened the subject with
the local Church – of the affectionate reminiscences of
the Saul of long ago, the Saul of their boyish days, with

which he won them all over, and then the arrangements for the few days' absence, the short voyage to Tarsus, and the reception of Barnabas in St. Paul's home.

Mr. Rackham in his commentary on the Acts judges that St. Paul was reluctant to go. He deduces this from the exhortation which occurs in the Bezan Text. This is an extraordinarily interesting manuscript of the Acts, which some people think is another original draft of the book. The Bezan Text suggests that St. Paul showed hesitation about going, and after the long stretch of years one can quite understand it. Moreover, he had made great progress in the mystical life; the great vision recorded in 2 Corinthians, when he was caught up into the third heaven, probably occurred about this time. Small wonder if for a moment he turned to his Master, like St. Peter on the Mount, and said, " Master, it is good for us to be here."

But if so, it was only for a moment. Barnabas told him of the great crowd waiting at Antioch, and Saul made one of the great decisions of history. A day or two afterwards he stood upon the quay of Antioch and faced the frown of Charon, the apostle of life face to face with the symbol of death.

CHAPTER VI

WE left St. Paul standing on the quay of Antioch. Before him the splendid city swept up the slopes of Mount Silpius in terraces of marble set in foliage. Above it frowned the sculptured head of Charon, the ferryman of the dead, and around lay the pageant of the city's life. The two friends took a house somewhere in the thick of the city and attacked the problem before them — the problem of how to bring the pagans, who had stood in an attitude of sympathy with Judaism but had never conformed to the law, and who were now praying for admission to the Church, into Christian unity with others who had been strict Jews and strict proselytes. It was the first delicate internal problem the Church had to face, and it was solved with complete success. Saul and Barnabas did a wonderful year's work. The results are best summed up in St. Luke's own words, the words in which he describes the result and conclusion of their labours. 'Now there was at Antioch, in the Church that was there, a body of prophets and teachers, Barnabas, Symeon (surnamed Niger), and Lucius (he of Cyrene), with Manaën (foster brother of Herod the Tetrarch) and Saul. As these were living a life of priestly service to the Lord and fasting, the Holy Ghost said, Separate me Barnabas and Saul for the work whereunto I have called them. Then they held a special fast and prayed, and laid their hands on them and dismissed them.' There you have, as a result of the Antioch mission, a Church, highly organised, equipped and endowed, living an ordered life of Eucharist, fasting and prayer : and this unity, order and consequent spiritual power were the result of only eighteen months' work among honest and good hearts ready to receive the Word and bring forth fruit with patience.

Between the day Saul landed and the day he was dismissed with all solemnity to make his first missionary journey, four events of great interest happened. The Church became a recognised body with a name, or rather a nickname. Herod Agrippa made a fresh attack on the Church of Jerusalem. The famine became acute in Palestine. And Barnabas and Saul went up to Jerusalem to administer relief to the starving Christians.

Let us take these one by one.

The word Christian was unquestionably given to the Church, not by angry Jews to whom the word Christos was of course sacred, but by amused pagans. I suppose there is no doubt that now for the first time the Church hired a city building for worship and instruction, and in this sort of way attracted the attention of the whole town. The names of some of the leaders too suggest men of consideration. Barnabas himself was a well-to-do and possibly well-known Cypriote ; Lucius (he of Cyrene) was probably a man with a circle of friends, and any new sect to which the foster brother of Herod the Tetrarch joined himself would rouse curiosity. It has often been pointed out that the word Christianus shows the catholicity of the Church ; the idea, ' a disciple of the Anointed One,' is Hebrew, the rendering of the Hebrew idea is Greek, and the form of the word is Latin. It is a

Hebræo-Greco-Latin word, and so bears a striking parallel to the title on the Cross.

The populace soon asked, " Who is the object of worship of this new body ? " And the usual answer was, " A man called Christos." Evidently Christos, not Jesus, was the word most often on the lips of the Church. The populace thought the word was our Lord's proper name, they did not understand that it denoted His office. Had they understood, they would have called us Jesuits instead of Christians ; and at once they made a pun upon the word Christos and turned it into a nickname. The word Christos is very like the word Chrëstos, which means amiable, worthy, often with a touch of ridicule. As soon as the people knew the sort of lives the Christians were living they dubbed them the Chrëstians, the ' awfully pious ' people, the ' goody-goody ' people. Very often in early MSS. and inscriptions the word is not Christianoi but Chrëstianoi. You can imagine the little street boys in Antioch, calling in derision, " Chrëstianos, Chrës-tianos, Chrëstianos ! "

The end of the year found the Church in Antioch busily engaged in collecting alms for the support of the Church in Jerusalem ; it was the middle of a period of bad harvests which more or less affected in different years the whole seaboard of the Mediterranean, and the attention of the Church was drawn to what was impending at Jerusalem by Agabus.

We must not be tempted into a long digression as to the status of the prophets in the earliest Church. In thinking of the earliest Church you have first of all to imagine a whole community of people charged with spiritual force which quickened any natural power they possessed ; psychical phenomena were common, which do not appear when things are at a lower level. Every mission to-day shows something of the same spiritual force, and the phenomena have reappeared in every age of the Church ; but in the earliest days under the impetus of the expectation of the Second Coming they were very plentiful. In various ways the Christians showed themselves to be super-men. Naturally, the gift of Tongues, in which the presence of some altogether inexplicable force was felt, and the gift of Healing, most greatly excited the mass of people ; but, above all, the Apostles valued the gift of Divine Insight which appeared in some who in meditation and contemplation exercised their intellectual gifts in the spiritual sphere. The real gift to the Church of this utterance by Agabus was not the knowledge that the famine was going to happen, but the suggestion which his words evoked that the various parts of the Church should be welded together by the exercise of practical charity. His prediction conveyed a suggestion which had the most blessed results in the history of the early Church.

The prophets became of great importance. They passed from church to church, possessing, more or less, Apostolic authority. Apparently, when they were present, the local ministry of external authority gave way to them. This floating ministry of Apostolic authority ceased in the second century, when it became general for each church to possess an Apostolic ruler. The wandering ministry, so to speak, settled down and became what we should call the bishops of local centres. By the third century, Origen tells us that instances of the truly prophetic gift had become rare ;

but it has not been withdrawn. Let us remember that it waits upon the Church on earth to be heard again, and that all great spiritual teachers possess it in some degree.

If there was any scarcity in the known world, the pressure of it would be sure to be felt in Jerusalem. Like all places of pilgrimage, Jerusalem contained a population vastly larger than the resources of the country could maintain ; when pilgrims for any reason ceased to come, multitudes were thrown out of work ; food must always have been dear there, the transport must always have seriously added to prices. A universal famine would mean horrible straits for Jerusalem, and the Antiochenes prepared a substantial gift. It was not a single collection made in church on Sunday, it was an assessment imposed by common arrangement on the whole congregation in proportion to their individual resources. It took some time to collect, and in the meantime Herod Agrippa I began a fresh persecution.

It was an ill day for the Church when Claudius added to the Tetrarchies of Batanæa Trachonitis, Abilene, Galilee and Peræa, already held by Agrippa under Caligula, the provinces of Judæa and Samaria. At this moment the contemptuous impartiality of Roman rule was the Church's greatest safety ; under the rule of Herod Agrippa I she was in the hands of a profligate religionist, a fervent adherent of Judaism. You remember how emotional the piety of Louis XV appears to be in the biography of Madame Louise of France. Herod Agrippa I, like Louis XV, was a person in whom there was a complete divorce between the religious and the moral senses. He had lived most of his life in Rome, but when

Ft

he was given Judæa he came there and charmed
the Jews by displaying the greatest assiduity in
the obervance of the law and in the exhibition of
external righteousness. With gratifying patriotism he
now attacked the Nazarenes. He had St. James, the
son of Zebedee, beheaded, and the brief line in which
the fact is recorded is a most striking illustration of the
contemptuous way in which the early Church regarded
the terrors of death. In contrast to it is the great
elaborateness with which the story of St. Peter's
Chains is told. Evidently here we have the whole
story without curtailment, as it was told to St. Luke by
St. Peter and by John Mark. Perhaps it has escaped
you that the deliverance took place only a few hours
before the moment fixed for the execution, and that
St. Peter was sleeping quietly. He was allowed to walk
straight up to death, and he looked it unflinchingly in
the face. If you will study the story you will see a
number of parallels in it to the story of St. Peter's
denials and to the story of the resurrection of our
Lord. He and the Church evidently had put the
stories side by side and delighted in the parallels and
contrasts. It is an extraordinarily vivid narrative. The
Bezan Text has an additional touch when, in describing
St. Peter leaving his prison, it adds, ' And they went
down the seven steps into the street.' The number of
the steps is just what an amazed brain would note and
remember, would mechanically count as the man went
down them. Remarkable too is the sense which is
preserved in the narrative that St. Peter was somehow
half in and half out of the body between the time he
was unconsciously sleeping and the time he came to
himself in the street and found himself alone. He had

noted every particular, and yet had somehow all the while been moving in another world. Taking all things into consideration, it is now again considered probable, after the opinion had been scouted for years, that St. Peter was smuggled down to Joppa and sent off to Rome at this point.

It was, I suppose, after this that Barnabas and Saul arrived in Jerusalem to administer relief in the famine. St. Luke suggests by his narrative that they stayed some time and administered the relief themselves ; this would mean a great deal of practical work, transport, storage, distribution. Only the elders are mentioned as having received Barnabas and Saul ; St. Peter, as we have seen, was probably not at Jerusalem, and all the Apostles may have been away, although considering the distress which was going on this seems very unlikely. The explanation probably is that the mission was one to the bodily needs of the Church, an affair for elders and deacons, not for Apostles, and so it is the elders who are spoken of. There is a touch of divine genius about the whole proceeding. The mother Church was now under a deep debt of obligation to the daughter Church, whose career she had been watching with such grave anxiety.

When they returned to Antioch the two friends took with them an interesting companion. The lady Mary, Barnabas' cousin (not, as in our version, his sister), was evidently one of the few wealthy disciples at Jerusalem. It is conjectured that hers was the house with the upper chamber, and hers the villa and oil-press of Gethsemane ; it is also conjectured that the young man who ventured into Gethsemane in his sleeping suit and a wrap, and who, when he was seized

as a disciple, left his wrap and fled in his sleeping suit
was John Mark, her son. Probably she entertained
Barnabas and Paul. Anyhow, they entirely captivated
John Mark. No doubt he had sat by open-mouthed
when Barnabas and Saul told exciting tales of the
work at Antioch. How infinitely preferable, he would
think, to the hum-drum life with his mother at Jerusalem! He persuaded his cousin to take him back to
Antioch, and his mother, glad no doubt to get him
away from a scene of late mostly associated with persecution and famine, let him go. He was a bright, enthusiastic, religious fellow, but no fit companion for Saul,
who at this period of his career must have been a rather
terrifying colleague. To work with Saul must have
been like working with one who had been raised from
the dead, and who possessed a knowledge of the life
behind the veil.

And now it was made clear to the minds of Barnabas
and Saul that they must make a first great sweep of the
Church's net, and it was made clear also to the authorities of the Church of Antioch. Saul was an Apostle
from the moment he had seen the risen Jesus outside
Damascus gate. Barnabas had come down from
Jerusalem commissioned by the Apostles with full
powers. Now, through a prophetic utterance in the
Church, God the Holy Ghost made it clear that Barnabas was also one of His Apostles, that He confirmed
and extended the authority conveyed to Barnabas by the
Twelve. The utterance came, we are told, in the
progress of a solemn service in which, after fasting
and while fasting, the Church exercised her priestly
function. That the central act of this service was the
Holy Eucharist there can, I think, be no manner of

doubt. The Church was now ordered to set apart her two great heads for the work to which they were called, and she obeyed. She instituted a solemn fast, and, after solemnly recognising the Apostolic character and office in her leaders by the imposition of hands, bade them depart in peace. After this, Barnabas and Saul are called Apostles, not because they were consecrated to the office by the laying on of hands at Antioch (St. Paul never appealed to this occasion for his commission ; he always insisted that our Lord Himself had made him an Apostle directly), but because now for the first time the Church formally recognised their Apostolate.

A parallel to this action occurs in the modern Church at an ordination of priests, when the priests who are present lay on hands with the bishop, not as channels of orders, but as conveying the Church's approval of and recognition of the ordination. How important this recognition of his Apostolate was, the events of after years showed to Saul. One of the greatest difficulties of his life was the constant necessity of proving that he was a true Apostle in face of the cavils of the Judaising Christians.

And now let us take our stand on the end of one of the great stone breakwaters of Seleucia. They are there still, and one breakwater is now called Paul and the other Barnabas. They form a long narrow outlet to the small artificial harbour and protect its shipping from the almost perpetual ground swell caused by the currents of wind which descend from the mountains on either side the port and work up the sea — the sea of swelling lapis lazuli with the curious glazed, solid look I have never seen anywhere else — lapis lazuli here and there flecked with snowy foam. Out through the narrow waterway comes a trading vessel under the pilot's care. Among the passengers are three men, none of them of imposing appearance ; one, a youth, looks excited and a little frightened ; of the others, one sits in grave pre-occupation, while his friend who is going home talks to old acquaintances among the merchants on board, and exchanges cheerful greetings with the sailors. And so, the wind freshening, the little ship, now clear of the docks, is caught in the swell and scuds north-west across the sea. Look at her long and hard, for she carries the Gospel of Christ now in the keeping of St. Paul the Apostle, and he is carrying it first to an island which is now governed by the rulers of the British Empire.

So we all embark now together on what Renan calls the Christian Odyssey. ' There had been nothing like this story,' says Renan, ' since Homer. It is so fresh, so inspiriting, it breathes of the sea ; it is the second poem which Christianity had given to the world ; the Lake of Tiberias and its fishing boats had been the first.' Very characteristic, graceful and trivial, and missing the soul of the thing altogether.

We had better finish this chapter with a sketch of the general method of the journeys : in the next we will begin to take the first journey in some detail. Generally speaking, St. Paul travelled by water or on foot; the land travelling being difficult and dangerous, he used the waterways whenever they were at his disposal. Three things determined the course of his journeys. 1. This difficulty of means of transport led to his working up the banks of rivers. 2. He chose places where he could work at his trade. 3. He

followed the path of Jewish emigration. The second
point suggests an interesting query : why did he make
such a point of supporting himself while he recognised
and strongly insisted on the principle that the ministry
should be supported by the Church ? His work must
have taken up a good deal of time ; he did the work
his father's workmen used to do, the rough labour he
had learned for custom's sake as a boy. His insistence
on maintaining himself gave an opening later on for
the insinuation that he did not dare to claim from the
Church the support she gave to a true Apostle. What
was the meaning of it ? I think it lay in St. Paul's
past history. I imagine he refused to allow the Church
to give anything to the murderer of St. Stephen. But
while this probably lay behind, on the surface, as
2 Corinthians shews, his attitude gave the impression
of a delightful little obstinacy ; he reserved to himself
the pleasure, he would say, of giving himself free of
cost to the Church. We can picture their trying to
break down his resolution, and how he shook his head
and persisted, and threw them off with some cheerful
phrase, and declared that he wanted the time his cloth-
weaving gave him for quiet thought, and so remained
master of the situation. His life then was that of a
wandering artisan, but of course we English have to
remember that in other nationalities manual labourers
are often cultured persons. English artisans are among
the least cultured in the world. St. Paul settled
down in a likely spot, worked at his trade and scattered
his ideas. Here the religious and commercial freemasonry of the Jews helped him ; this extraordinary
people, wherever it is properly organised, lives in a
close community in which everybody knows his

neighbour's concerns.   A Jew arriving in a foreign
city at once presented himself to the heads of the
community, and was at once welcomed and admitted
to the circle.

In the Middle Ages there was a long succession of
distinguished Jewish travellers.   Jews had then far
greater facilities of travel than other people, and to-day
the same close organisation still exists among the strict
Jews of Russia, Poland and the East.   St. Paul's programme in a new place never varied, and the regularity
with which the various acts of the drama developed
would have utterly crushed the spirit of anybody else.
He arrives at a city, the Jews give him a warm homelike
reception.   (I emphasise *homelike*, for there lies the
pathos of it.)   He starts his cloth-weaving.   The
Sabbath comes, St. Paul goes to synagogue like a good
Jew, everybody looks at him, everybody whispers that
the newcomer is a great acquisition, so interesting, so
cultivated.   At the end of the service, an official hopes
St. Paul will give them the privilege of hearing him say
a few words.   Paul gets up and begins a sermon on the
hope of Israel, a pleased thrill passes through the
synagogue.   ' It is going to be a Messianic sermon,
how interesting ! '

Then Paul tells the story of Jesus and the Resurrection amid that breathless silence of which the preacher
is only occasionally conscious.   At the end a babel of
voices ;   great curiosity about the supposed resurrection of Jesus ;   much cross-examination about the
evidences ;   much criticism of the argument from the
Old Testament.   In the week following, some live as
if they had never heard the sermon on the previous
Sabbath, others in various attitudes of interest or

criticism, or indignation, keep up a ferment about it. Some are touched and converted, others reject it all and are at first indifferent, then, when they find the preacher is creating a schism, furiously angry. All the old pleasant intercourse is ended, and St. Paul is forbidden the synagogue. He goes on teaching a group of Jews and Gentile proselytes in a private house, the latter bringing in complete outsiders. Gentiles begin to flock to hear him, the little Jewish nucleus is swamped and made socially as uncomfortable as can be. Then the whole place rises in arms against him. His life is in danger, he makes what provision he can for Christian teaching and worship, and has to devise a secret escape, promising to return when the storm is over. He gets into another city and begins to preach in the same way. Very soon he is pursued by Jewish opponents and the synagogues are warned. The Christian news spreads itself, and he finds a knot of inquirers waiting for him. Think of the martyrdom of such a life. He died a hundred deaths before they beheaded him in Rome. ' In deaths oft,' he says, in that defiant battle song of 2 Corinthians in which he sings of his five Jewish scourgings, the three applications of the bastinado, the stoning, the three shipwrecks, the twenty-four hours he was a castaway on the sea, his encounters with brigands, his fording of dangerous rivers, his constant danger from assassination, his ceaseless toil at cloth-weaving and preaching, the cold of winter and of rain, the trouble of having such poor thin clothes, the constant loss of sleep, the constant lack of proper food, and above and beyond all these external things the real, the increasing burden of his life – the care of all the Churches.

CHAPTER VII

A T the end of the last chapter we had despatched
Saul, Barnabas and John Mark to Cyprus.
We had watched the trading ship disappear
over the swelling edge of the lapis lazuli sea, and then
I had said something about the general character of
St. Paul's missionary journeys.

Now we go on to follow the first of them in some
detail. The Apostles landed at Salamis, and after
preaching there worked their way through the island
visiting all the Jewish communities until they reached
Paphos. Up to their arrival at Paphos nothing
occurred to mark a fresh step in the progress of the
Gospel towards the Gentiles. Barnabas, who was at
home in Cyprus and evidently a man of consideration,
was to the fore. Some knowledge of the Gospel had
already reached Cyprus. It had been spread to
Cyprus straight from Jerusalem after the persecution
of St. Stephen. Saul would therefore be regarded by
what disciples were already in Cyprus with immense
curiosity, and it would be natural for him to keep in
the background during the journey through the
island. The Gospel had evidently been presented in
Cyprus after the earlier fashion, which aroused less
opposition among the Jews than the later, and there
seem to have been no disturbances. But Paphos saw
one of the most critical and decisive scenes in the
history of the Church.

In order to understand what happened at Paphos,
you must remember that in those days all interesting
teachers in philosophy and science went on lecturing
tours, as people do to-day in the United States.
Indeed, before a man could get a Chair in Philosophy
at one of the Universities he must have made himself
acceptable as a lecturer in all the chief centres of
thought. Barnabas and Saul arrived in Paphos, their
reputation had evidently preceded them, and their
orations roused great interest in a town which had a
special reason for wishing to think itself cultured. For
the Proconsul of Cyprus had his headquarters at Paphos,
and the Proconsul was a remarkable man, highly educated and deeply interested in science and philosophy.
A Roman Proconsul was surrounded by a larger Court
than a modern Colonial Governor. In our day young
diplomatists begin at the Foreign Office, but in those
days they were at once attached to the train of a
provincial Governor, and picked up their first diplo-
matic knowledge in studying the administration of his
province. The Governor also found posts for his
friends about his person, and if he was a man of culture
he attracted to himself all the interesting and learned
people of the country. In the train of Sergius Paulus
there was a remarkable man. His name was probably
Etoimas Barjesus, but we will use the form with which
we are familiar, Elymas. Those were days, you must
remember, when no distinction was made between
astronomy and astrology, between science and magic,
between chemistry and alchemy ; also they were
days when the Eastern priesthoods possessed occult
powers of a remarkable character. Elymas was a
distinguished magician, deeply learned and with

extraordinary powers. Sir William Ramsay sums him up in the phrase, ' He represented the strongest influence on the human will that existed in the Roman world.' When St. Luke calls him a sorcerer and a false prophet that is what he means ; he does not mean that Elymas was a humbug and a scoundrel. Elymas was probably an extremely able and agreeable person. St. Luke means that in Elymas what spiritual force existed in the natural religions was present in a highly organised and concentrated form. Elymas was the epitome of what the Gospel came to destroy, the epitome of the strongest force against it existing in the world.

Sergius Paulus invited Barnabas and Saul to unfold their views at a gathering of interesting people at the Proconsulate. It was the first entrance of the Gospel into aristocratic Roman society. The invitation was a command and the Apostles obeyed. It was clear that for this occasion they must change places ; it was not the wealthy Cypriote, it was the Roman citizen who was in his proper place in the Proconsul's Court, and it was Paulus, the Roman of Tarsus, who took the lead at the Proconsul's gathering. The subject the Proconsul wished Paul to expound was the nature of God and His relation to human beings. Paul began ; the Proconsul was a sensitive, and he became growingly conscious that he was in the presence of a new spiritual force. The colossal, consecrated, sanctified, disciplined personality of Paul laid its spell upon him, and drew out of the polite crowd the only personality there worthy to cross swords with it, the personality of Elymas. It became a tremendous duel. Every power that the magician possessed arrayed itself against the

Gospel. He was a Jew by birth, versed no doubt in the Scriptures, and he fought the Gospel point by point. It was an extraordinarily dramatic conflict between Christ and Anti-Christ fighting for Paganism with Jewish weapons, and 'the strongest influence on the human will that existed in the Roman world' was soon struggling for its life in the drawing-room of the Governor's Palace. For this the penitence at Damascus, for this the two-year fast in Arabia, for this the eight or ten years' discipline and silence at Tarsus, for this the patient devoted mission work in Antioch. An extraordinary spiritual force possessed and issued from Paul. Through him our Lord worked on Elymas the sign He had worked on Paul at Damascus, and the narrative says, with the graphic touch of an eye witness, that the man went about seeking some to lead him by the hand. There was a paralysed silence in the room amid which he groped for help, none daring to touch him. The Great War has supplied us with instances of the temporary loss of eyesight from shock.

Sergius Paulus, says the Bezan Text, marvelled and believed God. I doubt whether that means that he accepted the Christian religion, in fact, I do not suppose the Apostles thought of offering him the Christian religion. But they had made a great demonstration of it before the aristocratic Roman world, and they had done all that they attempted to do ; they had won the battle, and remained in the eyes of Sergius Paulus and his circle masters of the situation.

But far more important than the effect which this scene produced on Sergius Paulus and his Court was the effect it produced on the Apostles themselves.

Our Lord, in the person of Paul, had seemed to lay claim to the whole Roman Empire. The Apostles had actually experienced the fact that they wielded a power able to conquer all that Elymas and Sergius Paulus, and that glittering circle of courtiers, men of letters and sycophants stood for. The Gospel had demonstrated its catholicity.

But it was desirable that they should leave Cyprus at once. The friends of Elymas would be powerful and unscrupulous. They took the first available ship. I think it probable that they landed at Perga on the coast of Asia Minor, not because they wanted to go to Pamphylia (when they got there they did not preach there), but because the first available ship was bound for Perga, and it was not safe to delay a moment. In acting thus they were obeying our Lord's precise injunctions to avoid martyrdom as long as they possibly could. It was, of course, the duty of the first disciples not to witness to the Faith with their lives if they could possibly help it. They had to remain alive as long as possible, and their great problem was how to combine unflinching courage and candour with adroitness and prudence. At a later period another great Saint had a similar duty – St. Athanasius, when he held the Faith in his hands and stood *contra mundum* ; and the story of his escapes is like a boy's book of adventure.

When the Apostles had landed at Perga and recovered their breath they said to each other, " What next ? " One thing was clear, they were the Missionaries of the Roman Empire, and so henceforth they must change places and Saul – the Roman citizen and henceforth to be known as *Paul* – must lead. And whither will Paul lead his friends ? Now about this there is a good deal of fresh evidence derived from two sources. First, from the discovery that the Epistle to the Galatians was most likely addressed to the Churches St. Paul founded on his first missionary journey, and that therefore its historical notes refer to this time ; and secondly, from our increased knowledge of the condition of all this country at that period through the researches of archæologists.

The facts are probably these. St. Paul seems to have said, " We will go to Ephesus and preach there, and from Ephesus we will go to Rome." There was no ship sailing from Perga to Ephesus at the time – there are periods in the year when the continuous north wind makes it very difficult to sail up that coast – so they decided to push across the country to Antioch, the Antioch which lay in Phrygia close to the Pisidian border, and there join the great trade route from the East to Ephesus. This new and exceedingly startling programme upset John Mark, who belonged, of course, to the more conservative Jerusalem type of Christian, and he went back to his mother's home at Jerusalem. Paul and Barnabas then made their rapid cross-country journey to Pisidian Antioch, and there all their plans were upset by Paul becoming seriously ill. This illness, which was either acute ophthalmia, or more probably malaria, with ague and dysentery, kept them for some time at Antioch. During his convalescence, in which he met with great kindness, Paul laid the foundation of the Church of Antioch, and for the rest of that journey had to content himself with the modest semi-circle of towns, Iconium, Lystra and Derbe.

That sounds, I know, like a series of unproved assumptions, and it is of course to a certain extent a hypothetical synthesis ; but this synthesis is the result of the long reflection of several learned people, and it seems to explain the facts as we now know them better than any other ; though, of course, some further discovery may upset it again. I won't take you through all the argument for this view, but I will note some of its points. When Paul and Barnabas decided to go straight across from Perga to Pisidian Antioch up country and over the Taurus they were attempting a difficult and dangerous journey, for it was not a recognised route and the Taurus was infested by brigands. It is therefore possible that St. Mark's nerve merely gave way, but if so, it is very unlikely St. Luke would have recorded it. St. Luke is an elaborate historian, everything he says has a point, and this reference to the return of St. Mark is most probably a very delicate reference to a divergence of view. That is the first point.

Well then, nobody would naturally go to Pisidian Antioch this way, and the Apostles evidently did not choose the route for Evangelistic purposes, because they did not preach on the way up : they took it as the most expeditious way of getting to Pisidian Antioch. That means that they wanted to get there very much, either in order to stay there or because it led to somewhere else. Now comes in the evidence of the Epistle to the Galatians. According to the Epistle to the Galatians it was only illness which kept them at Antioch ; they had meant to push on somewhere else ; and our knowledge of the topography shows that that big objective could only have been Ephesus ; and Ephesus was the starting point to Rome for all the East.

I ought to say a word more about the Epistle to the Galatians before going on. Who were the Galatians? Like some of ourselves they were Celts, who made a great invasion of Southern Europe three centuries before our Lord. A great body of these turbulent fighters crossed to Asia Minor, which they plundered right and left for fifty years. Then Attalus, King of Pergamum, fought them until he forced them to settle in a tract of country at the north of the great central plateau. Here they lived in three clans round the cities of Ancyra, Tavium and Pessinus, a bit of country which was consequently called Galatia. They continued very tiresome until the Romans, in the course of their universal conquests, suppressed them in 189 B.C. About a century before our Lord, Augustus allowed one of their princes, Amyntas, to govern a large kingdom comprising Galatia proper and a great deal to the south and west of it. When Amyntas died, this was reorganised as a Roman province and called the Province of Galatia, so that in St. Paul's day the word Galatia was being used in two ways : there was the original little old Galatia where the Celts had first settled, and there was the big Roman province of Galatia made out of the kingdom of Amyntas, of which the little old Galatia was only the north-east corner. You see the question : To which Galatia did St. Paul write his Epistle, the old mountain district of the clans, or the big Roman province in which lay Antioch Iconium, Lystra and Derbe ? Bishop Lightfoot held it to be the first, although there is no record of St. Paul ever having been there. Since his day most scholars have been converted to the belief that it is the second, and that the Churches whose tendency to relapse into

GT

Judaism gave him such keen anguish were these first begotten Churches of his, the Churchès of the first missionary journey.

Pisidian Antioch, really a Phrygian city on the borders of Pisidia, stood on the lofty range of the Sultan Dagh, 3,600 feet above the sea. It was a purely Roman garrison town — as much so as one of the big Siberian cities is a Russian town — and the cross-country route to it was rendered unusually dangerous just then from the fact that the authorities were taking strong measures to suppress the brigands with whom the whole mountain region was infested. There was a great and influential Jewish colony there. We have no record of the journey, but it is very probable that it involved some of the perils catalogued in 2 Corinthians xi.; at any rate it is now clear that after travelling rapidly through hot, malarious Pamphylia, St. Paul became violently ill. Further travelling was impossible, but further work was not. Notwithstanding the fact that he was so ill as to be an object for ridicule and con-tempt, he went with Barnabas on the Sabbath day into the synagogue at Pisidian Antioch and sat down. At the end of the service the rulers, according to courteous custom, invited the stranger to speak. I suppose every-one thought that the placid, serene, healthy Barnabas would speak. But no. The shrunken, fever-stricken, palsied little figure got up and mounted the platform ; there was apparently a buzz of surprise and amusement, for he made a gesture with his hand, evidently so sharp and authoritative as to get their sudden attention. Then he spoke. At last he came to his great warning. ' Beware, therefore, lest that come upon you which is spoken by the prophets. Behold, ye despisers, and wonder and perish, for I work a work in your days. A work which ye shall in no wise believe, if one declare it unto you.' The Bezan text adds, ' He became silent.' He made a profound impression. The Apostles did not stay for the usual questions and discussion, probably St. Paul was too ill ; but as they left the synagogue many sympathetic whispers reached them begging that they would continue this exposition on the following Sabbath. During the next few days there was much happy work, Jews and God-fearing proselytes (whose status I have already described) crowding the lodging of the Apostles. But much more than this, something caught the attention of the whole city. It was, as I have said, a typical Roman outpost, and I suppose the local religion was less strong there than in a native city like Iconium ; there may have been more wistful people hungering for a religion which would satisfy. But I cannot help wondering whether the ' something ' may not have been the ' stake in the flesh,' the illness, whatever it was, from which St. Paul was suffering. There is no doubt that it was something very conspicuous, and that the very greatest possible kindness was shown to him while he was in a state of physical disability which might have moved rough people to contempt. However that may be, a really astounding thing happened on the next Sabbath, when the whole world of Pisidian Antioch crowded the synagogue, as the Bezan Text says very truthfully, to hear Paul.

It goes on to say that Paul spoke at great length about the Lord. On the previous Sabbath he had preached on the history of the Jews, a preparation for the coming of the Christ, on the fulfilment of the

Messianic hope in the Death and Resurrection, and on the condition of the forgiveness of sins. It was his own edition of St. Stephen's Gospel, and, of course, all on Jewish lines of thought.

Now, in the presence of the immense Gentile crowd, not, remember, God-fearing proselytes, but sheer Pagans who had never entered a synagogue before, *he spoke at great length about the Lord*, by which I understand that he told the story of Jesus as we have it in the Gospels. A sense of enormous sympathy and response filled the atmosphere, and the Jews saw the middle wall of partition crumbling to pieces before their eyes.

Well, I really cannot think they will be severely judged at the last day ; it was enormously difficult for them ; the two strangers were subverting everything they held most sacred ; if these men remained and preached, all the sacred separation of Judaism would be gone. They repudiated Paul and all that he said ; their best controversialists denied the possibility of such a Messiah. Anti-Christ stood now embodied in the representatives of the chosen people, as he had stood at Paphos embodied in the representative of the natural religions. It was another turning point in history, and Paul and Barnabas turned to the Gentiles who stood breathless and open-mouthed at this extraordinary scene. My heart always goes out at this point, not so much to the marvellous St. Paul, transfigured by the Holy Ghost, and lifted right above the storm and stress on the wings of the Spirit, as to the dear St. Barnabas. It is impossible to over-praise the nobility, the Christian perfectness, of his fidelity to the great companion whom the Holy Ghost had put over his head, and who had led him into adventurous paths he would, I suppose, have never followed on his own initiative.

At last you see we have come to the gathering in of the first fruits of the Gentiles proper. Now for the first time the Gospel is offered to men who had had nothing whatever of preliminary contact with the teaching of the synagogue. It comes about, you will observe, in a typically Roman town, and the whole story of the preaching at Antioch would further convince St. Paul that at the moment the best hope of spreading the Gospel lay in the Roman world proper, and that the native populations, fiercely attached to their rude local cults, would be much less accessible than their powerful cultured masters who had realised that the world at that moment held no religion worth their acceptance, save one which in some ways curiously resembled certain aspects of Christianity, the religion of Mithras.

You must realise the extreme violence of the situation which had been created at Pisidian Antioch. St. Paul was at his weakest, physically, but spiritually he was at his strongest and most persuasive. Out of the Gentile mob there advanced towards the Church, as it were, a procession of souls ordained to eternal life. St. Luke can really find no other word. Their external note was joy ; they glorified God ; they were glad ; they were filled with the Holy Ghost. There and then they broke silence in the synagogue, and actually the same building resounded with the shouts of Jewish hatred and of Gentile praise, while between the two stood Paul racked with the pain of acute illness.

The weeks that followed were marked by the same

extraordinary contrasts. The new Church was in a
state of abiding bliss, the devotion of the converts to
St. Paul knew no bounds. They received him as an
Angel of God, they tenderly ministered to his sickness,
if they could they would have dug out their eyes and
given them to him. On the other hand he was still
subject to the jurisdiction of the Synagogue, although
he no longer went to its meetings. The Bezan Text
says the Apostles endured great afflictions and persecution. In 2 Timothy the writer recalls it : 'Thou hast
fully known the persecutions, afflictions which came
unto me at Antioch, at Iconium, at Lystra : what
persecutions I endured, but out of them all the Lord
delivered me.' No doubt at Antioch he was scourged
by the Synagogue, the first of the five times when he
received forty stripes save one.

But the Gospel spread throughout the region, and
the Synagogue was able to represent to the authorities
that Paul was a disturber of the public peace. The
Jews worked on them through the influence of the
aristocratic ladies attached to the Synagogue : another
Roman touch ; in a typical Oriental city this could
hardly have been. Ultimately, the Apostles were seized
by the coolly tolerant Roman power, always difficult to
move in such matters, and in all probability before
their expulsion from the city Paul was bastinadoed by
the lictors. He was three times bastinadoed before the
year 56, and it is conjectured that Antioch and Lystra
were the first two places, and that Philippi was the
third. This is estimated by considering that the Roman
Governors he met were favourable to him, that he was
therefore probably bastinadoed by the order of local
magistrates where there was no governor, that only

some of these magistrates had lictors, and that those of Antioch and Lystra had. But the strength of the love of the Church protected the Apostles and saved their lives, and they were merely put over the city border. As they crossed it they solemnly condemned the act of inhospitality, uttering against it the sentence of the Church, and went on to Iconium. And notwithstanding all the violence and suffering, they left behind them in Antioch a Church filled with joy and with the Holy Ghost, in the heart of which stood One greater than Paul.

CHAPTER VIII

Iconium was a city on the borders of Lycaonia, eighty-five miles away from Antioch in Pisidia. For the facts of the visit to Iconium we have an extraordinarily interesting new body of evidence in the recovered *Acts of Paul and Thecla* ; and I think the best plan will be to say a word about the *Acts of Paul and Thecla*, and then, without narrating the whole tale of the *Acts* as it exists in the extant document, use what is now considered to be the original and true form of the tale in our study of the work at Iconium.

According to Tertullian, who, as you remember, was a great African writer of the end of the second and beginning of the third century, the *Acts of Paul and Thecla* were put together by a presbyter of Asia out of love for St. Paul ; and as a punishment for his presumption in so doing the presbyter was degraded from his office. But of late years the presbyter's tale has been subject to critical examination, and it has been discovered that it cannot possibly be mere invention on the part of the presbyter ; Tertullian says he *compiled* it. Sir William Ramsay has pointed out a number of historical and local details in the story which could only occur in a contemporary document. The tradition too is universal in the East, and the Peak of St. Thecla is a feature in the landscape of Iconium. In fact, the reason the presbyter was so severely punished was that he had manipulated a true story for his own purpose,

which appears to have been to get St. Paul's authority
for what he believed to be true about the life of vir-
ginity. These *Acts* as they stand are a great glorification
of the virgin life.   I cannot stay to go through the
critical examination of the document and explain to you
why parts are felt to be genuine and parts not – you
will find this all most elaborately done in Sir William
Ramsay's *Church in the Roman Empire* (pp. 375–428).
I will merely as we go on introduce into the narrative
what is now thought to be true.

When the Apostles pursued their journey, after
pausing on the outskirts of Antioch to register solemnly
the fact that Antioch as a city had rejected the Gospel,
they took the Via Regalis, the splendid Imperial road
which had been made to join the Roman city of
Antioch to the Roman city of Lystra. This road runs
along the face of the range which is called the Sultan
Dagh, very much as the road from Assisi to Trevi
runs along the mountain range past Spello and Spoleto
and Terni to the end of the hills. The Via Regalis ran
through the new city which was growing up, Neapolis,
and on to Misthia on the shores of the big lake Karalis.
Here the mountain range ran down into a gap, and
through this gap a country road led from the grand
Imperial road to Iconium fifty miles away to the east.
At this juncture of the roads, according to the earliest
Paul and Thecla story, the Apostles found a friend.
A certain just man of Iconium had been warned in a
dream of the coming of the Apostles, and had travelled
all this great distance to meet them ; he is called
Onesiphorus in the present text ; that is thought to
be an addition, but it will be convenient to call him
Onesiphorus. Onesiphorus scanned the passers by –

the travellers to Lystra by the Royal road, and at last
he saw Paul coming – a small man with meeting eye-
brows and a rather long nose, bald-headed, bow-legged,
strongly built and full of grace, because, the account
says, at times he looked like a man, and at times he
looked like an angel. Happy in the possession of this
new-found friend, the Apostles now took the easy hill
route to Iconium.

Iconium is 3,370 feet above the sea, and its situation
is strikingly like the situation of Damascus. Both
cities lie sheltered by a mountain mass from the west,
and with illimitable plains stretching eastward, out of
which isolated mountains rise like islands ; in both
cases too the plains are barren, and the cities themselves
exquisitely luxuriant, watered by streams which issue
from the hills and ultimately lose themselves in lakes on
the distant plain.

Iconium was a Phrygian city in the extremest corner
of Phrygia. Lying as it did at the beginning of the
great Lycaonian plain, the world in general thought of
it as one of the Lycaonian cities ; but it was not ; and
it is a recently recognised proof of St. Luke's extraordinary accuracy that he speaks like an Iconian when
he says that St. Paul and St. Barnabas fled from there
to the cities of Lycaonia.

Iconium was very proud of itself. It insisted that it
had been there before the Flood, and that it was the
first city that had been rebuilt after the Flood. Greek
colonists had Grecised its legends, and one of the
traditions of the origin of its name which comes from
the Greek Eikon, an image or likeness, is that Prome-
theus made clay images there after the Flood to take
the place of the people who had been drowned. Another

is that Perseus had brought to Iconium the head
of Medusa on his shield, and that it is the head of
Medusa which the name commemorates. Iconium
was not a Roman city like Antioch, it was a Phrygian
city intensely devoted to Rome. It had not long before,
in a spasm of enthusiastic loyalty, accepted the name
Claud-Iconium in honour of the Emperor Claudius,
which is as if Toronto were by a decree of the legisla-
ture to rename itself Georgian Toronto. It held itself
haughtily aloof from the neighbouring cities of Lycaonia,
and there was some sharp borderland feeling about.

Such was the city to which "Onesiphorus" brought
the Apostles. According to the story, he installed them
in his house, and later on, when the Iconian Church
was formed, this house became the meeting place of
the Christian Ecclesia. The Apostles met with a great
success at Iconium ; the Gentiles did not invade the
synagogue and precipitate a conflict as at Antioch ;
and a great multitude both of Jews and of Greeks, that
is to say proselytes attached to the Synagogue, believed;
but the door had now been thrown open to the Gentiles,
and when it was gradually found that the Apostles
were receiving people who had had no previous contact
with the Synagogue, the trouble began again.

At Antioch the Synagogue had worked upon the
authorities through a group of devout aristocratic
ladies, but I gather that the purely Gentile movement
towards the Gospel was less widespread at first at
Iconium, and the Jewish rulers were able to stir up the
Gentile mob. There was a disturbance and some persecution, but, the Bezan Text adds, the Lord quickly
gave peace.

The Apostles now settled down to a long mission,

and laid the foundation of a devoted Church in which many of the signs of the Holy Ghost were apparent ; there were signs and wonders, and gradually a portion of the population became deeply moved. It is thought that the story of Thecla illustrates what happened often, when simple and naturally devout souls among the Gentiles laid hold of the word of God ; and that it explains some part of the deep resentment which the Christian teaching at once aroused. Let me now tell it. When Paul and Barnabas were finally separated from the Synagogue, the house of Onesiphorus became the scene of organised Christian worship, with, as the narrative says, Bending of the Knees and Breaking of Bread. In an adjoining house lived a wealthy and noble Iconian family. Their mansion overlooked the more modest house of Onesiphorus, and the chamber of one of the daughters was so placed that, sitting in her window, she was able to hear what St. Paul said. She was converted, and became completely fascinated by St. Paul. She gave up all her ordinary pursuits, and her mind gradually got alienated from the thought of marriage, for she was betrothed to the son of another wealthy house. Both families were in despair, the girl was plainly bewitched, and they set themselves to watch the ministry of Paul.

It seemed as though all the women and young people in the city were seeking personal interviews with Paul. It was a continuous stream. Thecla's lover watched the house and reported a constant succession of men visitors also. It is probable that Paul's preaching of social purity was misunderstood to mean a prohibition of marriage ; certainly it cut at a good deal that was customary in Iconium, and it

was complained that he interfered with the privacy of
family life.   At length they managed to stir up the
authorities, who imprisoned Paul on the charge of
influencing people by magical arts and causing
disorders in the city.   But Thecla was not daunted :
her story is curiously like the story of St. Clare.   At
night she bribed the porter at her father's palace, by
giving him her bracelets, to let her out.   She went to
the prison, and by giving the gaoler a silver mirror she
persuaded him to let her see Paul.   St. Paul proceeded
to give her a long and complete instruction in the
Christian religion, which had not concluded when she
was found still sitting at his feet by her mother and her
lover, and carried back to her own home, where, by
means of kindness and persuasion, they hoped to be
able in time to break the spell.   It was found impossible to substantiate a charge against Paul, but he was
scourged, and he was told that he and his companion
must leave the city.   Their enemies prepared a riotous
attack on them, and in the end the Apostles only just
escaped in time.   They fled to Lystra, not probably so
much with the intention of evangelising Lystra as of
waiting there for perhaps a year until the storm had
blown over and fresh magistrates had been appointed,
when they meant to return and strengthen the
organisation of the devoted and enthusiastic Iconian
Church.   Well, that is the story of Thecla in so far as
it affects St. Paul.   As I say, what I have given you is
supposed to be contemporary narrative, and to be the
true basis of the much more elaborate *Acts* ; and
whether true in detail or not there is no doubt that it
vividly describes the sort of incidents which accompanied St. Paul's mission to the Gentiles.

But you will like to hear what is considered to be the remainder of the original story. Thecla remained immovable. Every art was practised to try to make her forget Paul, but in vain. Having failed by kindness they tried severity. They brought her before the magistrates, who threatened to punish her if she would not give up her fixed idea and marry her betrothed. She still remained obdurate. Then they arranged that she should be allowed to escape, and after she had gone some way along the plains that she should be pursued and captured by her lover, who should carry her off to his house and wed her by force, with the hope that compulsory marriage might break the spell. She fled and was caught, and here the story halts, for we only know that she prayed vehemently and was in some way delivered. After painful wanderings poor Thecla reached Antioch searching for Paul, who, as we know, had turned when he reached the Via Regalis to the left instead of the right, and had gone to Lystra.

Unfortunately for Thecla, a great Festival was beginning as she entered the city, and the beautiful high-born girl had to face the big ribald crowds. A girl of her appearance unattended in an Eastern town of that period could not possibly be supposed to be respectable, and the President of the Festival, when he met her, offered her insult. Thecla protested that she was consecrated to the service of the great God – the position of a virgin devotee was understood by the people – but the President did not believe her, and Thecla, with the athletic energy so often displayed by Virgin Martyrs, tore his robe and pulled off his official head-dress. The President ordered his officials to arrest her. Thecla cried to Paul, begging him to help her ; but St. Paul, of course, was at Lystra.

Thecla was at once brought before the authorities, and her trial was an incident of the Festival. She was tried before all the spectators. She was charged with sacrilege ; she had assaulted the President and High Priest of the district while wearing his official head-dress. Thecla admitted the crime, and she was condemned to be exposed to the wild beasts who were to be displayed towards the end of the Festival. The whole city became divided over the case of Thecla. The women took her side violently, asserting that as a virgin devoted to the God she must be protected, even though she had knocked off the head-dress of the high priest ; and the greatest lady present, Queen Try-phæna, came forward to protect Thecla. Queen Tryphæna, who at this time was sixty years of age, was the mother of the King of Pontus. She did not get on very well with her son and was living just then in retirement at Antioch. Queen Tryphæna went bail for Thecla and took her to her own house. At last the day for the opening of the games arrived. It began with a procession of the wild beasts, and Thecla, who had meanwhile been living the life of a young lady in a palace, was put on top of a cage which contained a lioness and paraded through the city. The lioness, however, was amiable ; she put her tongue through the bars of the cage and licked the soles of Thecla's feet. After the procession Thecla returned to the charge of Tryphæna, to spend her last night on earth. That night Tryphæna dreamed ; her dead daughter appeared to her and told her to take Thecla to be her daughter. In the morning Tryphæna refused to give

Thecla up, until a posse of soldiers arrived to use force, and then Tryphæna took her by the hand, and, followed by all her household, led her to the stadium.

In the stadium the feeling of the people had partly changed. The men now wanted the spectacle, but the women still championed Thecla. A great body of women sarcastically cried to the Governor bidding them take them all and do likewise with them. Presently Thecla, who had been stript and bound with a cincture, was brought into the arena. She was fastened to a stake, and then she prayed, and the prayer given is thought to be genuine :

" My Lord and my God, the Father of our Lord Jesus the Messiah, Thou art the helper of the persecuted, and Thou art the Companion of the poor, behold Thy handmaiden, for lo, my shame is uncovered, and I stand in the midst of all this people. My Lord and my God, remember Thy handmaiden in this hour."

Then the bars were flung down, and the lioness bounced into the arena and went up to Thecla, but she recognised her and did her no harm ; they had made friends during the procession through the city. As nothing could be made of the lioness they turned a bear into the arena, but the lioness, who was spoiling for a fight, promptly attacked the bear, and Thecla remained unmolested. The President then proposed she should be torn asunder by being tied to two bulls, and this was arranged, but just as the preparations were completed Queen Tryphæna fainted dead away. By this time the people, all the while a little uncomfortable lest Thecla should be really a Virgin Votary under the protection of the Father God, had grown seriously alarmed. The release of the prisoner was demanded, and the authorities, with a great air of magnanimity, released Thecla to the people and commanded that she should be given her clothes again. She returned home with Tryphæna and converted her and her household to a very simple embryo Christianity. It is thought that St. Ignatius refers to the story in the Epistle to the Romans in the beginning of the second century, and it really seems likely that something on these lines happened as a result of the Iconium mission.

Meanwhile, St. Paul and St. Barnabas had reached Lystra. Lystra, now called Khatyn-Serai, the Lady's Mansion, lies in a secluded, well-watered, gently sloping valley. It is surrounded even to-day by foliage, and is an ideal spot for those who, like all Easterns, love quiet gardens and flowing streams. It is, and always has been, a quiet rustic town with nothing cosmopolitan about it. There seems no doubt that the Apostles went there really to be quiet until the storm at Iconium blew over ; they would probably not have gone farther if things had remained quiet at Lystra. There was no Synagogue at Lystra, and therefore, of course, very few Jews ; but among the Jews there was one delightful family, and with this family the Apostles probably stayed. It was a tiny family of those true believers who waited for the consolation of Israel. Only three people : an old lady, Lois, her daughter, Eunice, and her grandson, then a lad, Timotheus. St. Paul evidently soon won the heart and the imagination of the boy Timotheus. He was a gentle, innocent, very religious lad, a little over-sensitive and girlish, as might be anticipated. The example and companionship of St. Paul must have been infinitely

Hт

bracing and exciting to the boy, who, in the absence of a
Jewish environment, had been closely confined to the
atmosphere of amiable piety, which Lois and Eunice
breathed.   Paul grew to love Timothy with the tenderness of a great, strong nature for a gentle clinging one ;
but neither of them could have dreamt in these first
moments of association that a day would come when
Paul would lay his hands on Timothy and commit to
him the abiding elements of the Apostolic office.

St. Paul and St. Barnabas did not rest during their
detention at Lystra, but moved about among the
country folk and preached to them.   These people
apparently understood Greek, very much as the
people in Welsh Wales understand English ; they
could understand what St. Paul said, but their intimate
domestic language and the language of their religious
emotion was Lycaonian, which neither St. Paul nor
St. Barnabas understood.   The Apostles impressed the
Lystrians greatly, for the strength of their consecrated
personalities would find little direct antagonism in these
simple country folk, and all went happily and well until
the visit to Lystra came violently to an end in a tremendous crisis.   Before the gates of the town stood the
most venerated Temple in Lystra – the town had
probably been built in the vicinity of the shrine – the
Temple of Zeus-before-the-Gate.   As you know, the
gate of an Eastern city is always a halting and a
gossiping place, and when the principal building in the
neighbourhood is situated there, it would be more than
usually a place of meeting.   Now, apparently at the
entrance of the Temple of Zeus-before-the Gate a well-
known Lystrian beggar had his pitch.   The man was
a God-fearing proselyte, and as Paul preached to the

crowd in the space by the Temple and the gate he
became more and more conscious of the devout attention of the beggar.   At last there came a day when
Lystra was crowded by the peasantry, probably for a
great religious Feast and Fair.   It was such a scene as
you can still see all over Europe to-day.   As Paul
preached the air became more and more electric, and
the passionate adhesion of the lame beggar, who was
quite hopelessly crippled (St. Luke emphasises this
three times), became more and more apparent to Paul.
At some supreme moment of appeal he turned suddenly
upon the man, and concentrating himself upon him,
shouted in trumpet tones, " Stand upright on thy
feet," and the man sprang to his feet and stood upright
and strong before the crowd.

There was a babel of Lycaonian ecstasy ; all was
plain.   Zeus had himself visited his faithful people ;
the tall, majestic, silent stranger was, of course, Zeus,
and this energetic little man who did all the talking
and acting was Hermes, the God's messenger.   Zeus
had healed the beggar at his Temple door on this great
festal day.   The droll part of the story is that St. Paul
and St. Barnabas were blissfully ignorant of what was
going on ; they were probably occupied with the
recovered beggar, taking care that he was not killed
by the curiosity of the crowd.   But when they were
once more quietly in their lodging some messenger
rushed in and told them that the Priest of Zeus-
before-the-Gate had brought the sacrificial animals,
which had probably been already prepared for the
Festival, and was just about to offer them on the spot
where the miracle had been worked.

Here the human element in the Apostles manifested

itself. They were quite incapable of making quiet explanations, all their Jewish horror of idolatry waking up ; they rushed out of the city tearing their clothes in two, as witness against the abomination which was about to happen, and springing into the middle of the solemnity they stopped it with cries of horror. " We are not gods," cried St. Paul, " we are Evangelists, men bringing good tidings from the only true God, about whom you can learn nothing from these temples and ceremonies, which are all merely human notions ; the witness to the real God lies in the loveliness and fruitfulness of the world, those blessings for which you gather together to give thanks in these mistaken ways."

St. Paul stopped the sacrifice, but he left a puzzled, sore and sullen mob, quite ready to listen to Jews who, in the days which followed, came from Antioch and Iconium, and told the people that these men were dangerous sorcerers and impostors. There was a riot and a successful attack on St. Paul. They succeeded, as they believed, in stoning him to death, though as a matter of fact he was only badly stunned and insensible ; they took what they thought was his dead body to the gate, and probably threw it down in revenge on the spot where he had cured the beggar and stopped the sacrifice.

When night had fallen, so the Bezan Text says, Barnabas, Lois, Eunice, Timothy and others crept to the spot. It was the scene of Stephen's martyrdom again, and the devout men came to carry Paul to his burial. They found him living ; he rose to his feet and re-entered the city, and the next day he went thirty miles to Derbe. Such are the powers of the Grace of God,

CHAPTER IX

WITH the terrifying scene at Lystra, from which St. Paul escaped alive as by a miracle, the more dramatic incidents of his first missionary journey end. The Apostles escaped to Derbe, a small borderland town 30 miles to the south-east, and waited there until the turn of the year brought a change in the civic officers at Lystra, Iconium and Antioch. During this time they preached a mission to the whole town, and had a more peaceful and complete success there than in any other place. Being a frontier town, the Roman organisation and discipline were probably very good. Derbe was on the high road from Iconium to the Cilician Gates, the pass through the Taurus to Tarsus, which lay only 160 miles away. St. Paul must have looked wistfully along the road, but it was necessary to return over the ground and consolidate what had been done. On the return journey their work was purely domestic to the new-made Churches. Public preaching was impossible in Lystra, Iconium and Antioch. Their work is described under three heads : they established the new disciples in the faith, giving them a clear-cut body of doctrine to maintain and defend ; they instructed them as to the inevitableness of persecution – quite deliberately preparing them for martyrdom – and they gave each Church its local ministry.

Here for the first time – and the pathos of it will

strike you if you think – here for the first time St. Luke suddenly uses the first person, relapsing again directly into the third : ' And that through many tribulations we must enter into the Kingdom of God.' It is thought that this sudden use of the ' we ' means that the Church, and he with the Church, was suffering persecution at the time that he was compiling the Acts.

At this time the evidence seems to show that the ordination of presbyters was on the following lines. First, the body of brethren elected the presbyters and presented them to the Apostles, who retained the power of refusal. The presentation was made at a public service which had been preceded by a fast, and then with prayer the Apostles laid on hands. The Eucharist no doubt formed part of the service, and was placed in close juxtaposition to the ordination. Notice how, in the Apostolic age, a fasting condition of body was held to be not merely fitting, but spiritually necessary for any great critical function of the Church. And this would, of course, be a real fast, not merely arranging to have the service just before breakfast. The mind and spirit were prepared for the effort they were about to make by being given complete control over a body rendered more than usually submissive by the discipline of fasting. The New Testament suggests that fasting is an important element in the worship of the Church, that it is more than a fitting custom and more than obedience to an œcumenical custom. The spiritual force generated and diffused at the solemn Eucharist would not be what it is if the celebrant had celebrated after satisfying his body with a meal.

The account of the return visit to these Churches

suggests enthusiastic and moving scenes.   The converts and their teachers had grown touchingly attached
to each other, and the Epistle to the Galatians gains a
new interest and pathos for us when we remember that
it was evoked by the fact that these children of St.
Paul, his first begotten in the Lord, were lapsing from
the Catholic gospel into the Judaic Christianity which
was the reduced Christianity of that day.

From Pisidian Antioch the Apostles recrossed
Pamphilia to Perga, where they preached until the
sailing season drew to a close ; then, taking ship at
Attalia, the port of Perga, they set sail for the Orontes
and the Syrian Antioch, which they had left eighteen
months before.   The Church gave them a great
reception, and in a full assembly the Apostles told the
story of their first missionary journey.   At Antioch
they now re-established themselves and began to face
a great crisis in the Church.

The question at issue was this : St. Paul and St.
Barnabas had made the Church Catholic.   Had they
done so at the price of her unity ?   Were Jew and
Gentile to be distinguished within the Church ?   And
if not, should Jew give way to Gentile or Gentile give
way to Jew ?   In order to do justice to the difficulty we
must look at it, not from the point of view of St. Paul,
but from the point of view of the Church of Jerusalem.
All the first disciples were Jews, and they continued to
observe the law as St. Paul himself did.   So completely had abstinence from unclean meat, the keeping
of the Sabbath, and the separation from Gentile un-
cleanness symbolised in the rite of circumcision become
interwoven with what was best in their lives that it
really seemed impossible to abandon such practices.

The more truly they became God's chosen people by accepting their deliverance from sin through His Son their Messiah, the more truly did such observances befit their state. All that was strong, true, beautiful in Judaism had laid fast hold on their lives. Messiah had come not to destroy the law but to fulfil it. Cannot you imagine the fresh joy with which the best Jewish Christians entered into all the symbolism of their religion, giving something of a retrospective character to the sacrifices, and for the rest filling out the external forms of religion with a new spiritual force and meaning ?

Our Lord had not announced the abolition of the law : He had said that not one jot or one tittle of it was to pass away. Armed with such a dictum as that, the Jewish Christians had, they thought, an invincible weapon. Yet in the power of the Holy Ghost a situation had developed which plainly threw all this into jeopardy.

You remember the stages by which it had been reached.

1. The twelve appoint to an office in the Church Nicolas of Antioch, a circumcised proselyte.

2. The preaching of St. Stephen had suggested the transience of the Temple and the customs.

3. Philip the Deacon had baptised the Samaritans – circumcised schismatics.

4. Also an Ethiopian eunuch, excluded from the covenant by his condition.

5. St. Peter had admitted at Cæsarea uncircumcised proselytes.

6. At Antioch a Church had arisen, the strongest outside Jerusalem, largely composed of them.

7. And now St. Paul and St. Barnabas had created Churches, the majority in which had been pure Pagans with no previous link with the synagogue.

Now all this had happened, while a strict Judaic party was forming itself for the protection of the law and the customs within the Church of Jerusalem. No doubt these people hoped, when uncircumcised proselytes had been admitted to the Church, that soon the influence of their Jewish brethren would win them over to the law and the customs. They would be prepared to be patient about this, but they would be quite clear that until the Gentile converts obeyed the law as our Lord Himself obeyed it they could not be regarded as full Christians. It was now reported that exactly the reverse was taking place, and that Jewish Christians were beginning to discard some of their previous practices and avail themselves of their new liberty. This, to the strict party in the Church of Jerusalem, was little short of apostasy ; there was imminent danger, so they would argue, that the religion of Christ, instead of being the fair flower of the Jewish dispensation, would become an indiscriminate cultus in which Judaism would be lost. Prominent in the alarmist party was a group of Pharisees who had been attracted to the faith mainly by the venerable personality of St. James, our Lord's relative, who, to use an anachronism, was Bishop of Jerusalem. St. James must have been a very remarkable person, for although, no doubt, we must discount a good deal from the legends which surround his name, still they undoubtedly give the general impression which he made. St. James is said to have inspired universal awe by his bearing, dress and mode of life. He wore no woollen clothes ; he was clothed from head to foot in white linen. On his head he bore the golden headplate of the High Priesthood. He alone, of all the Jewish people, was permitted to enter the holy place, for his sanctity was so great that the Jewish people overlooked his Christianity. He led a celibate life, he was a vegetarian, he spent so many hours in prayer within the Temple that his knees grew hard and stiff. He was popularly called the rampart of the people. Much of this, of course, is pious romance, but it is the poetising of the general aspect of a very remarkable man. St. James naturally used his influence to conciliate the Pharisees. In doing this he had no doubt insisted upon the fact that our Lord did not come to destroy the law but to fulfil it. He would dwell upon the scrupulous care with which Jesus had observed the precepts ; he would assure his converts that adherence to the new faith in no way withdrew them from the discipline of the old. The result of his success was the strengthening of a well-knit conservative party, which far outstripped him, if not in zeal for the law, certainly in intolerance of wider views.

At this moment it was this Pharisaic party in the Church which was its greatest danger. Its zeal for the law had loosened any real grasp it had ever had on the fundamental idea of the religion of Christ, the personal relation between Jesus and His disciples, and it was working busily towards a schism. It was well organised, and it arranged a mission from the Church of Jerusalem to the Church of Antioch, for which the approval of the Apostles at the capital was obtained.

When the missioners arrived and began to teach, they assumed that half of the Antiochene Church was still in an imperfect state of discipleship, and asserted that full Christian membership required circumcision and the observance of the law of all who desired salvation. The Church was thrown into the wildest excitement and confusion. The Greek word translated *dissension* is the word for civil strife or sedition. St. Paul and St. Barnabas challenged the truth of the statement. According to the Bezan text, St. Paul maintained that each should remain in the state in which he was when he believed. This we are told he affirmed vehemently, and we can well believe it. There was a complete division for the moment, and the corporate life of the Church of Antioch came to a standstill.

The Church of Antioch requested St. Paul and St. Barnabas with certain others to go to Jerusalem and lay the whole matter before the Apostles. At the same time, according to the Bezan text, the Pharisaic preachers charged St. Paul and the other teachers to go up to Jerusalem to be judged before the Apostles and presbyters. St. Paul evidently hesitated ; he had received his Apostleship from our Lord Himself, and he was exceedingly fearful of seeming to defer to his brother Apostles as though they were not merely his equals but his superiors. But our Lord reassured him and told him to go. " I went up," he says, " in accordance with a revelation."

It was a great moment ; feeling ran very high indeed. Among those whom St. Paul chose to take with him was Titus, an uncircumcised Gentile. St. Paul was devoted to Titus, and it is delightfully characteristic of St. Paul to have taken him at this juncture to Jerusalem. He took him as a sample of the work which had been placed in his hands. He felt that Titus was a living proof of the rightfulness of his contention, and he thought that the Church of Jerusalem would be unable to resist the charm of the young Gentile Christian. But St. Paul underestimated the strength of the opposition, and poor Titus had reason for once in a way to regret the enthusiastic affection of his master.

The departure for the Jewish capital was a great occasion, the Church going down to the port to give the embassy a good send off. And the scene on the great stone quays, now called Paul and Barnabas, is not one of the least touching in history, the vessel going out between two long lines of cheering Gentile Christians, every man and woman filled with passionate devotion to the two splendid figures on the deck on their way to fight the battle of Christian charity and the Catholic Gospel.

The Apostles made a slow progress to Jerusalem. They visited the Churches of Phœnicia and Samaria by the way. At Sidon, Tyre, Ptolemais, Cæsarea and Sebaste they described the first missionary journey and its results. Everywhere the story was received with thankfulness and delight ; the journey was a triumphal progress, and St. Paul and St. Barnabas arrived at Jerusalem approved and acclaimed by all the northern Churches. It was a dramatic moment. To the Apostles, who had lived and walked and talked with Jesus, and who desired for themselves and their posterity such a life of obedience to the law as Jesus lived, comes the Apostle of a few years' standing, once the bitter persecutor of the Church, to demand for his new Churches in the northern cities complete exemption from the Law he had once so cruelly defended.

The Church of Jerusalem received him with all

honour. There was a meeting of the whole Church. St. Paul and St. Barnabas, I imagine, amid that breathless silence before a storm in which the whole atmosphere is electrical, told the story they had already told at Antioch and in Phœnicia and at Samaria.   In the Christian assembly, admitted to its fullest privileges, sat Titus, the young Pagan, who had become a splendid Christian.   Paul and Barnabas ended.   Then the Pharisaic teachers, the Bezan text says, the same who had charged them to come up to the presbyters, rose in their places and deliberately made the dogmatic statement : " It is necessary to circumcise all these people and charge them to keep the law of Moses." Nothing of moment was said or done that day ; it was felt that there must be much prayer and reflection before a decision could be come to, and the assembly was dissolved in the usual manner. But in the course of the next few days a serious disturbance arose. When it was generally known that Titus, who had, I suppose, received Holy Communion with the Jerusalem Church at the solemn reception of Paul and Barnabas, was an uncircumcised Greek, the indignation of the strict party knew no bounds, and they demanded that, since this had occurred, Titus should be made to submit to the law at once.

When St. Paul tries to describe this incident in the Epistle to the Galatians, his feelings so overcome him that his grammar goes to pieces, and it is impossible to say for certain what happened. The translation in the text of the Revised Version says that Titus was not made a Jew, the translation in the margin says he was. Commentators differ : Sir William Ramsay is on one side ; Mr. Rackham on the other. I think I believe that St. Paul felt it best to give way, and that Titus was circumcised. It seems to me that probably the other Apostles said to him, " This has so affronted some of the Church here, this discovery that they were un- awares communicating with a convert from Paganism, that we advise you to show them that the affront was not intended : this need not form a precedent ; the case is exceptional " – and that St. Paul consented.

If he did not give way, why his agitation and con- fusion in the Galatian letter ? Why does not he say so triumphantly ? There can be no doubt that in Galatians ii. 3, he is describing one of the bitterest moments of his life. The incident, however, was not all loss ; it threw St. Paul and St. Barnabas into close contact with the other Apostles, and in the Galatian letter St. Paul alludes to private interviews which are not mentioned by St. Luke in his description of the Council of Jeru- salem. It must be remembered that the Book of the Acts is an eirenical book, and, although the private interviews made for peace in the most noble way, still it was probably wiser to confine an official account of the matter to the official acts of the Church as a body. There is one omission in the Book of the Acts to the meaning of which we have no clue – the omission of the name of Titus. Titus was evidently a very im- portant person in the entourage of St. Paul. It may be that he had been an object at this time of so much bitter feeling that it was best to omit all reference to him. But Sir William Ramsay makes another sug- gestion : he thinks it probable that St. Luke does not name him because he was a near relation of his – that he leaves out the name of Titus as he leaves out his own name. There is really, as Sir William Ramsay points

out, a great beauty in this incident. The beauty is
rather obscured by the careful and anxious way in
which St. Paul is obliged, all through his account of it,
to emphasize his co-equality with the other Apostles,
which gives to his written words a rather ungracious
look. But, as Ramsay says, he might quite well have
taken up an attitude of superiority and said, ' I was
sent up here, not by the Antiochene Church, but by
direct command from the Lord Himself.' As it was,
he, on his side, patiently, faithfully told the whole
story of his life-work, submitting every detail of it with
quiet care to St. Peter, St. James and St. John ; and
at the end the three Apostles said to him, " The only
advice and instruction we have to give you is that you
continue to do what you have been zealously doing."
It was quite clear to the three that our Lord had put
St. Paul in command of the spread of the Gospel in the
Gentile world. They divided the mission field with
him, and from henceforth the two names stand side by
side indissolubly connected in the mind of the Church –
the holy Apostles Peter and Paul, not memories, but
living presences in the communion of Saints, before
whom every morning many Christian priests as they
go to the altar pause and submit themselves in all
humility, asking the help of their prayers as they
confess their sins to God.

The three made one great request of the Apostle of
the Gentiles. Jerusalem was a hard place for poor
people to live in, and the poor of Jerusalem were
largely helped by the alms of the Jews of the dispersion. St. Peter, St. James and St. John asked St.
Paul to organise collections in the Gentile Churches for
the Christian poor of Jerusalem, who were, of course,

now cut off from the alms of the Jews of the dispersion. This charity, they said, will be a bond of unity. St. Paul agreed with enthusiasm, and, as we know, he gave himself to the work with the greatest zeal and perseverance.

At length the day arrived for the council. I do not suppose that the Church possessed any very large building, but it assembled in the largest. Probably it was an oblong room, at the upper end of which the Apostles and Presbyters who formed the Council sat in a semi-circle facing the lay members of the Church who had been selected to hear the debate and witness the scene. In the centre facing the people would be the first Cathedra of an Apostle in the Succession, St. James's chair of dignity as the Apostle who governed the local Church ; and I picture St. Peter and St. John on one side, St. Paul and St. Barnabas on the other. The Council began by hearing the arguments of the strict party. There was evidently a very keen, hot debate, in which the Apostles did not intervene. They bided their time until the disputants had thoroughly talked themselves out, then when they had sunk back in their chairs breathless and spent, and with the sense of reaction upon them which is the result of talking oneself out, it was found that St. Peter had risen, as the Bezan text says, in the spirit. This assertion is a useful reminder that the leaders at the Council of Jerusalem were on a much higher spiritual plane than the majority of the leaders of the Church.

" When God was ready to admit Gentiles to the Church," said St. Peter, " He chose that they should be admitted by a leader of the Church of Jerusalem – by me. It was I, not Paul, who opened the door of

Faith to the Gentiles in the case of Cornelius. On that occasion," continued St. Peter, " God showed that the distinction between Jew and Gentile had now been done away. On that occasion God showed that He distinguished men by the condition of their inner life, and He proved to us that the hearts of the Gentiles in the house of Cornelius were fit to receive grace by visibly bestowing the Holy Ghost upon them.

" We must not therefore deny that God is willing to save the uncircumcised while they remain in uncircumcision. To insist now that circumcision is necessary to salvation is to deny what God has done. And do we still trust to our circumcision for salvation ? Have not we recognised that it is part of a system which was failing to save us ? If we are saved it will be by the same process by which an uncircumcised man can be saved, and by that alone – by the grace of the Lord Jesus."

He sat down, and there was profound silence ('after,' adds the Bezan text, 'the Presbyters had assented to what St. Peter had said'). The silence was broken by St. Barnabas, who very tactfully had been asked to speak before St. Paul. No doubt, taking up St. Peter's points one by one, St. Barnabas illustrated them by what he had seen in the Gentile Churches. Then St. Paul spoke, and you can imagine what it must have been not so much to hear as to feel St. Paul getting it home to the hearts of the Judaic Christians what his mission among the Gentiles was like. Then there was a long pause, and every man in the room was conscious only of one figure – the venerable figure in the centre, which had not moved during all this time.

It

At length St. James spoke :

" Brethren, hearken unto me. Symeon has told us at length how God first visited the Gentiles in his presence to take from them a people for His name. And the prophets looked forward to the day. Amos was contemplating the kingdom when its fortunes were at a low ebb, but God had an immutable purpose for Zion – it was to be raised up again, that in a new Messianic kingdom God should dwell for ever, and in this kingdom all who seek after Him will find Him ; it will become the rallying place of the world. For all the Gentiles belong to God, and the prophet saw that the time would come that they would flow into the kingdom of God, for this, as Isaiah in another place shows, has been God's eternal purpose.

" And so I judge, speaking as presiding Apostle in Jerusalem, and also as representing the brethren who are zealous for the law, that we do not disquiet the Gentile brethren, but that we enjoin them to unite with us in four things, in abstaining from contact with idols, from fornication, from things strangled and from blood, the last two requirements bringing their daily customs sufficiently into harmony with ours to make real brotherly intercourse possible. Do not let us fear for the honour of Moses. Throughout the world, in every synagogue, the law will continue to be read every Sabbath day."

The Apostles had lifted the whole assembly above the plane of controversy to the plane where the Holy Spirit operates. When St. James was silent the Presbyters with one accord gave their assent, and the heart and conscience of the whole assembly went with it. And so you and I were saved.

CHAPTER X

You remember that in the decrees of the Council of Jerusalem four obligations were laid upon the Gentile Christians. The first two insisted that there could not be two levels of morality in the Church ; that in the matter of idolatry and sexual impurity the converts were to accept the Jewish rule until their gradual assimilation of the teaching and grace of our Lord had formed the Christian principle of living in their hearts. Many people think that by fornication is meant continuance in the Gentile view that marriage is permissible within degrees of relationship in which it was forbidden among Jews. But although this is no doubt involved, I expect we must give the word its usual wide sense. It is difficult for us to realise the fact that the Pagan religion of the period was, generally speaking, quite useless as a restraint upon sensual passion – that the requirement of purity for everybody was an amazing and unheard-of thing to the Gentile converts. The Church being now Apostolic and Catholic, these two rules secured to her the note of Holiness. Then the third and fourth requirements, abstinence from things strangled and from blood, were the Council's solution of the problem of unity. It would have been really demoralising for the Jewish Christians to have abandoned at this stage their special customs, so the Gentiles were required to keep the two chief rules about food. This would enable Christians to eat together in peace and comfort.

You notice how very tactful the decrees were — they imposed four Jewish rules upon the Gentiles, but they said nothing about circumcision or the obligation to keep the law of Moses. The decrees were embodied in a conciliar letter addressed, not to the Gentile Christians generally, but to those of the Province of Syria where the dispute had arisen. The letter is contained in Acts xv. 23–29.

It was conveyed to Antioch by delegates chosen by the Church of Jerusalem. Men of distinction were chosen. Judas Barsabas was a Hebrew, probably the brother of Joseph Barsabas, one of the two selected for the Apostolate when the lot fell on St. Matthias, one, therefore, of those who had been converted by Our Lord Himself, probably a member of a now long-established Christian family ; and Silas or Sylvanus, evidently a Jew of the dispersion, a man with a Latin name and the Roman citizenship, one therefore able without difficulty to enter into relations with Gentiles. Judas and Silas were both prophets.

Armed with the letter, the delegates proceeded to Antioch with St. Paul and St. Barnabas. At an assembly of the whole Church they delivered it publicly to the heads of the Church. It was received with great joy and exultation. After the excitement had abated Judas and Silas delivered charges to the Church. In their charges they were lifted to the plane of prophecy, and again the prophetic outburst was received with joy and thankfulness. The whole scene illustrates the heights of blessedness on which the earliest Church lived.

They appear to have preached a mission in which they delivered the Gospel as preached by the original

Apostles and so corrected the mischief the Judaisers had wrought. At the end Silas remained in Antioch. I imagine it was thought well that a member of the Jerusalem Church should remain on at Antioch — a kind of ambassador to allay any possible misunderstandings. But the Council of Jerusalem, although it secured the unity of the Church, did not bring peace. In the present state of human nature great questions cannot be raised and disposed of so quickly. The Judaisers, who had been temporarily silenced in the Council, could not yield their point, and one sympathises very sincerely with them. St. Paul became to them the enemy, the arch-apostate, and they gradually developed a relentless hatred of him. His conflicts with the Jews he could bear with equanimity — they were in the nature of things ; but the conflict within the Church was exquisitely painful. The Judaisers started an organisation to oppose St. Paul, and wherever he went its agents followed him. Not content with trying to set converted Jews against him, they sent missions to his Gentile churches in his absence, and, as the almost heart-broken letter to the Galatians shows, they upset his work in the Churches of the first missionary journey.

And even among those in high places in the Church there were episodes which showed how enormous the difficulty was which the Holy Spirit was slowly overcoming. St. Peter himself came to Antioch not long after the council. We can imagine how completely carried away St. Peter would be by the love and fervour in this splendid mission centre. Without any hesitation he lived freely and happily with the Gentiles. But presently a group of the strict party came down with letters commendatory from St. James. St. James's object was, I suspect, eirenical ; I imagine that these were the more reasonable of the Judaisers and it was hoped that a *modus vivendi* with them could be found. But they lived as strict Jews, and St. Peter, probably from a desire not to exasperate them at a hopeful moment, drew back and resumed the Jewish separateness. A certain number of convinced Catholics in the Church of Antioch, even St. Barnabas himself, seem to have thought this expedient for the moment. But St. Paul was displeased, and in the assembly of the Church frankly expressed himself. He knew what St. Peter's real feelings were, and what his actions had been, and he insisted on making both clear. This is always spoken of with bated breath as a very sad and painful affair, but it was probably nothing of the sort. Two lovable, frank and high-spirited men had a strong difference of opinion in the presence of the Church. Would to God there had never been a greater scandal in the Church than that ! But a really painful episode followed it — the separation of St. Paul and St. Barnabas. It was really painful, and yet I believe the Holy Ghost to have been its author. It was really impossible for St. Barnabas to spend his whole life as second in command ; he was too big a man, his whole nature would have suffered. He had been St. Paul's champion and his leader ; then with superb humility he had changed places with him. There is really no character in all the history of the saints more noble, generous and loving than St. Barnabas. He was a very perfect Christian gentleman. But the position could not be maintained indefinitely, and if it had not been sharply broken it would not have been broken at all.

You remember how the first stage of the second missionary journey was planned out and the Apostles parted company over the young cousin of Barnabas. Mark had now accepted fully the programme of the Church. He had not been caught by the Judaizers ; but his abandonment of the first journey had evidently been not altogether on questions of principle, it had betrayed certain weaknesses of character. Besides, although St. Paul and St. Barnabas were at one in principle, recent events had shown that they did not entirely agree about matters of expediency. As we know, the estrangement from St. Barnabas, if indeed it ever amounted to that, was not of long duration. In 1 Cor. ix. 6 St. Paul quotes him as of one mind with himself, and later on St. Mark had entirely regained his affection and respect. It is impossible to say which of the two saints showed the better judgment at this moment. But it was no doubt much the better plan that each should head a mission of his own. St. Barnabas sailed for his own country where the appeal to the Gentiles had yet to be made, and St. Paul took the best of subordinates in choosing Silas and went by land through Syria and Cilicia towards Tarsus. St. Luke suggests that the sympathy of the Church of Antioch was rather with St. Paul, but of course St. Luke is not quite an unprejudiced witness. The frankness with which he records the difficulties at this juncture is very inspiring, and it is a pity the historians of the later Church have so often failed to follow his example.

St. Paul and St. Silas probably followed the coast line along the flank of the Amanus range and round the head of the Gulf of Issus to Tarsus. Our thoughts

go back to the little boy with the thin white face and
the tumbling dark hair on the roof top long long years
before – the boy who had dreamt of the conquests of
King Messiah but had grown into a disillusioned
young man who knew it could never be, and then had
become a broken-hearted young man who realised that
it might have been had he not slain the messenger
ordained of God. Now, in middle age he enters
Tarsus, carrying within him the Master who had
solved the problem, and bearing in his hand instructions of the Holy Ghost which enabled Jew and
Gentile to eat of the same bread and drink of the same
cup in Christ Jesus Our Lord.

And now, having set the Church of Tarsus in order
and at rest, St. Paul makes for the foothills of the
Taurus towards the great pass of the Cilician Gates –
that awful rent in the mountains which he had gazed
at with boyish curiosity from the house-top long ago –
then the gates of the unknown, now the gate through
which he was to reach his dear churches in Lycaonia
and Phrygia. And so these two wayfaring Jews trudge
northwards up and up through the windings of the
frightful chasm. The limestone cliffs are in places but
twelve paces apart, high above them the pine trees
fringe their summits and veil the gorge in darkness.
It is one of the dramatic facts of history that those two
men were on their way to bring a crusading army down
through the gorge in the far-off centuries – an army
which, as it wound its glittering way through the gloom,
imprecated the horror of the place and called it the gates
of Judas, an army which had made the oft-repeated mistake of drawing a sword to advance the cause of Christ.
And now the Taurus summits lay behind them, the

travellers descended to the plateau of Lycaonia, and
St. Paul re-visited in succession, Derbe, Lystra, and
Iconium.   At Lystra he found that Timothy had
realised his fondest hopes.   Of his sweetness and
goodness the Church could not say too much.
Timothy's devotion to his Leader was only less strong
than his devotion to his Lord, and St. Paul, who had
permitted no human affection to lodge in his heart
since he had given it to Jesus, now for the first time
felt the joy of that ideal human love which flows from
the consecrated relationships of the Church.   He was
beginning very strongly to feel the importance of
educating a school of disciples out of whom his own
successor could be chosen, and it was decided, God
alone knows at the cost of what agony to the women in
the little house at Lystra, that Timothy should accompany St. Paul.   Among all the sacrifices which have
been made for Christ, none will rank higher at the
Judgment than such a sacrifice as Eunice made.
Timothy was an admirable domestic chaplain, he possessed the tact, sweetness, charm and self-effacement
necessary for that almost intolerable post.   He lacked
the inspiration needed in a chief, he wanted courage
and incisiveness, but he was unequalled as a sub-
ordinate.   It was important that the Apostles should
be men of unyielding will and strong personality, it
was equally important that their immediate successors
should be by nature plastic and unoriginal, conscientious meek disciples – the transmitters of a
tradition.   Do not despise the Apostolic Fathers because they are unoriginal ; they were unoriginal in
the providence of God.   There was a problem to be
solved about Timothy.   Timothy was a Jew who had

been brought up where there was no Jewish organisation, and the requirement of the Law had never
been fulfilled in him.   St. Paul felt it would be an
affront to Jews if he took in his train an uncircumcised
Jew, so Timothy was brought into proper relation with
the old Covenant.   It is a typical illustration of controversial malice that when the Judaisers afterwards
arrived in Galatia they laid hold of this in order to
convict St. Paul of inconsistency.   " He has no prin-
ciples at all," they cried, " he is a mere man-pleaser ;
when it suits his purpose he can preach circumcision
like the rest of us."

Evidently the whole question was even then before
the Galatian Churches, and it was part of St. Paul's
duty to get the decrees of the Council of Jerusalem
accepted.   They were gladly accepted, and, as St. Luke
says, the Churches were strengthened in the faith and
increased in numbers daily.

Now we reach a critical day in the history of St.
Paul – the day he left Pisidian Antioch to break fresh
ground.   The time, he felt, had now come for him to
carry out what appears to have been the intention
frustrated by his former illness at Antioch, and go to
Ephesus, probably with a view to Rome.   It is thought
the Apostolic party went first to Metropolis, a place
from which a road then ran in almost a straight line
along the higher ground to Ephesus, 200 miles away.
But at Metropolis a startling thing happened ; the
missioners received a conviction that they were not to
preach anywhere in the big province of Asia, which
seemed such a likely field for the Gospel.   They believed themselves to be so guided by the Holy Ghost.
North-east of the province of Asia lay the populous

province of Bithynia, stretching along the south-
eastern side of the Sea of Marmora, the Bosphorus and
the Black Sea.   For this they now made, striking across
Phrygia in silence, probably to Cotiæum, 80 or 90
miles north-west.   Bithynia was ripe for the Gospel.
Sixty years later the Governor Pliny wrote that Christianity was so prevalent there that the old worship
was falling into neglect.   But it was to be evangelised
by St. Peter, not by St. Paul.   Again the missioners
were stopped on the frontier of Bithynia.   They made
a strong effort to enter the country, but the Spirit of
Jesus, we are told, forbade them, they were forced to
turn west, and they proceeded still in silence from
Cotiæum to Troas on the coast, 200 miles away.   We
wish we knew through what human instrumentality
these impressions were given.   It must be supposed
through the prayer activities of Paul and Silas.   It was a
strange discipline.   It is clear that they travelled for 300
miles without attempting to make a convert.   They were
being taught a severe lesson of their complete dependence upon God.   And now we see the brave group
clearly once more.   They have sighted the Ægean,
where it washes the base of Mount Ida, and they are
tramping cheerfully along the lovely road cut in the
flank of Ida above the purple and sapphire sea, now
descending to the shore, where the snowy surf breaks
upon the pebbles, now crossing the torrents which
rush down the mountain slopes, now lingering awhile
in the hanging woods of oak and chestnut, where the
parting branches grant a vision of the sunlight on
the waves, and Lesbos, like a dream island in the
quivering noon-day light, hanging between earth and
heaven.   Troas ; it was a port on one of the great

routes then, like Marseilles, Brindisi and Alexandria to-day.

Here the party halted and discussed the extraordinary situation. They must either cross the sea or go home, work having been forbidden for the moment in Asia. Then came the dream to St. Paul. The man of Macedonia stood before him and eagerly entreated him, " Come over and help us."

Next day four men, with a look of fixed resolve in their faces, were down at the harbour booking passages across to Europe. Among them was the Evangelist, St. Luke. It is generally supposed that St. Luke had been in the company of St. Paul for a long time. A study of the ' we ' passages in the Acts shows that there were occasions on which he was evidently present, but which he describes in the third person ; already there has been one use of the ' we ' ; it occurs, you remember, at Pisidian Antioch, and according to Codex D, the Bezan Text, the first person is used much earlier in the scene at Syrian Antioch, when Agabus prophesied the famine. It seems probable then that St. Luke was in touch with St. Paul, at any rate off and on, all through his ministry.

He was a Gentile. He is distinguished in Colossians from those of the circumcision, and his name is the Greek contracted form of the Roman name Lucanus. He was probably an inhabitant of one of the Greek cities of the Empire who enjoyed the Roman citizenship. His characteristics, it has been observed, are Greek, his literary ability, his versatility and his love of the sea. He was a physician. Among the Romans the medical profession did not rank high, and the great families kept a doctor as they kept a barber.

But it was far otherwise among the Greeks. The study of medicine ranked in the Greek Universities with the study of philosophy. St. Luke held in his world the same social position which an able physician holds in our world. We know he was able because he was a traveller. He evidently knew the sea-board of the Mediterranean quite well, and only professional men of repute travelled in those days when few travelled for pleasure. St. Luke's travels were like those of Browning's Karshish. He was evidently, from his style, a University man, and there are three probable Universities. He does not mention Alexandria, so this is least likely. He evidently knew Athens, so this is possible ; but most probably he was educated at Tarsus. Renan and Ramsay think he was a native of Philippi, but there are touches in his story of what happened at Philippi which make against this. On the other hand he was evidently left in charge at Philippi and stayed there for years, and that is surely the reason why the ' we ' passages begin just as the party is going to cross to Europe ; it is in order to make it clear to his readers that this was the moment of his own arrival at Philippi. St. Luke modestly brings himself forward in this way, at the last possible moment. And there is a note of patriotism in his account of Philippi – he makes the statement, which would have been disputed by its rivals, that Philippi was the first city of the region.

He may then have had ancestral links with Philippi, but he had probably been born and brought up in one of the eastern cities. There is a tradition that this was the Syrian Antioch, but more probably, from the remarkable knowledge he shows of the locality, it was

the Pisidian Antioch, and tradition has confused the
names. The account of St. Luke which best groups
all statements and hints is that he was an able physician
of Pisidian Antioch possessing the Roman citizenship
and descended from a Philippian family, that he had
travelled and lectured in the Empire and had been at
the University of Tarsus, that he was a God-fearing
proselyte who was converted by St. Paul during his
retirement at Tarsus, that he went to the Syrian
Antioch with St. Paul when Barnabas came to summon
him thither, and that from that time onwards he was
more or less attached to the person of St. Paul. If
this be so, when they reached Pisidian Antioch and
St. Paul fell violently ill, St. Luke found himself at-
tending his spiritual master in his own home circle.
From this time onward he took what care he could of
St. Paul's wretched health. His family connection
with Philippi would make it desirable to leave him
there in charge, and the selection, at moments of hesitation in St. Paul's career, first of Pisidian Antioch and
secondly of Philippi would be largely due to the providential circumstance that his devoted friend had links
with both. St. Luke was a man of great literary taste,
and of great power as a historian – a historian who
knew how to select his materials for the picture he
desired to paint. Early in his Christian career he felt
himself called to be a chronicler of the Church, and
part of the impedimenta of a Pauline journey was the
growing packet of priceless notebooks in which St.
Luke collected his material. He was a painter in
words, not in colour. I fear there is nothing to be
said for the tradition that he was a painter. It appears,
without any clear pedigree, in the ninth century.

The Apostolic party had a good passage to Neapolis. They did the 125 miles in two days, and after climbing the winding mountain road which leads up from the port over Mount Panigæus they found themselves, at the end of a ten mile walk, on the edge of a fertile plain with the Roman colony of Philippi before them. It was a Virgilian landscape, a realisation of the pastoral poet's dream, and we will leave St. Paul crossing the flower-strewn meadows towards the town, the flower-strewn meadows from which Persephone was rapt away to be Queen of the Nether World.

CHAPTER XI

We left St. Paul, St. Luke, St. Silas and St. Timothy crossing the flower-strewn meadows from which Persephone had been snatched away, towards the Roman town of Philippi. The present geographical distribution of nations and the great modern facilities for travelling by land tend to exaggerate for us the importance of the step which St. Paul took when he crossed from Troas in Asia to Neapolis in Europe. We must remember two things. First, that Europe in the guise of the Roman Empire had overflowed into Asia, and that there was very little difference between what St. Paul found in the province of Asia and what he found in Macedonia. For the West had crossed the Bosphorus, and the Taurus Mountains, which little Saul had known so well, divided West from East. The province of Syria, south-east of the Taurus, was known then as the first province of the East.

And secondly, we must remember that in those days the sea united rather than divided. Communication between the various towns of the sea-board of the Mediterranean was safer and more expeditious than communication between the coast and the interior. It was the pre-war Turk who fixed the great division between East and West at the Bosphorus, and if the European lands which he ruled were not such a desolation and therefore such a negligible quantity, it

would be realised that the division is west of the Bosphorus – practically on the eastern shore of the
Adriatic.

St. Paul was now in Macedonia. To call the
Macedonians Greeks is like calling the Scotch English.
The Macedonians were a rough, hardy folk who, in
the palmy days of Greece, were reckoned barbarous.
Then they had their day. They shattered the Greek
power, they conquered the Persian Empire and
leavened the whole civilisation of the period. It was
a long time before Rome conquered them, and when
she did she broke up the country into four districts
with the object of breaking the Macedonian unity and
making the tough province easier for the Empire to
digest. The Macedonians, as we all know, are as
difficult to manage to-day as ever they were. They are
simple, sturdy, faithful and affectionate, and even in
the scanty references to them in the Acts all this
appears : the people were sturdy and turbulent, the
women free and independent, ready to take speaking
parts in public life, and the Churches were simple and
warm-hearted. St. Paul loved the Church of Philippi
beyond all his Churches.

Philippi had once been important as a gold-mining
town, but the veins of gold gave out a hundred and
fifty years before St. Paul came there, and it would
have sunk into unimportance but for an accident. The
Philippi of St. Paul's day was born of the great battle
in 42 B.C., when Brutus and Cassius fought Octavian
and Antony and the future of Rome was decided.
The triumvirs made Philippi a Roman colony in
gratitude for the victory and settled it with soldiers;
and it received a reinforcement of military settlers
    Kт

eleven years later, after the battle of Actium. It was therefore a Roman, and an intensely Roman, town — a Roman town planted in a part of the Empire where the inhabitants were stubborn and independent, where religion was singularly pure and therefore real. It was, I suppose, an exceedingly good specimen of a town of the period. Its rejuvenescence having been so recent, and its atmosphere so Roman and military, very few Jews had been attracted to it.

The Apostolic party seems to have made its way to an inn and spent some quiet days in examining the neighbourhood and getting some impressions of the religious forces at work there. They found that there was no synagogue, but that the Jews had a *proseucha*, a simple enclosure on the bank of the river a mile from the town. If there was no synagogue the Jews always liked to arrange a praying-place near a river so as to be able to use the running water for their ablutions.

One always associates this *proseucha* with St. Barnabas, Pimlico. You remember that the Protestant Lord Shaftesbury once said that he should be happier worshipping with Lydia by the river side than in the gorgeous shrine of St. Barnabas. And no doubt he spoke truly and would have been quite comfortable in the *proseucha*, for Protestantism, in its dislike to the historical development in Christian worship, has returned to the arrangements of the synagogue, and the *proseucha* was even simpler than a synagogue, it was merely an enclosure open to the sky.

On the Sabbath at the time of morning service the travellers walked across the meadows, as St. Luke says, ' to river ' — he lived there afterwards for years and

he says ' to river ' with the local familiarity which
leads us to say ' to town.' They found the *proseucha*
and a nice little party of ladies – a few Jewesses and
the rest God-fearing proselytes. The entrance of four
unknown and interesting-looking gentlemen must have
been a delightful variation in their rather dull Sabbath
morning meetings, for they were in the position of
a Friends' Meeting which is but rarely favoured with
the presence of a ministering Friend. After prayers
they no doubt hoped for a sermon, but the four gentlemen preferred conversation, so they all sat down and
made friends, and there was general talk. It soon
became clear that St. Paul was the most interesting
person in the party, which gradually became a semi-
circle of listeners round him. In the semi-circle sat
a woman who became one of his dearest and most
devoted friends. Lydia was a very rich tradeswoman
who had a flourishing business in the town. She was
not of gentle birth, and she was called by the name of
her native country, which probably means that she
was of a freed family. She was a native of Thyatira
in Lydia, and she had a big shop for the sale of dyed
goods. Lydia was, no doubt, an important member of
the little group in the *proseucha*.

She was a God-fearing proselyte, not a Jewess, and
she was one of those naturally Christian souls who
recognise the Gospel as being the way, the truth and
the life as soon as they hear it. One wishes St. Luke
had not been so compressed here. He tells us nothing
at all about the steps of the work which now began in
connection with the *proseucha*. So far as that little
group was concerned, the adhesion of Lydia had made
everything easy for St. Paul, and before long she and

all her family and household received Holy Baptism.
Lydia's first effort when she became a Christian was
to try to induce the missionaries to leave their inn and
come and stay with her in her comfortable house.
St. Paul evidently tried hard to get out of it and resisted the invitation for a long time, but Lydia made
such a personal point of it, and insisted with so much
force that her house was the one and only place suitable
for the assemblies of the future Church, that at last
St. Paul gave in, no doubt to the satisfaction of St.
Luke, St. Silas and St. Timothy.   It is a real pleasure
to believe that Lydia made them all thoroughly comfortable.

Lydia became a pillar of the Apostolic Church.
There seems no doubt that most of the pecuniary help
St. Paul afterwards had at times came from Lydia.
St. Luke remained in her household when St. Paul
went on, and there he organised and governed the
Church of Philippi.   I always hope it is Lydia whom
St. Paul addresses as ' true yoke-fellow ' in Phil. iv. 3,
because she really deserved something nice from
St. Paul.

Very soon it became known in Philippi that two
Jewish proselytes were at work.   The Romans gave
complete tolerance to all recognised cults, of which the
Jewish was one, and at first they would be undisturbed
by the news.   Gradually it became clear that this was
Judaism of a new pattern.   It began to do what was
sternly forbidden in a Roman colony, to upset civil and
domestic life.   St. Paul's tremendous personality, too,
began to be noticed, and the usual catastrophe when
it came was the result of one particular episode.   There
was a poor girl in the town who was probably the slave

of a corporation of priests.   Hers appears to have been
one of those cases of double personality of which we
now hear so much.   In pagan days such unfortunates
were trained to exhibit their powers and turn them to
account.   In one of her states this girl was a ven-
triloquist, and she could throw her voice here and there.
Probably she could talk several languages which she
really did not know, and she was also clairvoyant.
She became possessed by the idea of Paul, her perverted
mind fastened on him, and do what they would the
travellers could not shake her off.   Day after day she
waited for them when they were going ' to river ' to
teach and baptise at the *proseucha*, and followed them
through the meadows crying monotonously and end-
lessly, " These men are slaves of the Most High God
who proclaim unto you the way of salvation."   This
does not mean any discernment on the girl's part as to
the Law or the Gospel.   There was a general belief
in a supreme God and a deep longing for a saving relation to Him.   The thought, as we saw in the case of
Thecla, of a person sworn to the service of a particular
god, and living under his protection and inspiration,
was quite a common one.

So the persistence of the poor hysterical girl was
merely annoying and saddening.   At last Paul felt he
must try to deal with her case, and he turned and
waited for her and brought all the force of his great
consecrated personality to bear on her trouble.   The
girl was cured, but with the cure her value disappeared.
She lost all her old powers, and the incident brought
the gathering displeasure of Philippi to a head.   The
storm broke.   If her masters were, as is probable, a college of priests, that explains the tumult they were at

once able to raise. It may have been a court day that day, but at any rate, on the first court day when the sessions were on in the Town Hall, Paul and Silas were seized and dragged before the authorities. The charge was that, under the guise of Judaism, which was a *religio licita*, they were introducing a new unlicensed religion. It had probably become clear that St. Paul was forbidding his Gentile converts to worship the Emperor, and his accusers laid stress on the fact that he was a preacher of disloyalty to Rome. This was enough to throw Philippi – a military colony with a passionate devotion to the Empire – into a frenzy. There was a violent scene, and St. Paul and St. Silas were stripped naked in public and bastinadoed by the lictors.

Here a very interesting question arises. Why did not Paul and Silas plead their Roman citizenship until next morning ? It is absurd to say that it would have been useless in the tumult. The lictors could have heard them speak, and the two men could have stopped the lictors with a word. Why was it not spoken ? It is impossible to say for certain, but I imagine St. Paul deliberately endured the whipping as an act of penance for the past, reserving to himself the power of interfering if the suffering seemed dangerous to life. It was either that or that they both determined to get the advantage at Philippi which an unlawful whipping would give them.

After the whipping the preachers were taken to the prison. The prison, probably, was part of the citadel, and on the steep side of a hill, and it was in charge of an officer who was not a mere warder but a man of some position. The governor put Paul and Silas into one of the worst dungeons – probably a dungeon excavated in the side of the hill without air or light. They were dragged in torn and bleeding, their wounds unattended to, and fastened into the *nervus*, a horrible instrument for keeping the body in a constrained position. We must not let our sense of the wonderful spiritual and moral elevation of the Apostles lead us to forget the fearful bodily sufferings they underwent. At midnight St. Paul and St. Silas sang their matins and lauds, and all through the prison the miserable inmates were listening to the strangely solemn and sweet sounds of the Christian worship. Suddenly there was a violent shock of earthquake. We must not suppose it did what no earthquake can naturally do ; its action was quite normal – the foundations were shaken. The doors would be held merely by wooden bars. These were swung down and the staples of the chains with which the prisoners were fastened were loosened in the general shifting of the walls. The usual earthquake terror seized everybody. The governor rushed into the courtyard, and seeing black gaps in the hillside where there ought to have been doors, and hearing no sound, supposed all the prisoners had escaped. Roman-like he determined to kill himself and avoid the disgrace of being executed, but a loud, clear voice rang out of the darkness, " Do thyself no harm, we are all here, everyone." The governor shouted for lights and then sprang with his torch into the prison, trembling with fright, and fell before Paul and Silas in a complete nerve collapse. He gathered himself together, probably after St. Paul had addressed some vigorous hopeful words to him, and brought St. Paul and St. Silas out into the courtyard. Then he secured

the rest of the prisoners, as the Bezan Text tells us, and
after order was restored he came back to the missionaries and said to them, " Sirs, what must I do to
be saved ? "   Remember again that paganism had prepared a way for the Gospel by familiarising people
with the thought of men who were devoted to a God
and his messengers to the world.   It was plain now to
the governor that Paul and Silas were such.

The events of the night were truly extraordinary.
The whole family and household of the governor
gathered round, and then and there Paul gave them an
outline of the Faith.   Afterwards they were brought
to the governor's house and their wounds were dressed
and supper was given to them.   Finally, and probably
after more instruction and some examination, baptism
was administered, and by morning the house of the
governor was a Christian Church.

Philippi must have filled St. Paul with hope.   The
next morning he was evidently in high spirits, and he
became the hero of a comedy which St. Luke describes
with a keen relish for the situation.   I am sure St. Paul
thoroughly enjoyed throwing the bombshell of his
Roman citizenship among the town authorities.   He
must have had some difficulty in keeping grave when
the mayor and corporation, all the Dogberrys, all the
Verges, of Philippi came to the prison to beg him to be
so good as to come out of the exceedingly uncomfortable quarters from which he had declined to budge.
It was comedy, but a strong purpose underlay it all.
St. Paul was securing for his new Church an immunity
from trouble for some time to come.   Philippi was one
of the very few places St. Paul left with dignity.   He
took his time, made arrangements for the government

of the Church, and left St. Luke behind, notwithstanding his sore need of his services, to set the little
community on its feet : then he took the marble-paved
Egnatian road to Amphipolis, passing between the
fields of flax under the shade of the plane trees which
lined the way.

Between Philippi and Athens St. Paul worked in two
cities, and for some months in each — Thessalonica and
Berea. Thessalonica was a great commercial city, and
Salonica, as it is now called, remains a great commercial
city to-day. In both Thessalonica and Berea St. Paul
had great success, and in both places many of his converts, Jews, proselytes and pagans, were among the
richer and more educated people of the town. The
remarkably prominent position which women held in
Macedonia is suggested by the report of the work in
both places. St. Paul made important converts among
the influential devout ladies. Mr. Rackham also finds
in the two reports a suggestion of the secret of Greek
history, the conflict between democracy and aristocracy. St. Luke, he says, seems to be comparing
the attitude towards Christianity of the two parties —
the democracy of Thessalonica and the aristocracy of
Berea — and the comparison is much in favour of the
latter. At Thessalonica it was the great success which
sowed the riot, and the upshot of it appears to have been
that the magistrates undertook not to take punitive
measures against the Thessalonian Christians if they,
on their side, would undertake to prevent St. Paul returning to the place, and that it was thought wise to
give the undertaking. St. Paul was evidently kept
from Thessalonica for some years by what he describes
as a device of Satan and it is to this that we owe the

first two letters of his which we possess. The riot at Thessalonica had very evil elements in it ; the hostile Jews got hold of the off-scouring of the city and used them as confederates. Their cry, too, is interesting : ' The men who have turned the world upside down are come hither also and Jason has harboured them.'

Christianity had now caught the attention of the Empire, and the situation was becoming more acute. The accusation is getting precise and very full of menace for the Church – they are acting in defiance of the decrees of Cæsar, saying that there is another Emperor, one Jesus. During the riot St. Paul and St. Silas were kept securely hidden, and when there was a lull they were conveyed away under cover of darkness to beautiful Berea, forty miles away. Here they found a colony of Jews, so spiritually minded that the rupture did not come when it was clear that the Gentiles were to be included in the Gospel. Probably the Gentiles of Berea were very good specimens of pagan fair-living people.

Peace at Berea was preserved among all those with whom the Apostles came into contact, and they were mainly of the educated class. When a movement against them among the peasantry began to assume dangerous proportions, the brethren sent St. Paul on his way to Athens with a strong detachment of Christians to protect and help him. Silas and Timothy were left behind to develop the Church. St. Paul was evidently again very ill. He had completely exhausted himself, and he was probably suffering from recurring attacks of malarial fever.

The convoy brought him safely to Athens and left

him there.   He sent a message back to say that Silas and Timothy must come to him at once.

And so, utterly broken down, weary and alone, we leave him face to face with the great Athene of the Acropolis and the severe and awful beauty of the Parthenon.

CHAPTER XII

St. Paul had not, as Renan remarks, been a few days alone for a long time. His life had been as a whirlwind, and he had always had subordinates and secretaries at his elbow ; but now he had a few unoccupied days to spend all by himself, and when he was a little rested he began a series of solitary walks through Athens in which he surveyed with some curiosity, and much deep reflection, the most elaborately beautiful city the world has ever seen.

I remember that the first impressions I received of the marble cities of the South was that the outsides of buildings and the appearance of the statues in the South are like the objects in the North which are carefully treasured in museums. Everything out of doors in England is blackened and beaten by the weather, and the first impression you must get of this Athens of the days of St. Paul is the unspoilt smooth detail of white marble, the gleam of bronze and the glitter of gold untouched by the action of wind and rain, relieved here and there by the black spires of cypresses, the white and rose blossom of oleanders, and the sheen of laurels, all flooded by a blinding white light which seems to come, not only from the sun, but from every yard of a blue translucent sky.

We are naturally accustomed to think that, before the Advent of our Lord, Jerusalem was the religious capital of the world. That is true in the sense that it

was Jerusalem which enshrined the set of religious
ideas which were destined to survive as the fittest, and
which formed the seed-plot of the religion of the
future. But in the estimate of the world of that period,
Jerusalem had only the sort of importance which at-
taches to Mecca to-day ; in fact, I suppose Mecca
counts for more. No, the religious capital of the
world then was Athens, and it was also the intellectual
and the artistic capital. When the Romans conquered
Greece, Athens led the captors captive, and Greek art
and literature became the idols of the Empire. All
young men of fashion came to the University of
Athens, where they read or idled as they pleased.

I want you first of all to do justice to the religion of
Athens. The world looked to Athens for a very cor-
rect and a very reverent expression of religion. It
was the centre of authority of the Greek mythology,
and the Greek mythology was generally accepted as
the most authentic account of the gods and their
history. You must often have asked yourselves what was
the exact relation of the heathen mythology to truth :
was it all ignorant delusion ? The answer is, Not altogether, if we believe that there is a spiritual universe
with its hierarchies of personal forces, all the creatures
of the one God. Athens worshipped the various personal forces of the spiritual universe. The simpler folk
regarded them as a multiplicity of gods, the more learned
as poetical embodiments of various aspects of the One
God. Athens also guarded the traditional account of
them, in which the forces for which they stood as
symbols were described in the shape of fables which
had been handed down through centuries, narratives
of the doings of individuals.

The attitude of Athens, then, in the days of St. Paul, recognised the truth of things more fully and clearly than does, say, the anti-clerical majority in France to-day. The man who sincerely worships God under the symbols Zeus, Pallas Athene, Hermes and Aphrodite, is less ignorant of and has a firmer grip of the essentials of life than the man who does not worship God at all.

Athens at the time of St. Paul's visit kept up all the old religious forms with reverence and pride. There were more festivals, processions and solemnities than there are in Rome to-day. But it was becoming impossible for cultivated men to believe in the old stories of the gods, and they were falling back for satisfaction upon mysterious experiences through clairvoyance and the exercise of other little understood powers, or upon philosophies which politely acquiesced in the complex religious customs as part of the necessary plant of social life, but whose interests were purely practical and ethical, and whose aim was the attainment of the true end of man – the blessed life.

Athens was both the holy ground and the headquarters of philosophy. Socrates, Plato and Aristotle had lived and taught there, and visitors to Athens went with reverence and awe to see the Academy of Plato, the Lyceum of Aristotle, the Porch of Zeno, the Garden of Epicurus ; and then they turned to take part in some of the reverent and stately religious functions on which the whole city devoutly prided itself, undisturbed by the fact that the thinking world had long outgrown their symbolism, although it fully recognised their utility.

Of the various philosophical schools of that day

two only offered a reasoned guide to practical life. Two only therefore counted in the development of the human race, and these two schools were, for the same reason, the schools which encountered St. Paul, the Epicureans and the Stoics. The Epicureans said that they believed in the gods, but that the gods lived in a remote sphere and were not concerned with the government of the world. For the rest they were practically materialists, who held that the world, and mankind with it, is composed of indestructible material, the combinations of which are perpetually being dissolved and re-arranged. They believed therefore that human personality is destroyed at death and that there is no hereafter. As practical guides to life the Epicureans preached a cheerful common sense, prudence and moderation, and the end they proposed to the human race was a condition of delicate comfort and pleasure. They were not sensualists, they were clear-sighted enough to see that sensuality is a fatal mistake in the pursuit of true comfort and peace. They held up as the highest good a serene happiness attained by bodily temperance, the cultivation of the mind and imagination, and social intercourse. The majority of well-bred Englishmen to-day who do not practise religion are Epicureans.

The majority of well-bred Englishmen who do practise religion are not really Christians ; they are Stoics. The Stoics preached virtue, not merely for our sakes, but for its own. They believed in the supremacy of duty, law and virtue, and their hero was the man who had risen superior to passion and to circumstance, and who had attained to perfect self-mastery. Unlike the Epicureans, who banished the gods to Olympus,

and who did not really believe in them, the Stoics
profoundly believed in God ; they had a somewhat uncertain grip on immortality, and they held that all
things happen according to an original Divine intention.

That sounds, as far as it goes, admirable, but as
a creed it was vitiated by the fact that the Stoic did
not believe in the Divine transcendence, that is to say,
that God is above and beyond the universe, holding
it in His grip. The God of the Stoic was rather the
universe itself, and we parts of Him rather than His
creatures.

And if you pressed the Stoic you found that, after
all, spirit to him was not really more than a refined
form of matter—in fact, that he was a pantheist, and
pantheism, remember, after all, is only materialism expressed in a curious love poetry. Still, the Stoic was
better than his creed – under these conceptions he
made a real personal venture towards God, and met
with the response of our Father in heaven ; consequently in feeling and practice the good Stoic was
a theist. As a consequence of his belief that all souls
are fragments of the pervading Divine Spirit, he taught
that all men were brothers, and he had the grand conception of the world as the City of God. Nevertheless,
Stoicism failed to produce either a brotherhood or the
spirit of brotherhood. It was the nurse of self-
sufficiency and rigidity. It had no sense of sin and so
it estimated man wrongly. After all, the Stoic had not
fully found God ; when he thought of God he really
thought of nature.

Such were the moral and religious forces at work in
Athens during the days when St. Paul, tired, sick and
restless, wandered alone through the wonderful streets.

Above and beyond them stood the Acropolis, like a glorified Edinburgh Castle, a crown of matchless buildings of which the Parthenon was but one. The streets were crowded with temples, altars, statues and busts to a degree almost unimaginable. It was easier, Petronius said, to meet a god than a man in Athens, and another writer speaks of the city as being, the whole of it, one altar, one sacrifice and votive offering to the gods.

The Romans had already carried away some of the best statues to Rome, and to others they had done unutterably barbarous things. They had knocked ancient Greek heads off the figures and replaced them with modern Roman heads. In some places modern Proconsuls replaced ancient heroes on their pedestals. There were multitudes of tasteless modern statues also to be seen ; the art of the period was atrociously bad. Nevertheless, many of the matchless old statues were still in position.

Dean Farrar describes the general effect in a characteristic passage. ' There were statues by Pheidias and Myron, and statues without number of the tasteless and mechanical copyists of the period of the Empire, statues of antiquity as venerable as the olive-wood Athene which had fallen from heaven, and statues of yesterday, statues colossal and diminutive, statues equestrian and erect and seated, statues agonistic and contemplative, solitary and combined, plain and coloured, statues of wood, and earthenware, and stone, and marble, and bronze, and ivory, and gold, in every attitude, and in all possible combinations, statues standing like lines of sentinels in every street.'

It was impossible to get out of the way of the

Lt

Athenian religion, to walk out into the streets was like walking into church, and St. Paul's spirit was provoked and embittered ; the beauty, insistency and earnestness of this tremendous demonstration of paganism filled his soul with a holy jealousy. He had meant to be silent and quiet for a few days, but in such a place it was impossible. He began to reason both in the synagogue and in the Agora. The Agora was the sacred central place of the city, the point which focused its life – it combined the functions of the Exchange, Bond Street, and Hyde Park. It was crowded by business people in the morning, it contained all the best shops, it was also surrounded by the most important of the civic buildings, and the senators and magistrates passed constantly to and fro. In the afternoon the fashionable folk came and lounged there, and chatted, or read the news, or listened to some fresh exponent of some novel fad or craze, who came to bid for an audience under one of the great porticoes or arcades. These porches were the recognised gathering-place of lecturers and students, and the most celebrated of the porches in the Agora at Athens was the Painted Porch, the Stoa Poikile, adorned with ancient frescoes, which had been the scene of the labours of Zeno, and which had given its name to his followers, who were called the Stoics, or the frequenters of the Porch. St. Paul's appearance, nationality, manner and message were all sufficiently strange to Athens to get him a large and curious audience. The people who met him told their philosophical guides of this strange little man, and Paul soon found himself crossing swords with Stoic and Epicurean teachers. Generally speaking, his audience quite failed to understand him.

Christ crucified and risen, offering pardon and the gift
of the Holy Spirit, seemed to the Athenians, who
were entirely contented with this world, a farrago of
nonsense.   Paul is only a seed-picker, they said con-
temptuously, as they broke off in groups and turned
away. ' Seed-picker ' was a slang Athenian term for
a man who had picked up scraps of learning and
chattered them ; it was also used of shoplifters and
area sneaks.   But the crowd that remained took
St. Paul more seriously, they listened laboriously and
with much confusion of mind, and caught as the two
key-words, Jesus and Anastasis or Resurrection.
Evidently, they said, the speaker is the slave of
new deities, whose cult he is obliged to propa-
gate.   These deities, they contended, are a pair,
male and female.   The male is called Jesus, and
the female Anastasis.   They mistook the word Anastasis, Resurrection, which is feminine, for a goddess.
It is interesting to notice that these very clever people
at Athens made one of the most stupid, muddle-headed
audiences St. Paul ever addressed.

The strange preacher, however, did not content himself with preaching the new deities, he attacked the
old, and that could not be permitted in Athens, or indeed in any city of the period.   No violence of any
sort was used, but one day, when the court of the
Areopagus was sitting, St. Paul was quietly arrested
and placed before it for examination.   The Areopagus
at Athens corresponded to the Senate at Rome, and its
permission was necessary before any new religious cult
could be introduced into the city.   The hill from which
the court took its name, as having been its ancient
meeting-place, lay to the south of the Agora, and our

English version gives the impression that St. Paul was taken to the top of it and induced to address a large crowd from there ; but this is probably not the case. He was evidently on his defence before the court, and the court would not have proceeded to the top of the hill to hear him.   It is more likely that the Areopagus was sitting in the Parliament House in the Agora, the Stoa Basilica, and that there St. Paul was taken and examined in a crowded court.   You will have noticed the great courtesy with which the enquiry was conducted.   On this occasion St. Paul suffered nothing more than a little derision.

St. Paul began in the traditional way : " Athenians," and proceeded to pay them a somewhat double-edged compliment.   " You are certainly," he said, " exceedingly religious, for among the objects of your worship I have found an altar inscribed to an unknown god.   What therefore you worship in ignorance this set I forth unto you."   We know from other sources that there were at this time altars at Athens inscribed to unknown gods ; and this was probably an altar erected after some pestilence or calamity which the Athenians had felt unable to trace to the action of any known deity.   St. Paul's sermon aimed at lifting his hearers' thoughts from the god whom they thought of as immanent in nature – of whom they were part, and whom they could represent externally in many graceful ways – to the Omnipotent and Eternal, who holds us all in the hollow of His hand, who can neither be embodied in any image nor cajoled by His creatures. In a few strong strokes he describes the Athenians as having been pleasantly occupied with the gods of their invention until suddenly a veil had vanished ; the

Omnipotent and Eternal had manifested Himself, thereby convicting men of blindness and sin, and commanding them to repent in view of a judgment, in which the judge should be one He had lately raised from the dead. At this a section of the audience burst out laughing, and said, " Really what preposterous nonsense ! " Another section said, " Most interesting, *most* interesting ; we should like to hear more another day, thank you — thank you so much for your nice explanation ; let the hearing be adjourned to another day." The Areopagus, who probably thought St. Paul a little mad, agreed to this. Mr. Rackham also thinks that the word used for *departed* suggests that they gave a quiet intimation to St. Paul that he had better leave Athens.

Nevertheless a few believed : Dionysius, who was a member of the court of the Areopagus, a woman named Damaris, and a few others.

It was apparently a humilating failure and yet——

' Ah, beautiful and chaste images,' cries Renan, ' fine gods and fine goddesses, tremble. See the man who will raise the hammer against you. The fatal word has been pronounced, you are idols. The mistake of this ugly little Jew will be your death warrant.'

It is St. Luke, not St. Paul, who calls the images idols in the Acts, although no doubt St. Paul did so also. They were not idols before St. Paul called them so, but they became idols when he so named them, for idolatry means clinging to a worn-out, superseded conception of God. A man is an idolater when he has the knowledge and power to enable him to rise to a higher vision of God and he refuses to do so. It is no doubt very sad that so much pre-Christian art was destroyed

just as the Incarnation was redeeming all the visible
world, enabling it once more to dedicate its material
beauty to the glory of God. But it was necessary to
demonstrate in an unmistakable way that the power of
the old religion was broken and its day gone.

And more than that ; if pagan art had not been
destroyed, Christian art could never have come to the
birth. Had men continued to think that the graceful
outline of the human form is all that art can represent,
Fra Angelico would never have been inspired to paint
the grace of the Holy Spirit, or Raphael the mystery
of the Incarnation. It was a stern necessity, but
I think a real one, which resulted in the head of every
one of the pictures on the walls of the glorious Egyptian
Temple of Edfu being defaced before the temple was
used for Christian worship, and which has led to the
noblest art of pre-Christian days being gathered up
into a splendid captivity in the halls of the Vatican
under the footstool of the Papal Throne. " They are
the idols of the ancients," said worthy but rough old
Adrian VI when his attendants led him through the
sculpture galleries, and he had the Belvidere walled up.
No doubt, in a subtle sense, the Pope was right ; it
was beauty of form that Greece had worshipped and
little else.

CHAPTER XIII

APPARENTLY Paul was still alone when he left Athens. The movements of Timothy and Silas at this time are not easy to follow. They had been left at Berea, and St. Paul had sent back a message to them by the people who brought him to Athens, telling them to join him immediately. Only Timothy seems to have come, and by the time he arrived it became clear to St. Paul that an Apostolic delegate was necessary at Thessalonica. He seems to have sent him straight back to Thessalonica and went on alone to Corinth. After a time Silas and Timothy rejoined St. Paul at Corinth, and the news Timothy brought of the condition of the Thessalonian Church induced St. Paul to write the First Epistle to the Thessalonians.

Corinth was fifty miles from Athens, and by far the quickest way to reach it was to take ship to Cenchrea on the Saronic gulf : the voyage took about five hours.

The change in the moral and intellectual atmosphere was, says Mr. Rackham, like going from Oxford to London – which, in a sense, is true, but Athens and Oxford are much more alike than Corinth and London. Corinth was a brand new city. Old Corinth had been entirely destroyed by the Roman general Mummius in 146 B.C. But so magnificent a site for a city could not long lie neglected. Corinth was like an immense Llandudno. It lay at the foot

of a fine bluff corresponding to Great Ormes Head,
the Acrocorinthus, and it stretched across the flat
isthmus from gulf to gulf, as Llandudno lies between
its two seas, or as Interlaken lies between the Lakes
of Thun and Brienz.

Now a canal has been cut across the isthmus ; then
they had a wonderful plan of hauling ships across on
dry land, and this was the quickest way from Asia to
Rome.

Although the Corinth of St. Paul's days was the
biggest city he had worked in up to this point, except
Syrian Antioch, Julius Cæsar had founded it anew as
a Roman colony only a hundred years before. It was
a thoroughly cosmopolitan city, there was no old
established community to give it local colour and tone,
and like Suez, Port Said and San Francisco, and those
delightful South Pacific Islands Stevenson describes, it
contained the seafaring scum of the world, and the sort
of scoundrels who subsist on their violence and vices.
Although the former population of Corinth had been
scattered at the destruction of the city, it had unfortunately left its religion behind. On the Acrocorinthus stood the far-famed Temple of Aphrodite
Pandemos, which possessed a thousand votaries who
were dedicated to vicious lives, sexual action being made
the expression of devotion to the goddess. The city
at this moment presented an appearance which may be
paralleled still in the western cities of America. There
were many magnificent new buildings, but here and
there they stood beside the huts of wood and thatch,
which the earlier settlers in the new colony had used.
Here and there through the city, too, were the remains
of the temples which Mummius had burnt down ;

the stained and calcined marble columns and capitals
stood clear cut against the blue sky, and were in
striking contrast to the ostentatious luxury of the new
buildings.   These old temples were objects of much
curiosity in St. Paul's day, and he would often find
country folk standing agape in front of them.   They
provided him with one of the most interesting illus-
trations in his letters.   He is describing the work that
he had done at Corinth under the figure of a building.
He is the master builder, he has laid the foundation,
other than which no man, who sets his hand to this
task, can lay — Jesus Christ — but in every building reared
upon this foundation both the character of the builder
and the materials he has at his command become
apparent.   It is possible to construct a glorious or
a mean building on the one foundation, like the grand
new buildings of Corinth and the wattle and daub huts
which still stood side by side.   But in the end, just as
the fires of Mummius had tested the building material
of old Corinth, so the day of the Lord will demonstrate
the value of what each man has built, because on that
day it shall be revealed by fire, which shall try every
man's work of what sort it is.   And the work of eternal
value alone will abide, and it will remain like the old
marbles of Corinth which defied the flames of Mummius — a possession for ever.   St. Paul adds a further
thought which, like many of his finest thoughts, is so
compressed as to be difficult at first sight to understand.   ' If any man's work shall be burned,' he adds,
' he shall suffer loss, but he himself shall be saved yet
so as by fire."   He is, of course, throughout the whole
passage, only contemplating the condition of the
saved — their relation to their work ; and in the case of

a man whose work must partly be destroyed but who himself is saved, he pictures him as if he were shut up at the last day inside the building he has erected, which is then set on fire. As the building burns, the rotten parts are destroyed, but the good parts remain, a framework, through the gaps in which he can escape to safety.

St. Paul, as we know from the First Epistle to the Corinthians, was still very unwell and exceedingly depressed when he came to Corinth. His sensitive temperament had been shocked by the failure at Athens, and he surveyed the exceedingly important, but terribly unpromising, mission-field at Corinth with dismay. The city contained 700,000 people, of whom 400,000 were of the slave class — a class without religion or morals. The state of the town was so bad that ' to play the Corinthian ' was a slang term for noisy profligacy, and a drunken Corinthian was a favourite farcical character in Greek low comedy. As usual, St. Paul went to the Jewish quarter and entered it in the character of a travelling artisan. He was advised to consult a skilled tentmaker named Aquila, who had lately established himself at Corinth and who probably was looking out for hands. So he went drearily to the house of Aquila, and — there seems no doubt about it — found two devout and simple Christians. It is, of course, possible that Aquila and Priscilla were two devout, clear-souled Jews, who quickly accepted the Gospel message from St. Paul, but there is no record of their conversion and baptism, and the reason for their presence in Corinth makes it likely that they were already Christians when St. Paul met them.

Aquila was a Jew of Pontus, in Asia, who had settled in Rome, where he had a tentmaking business. Tentmaking was, of course, in those days of constant travel without railway trains, a very big industry indeed. It is probable that it was at Rome that Aquila met his wife, Prisca or Priscilla — both names are Roman, and they both occur in the cemetery of the Acilian Gens, so it is possible that they were freedmen of that family. A more interesting suggestion, and one which has the support of Dr. Hort, is that Priscilla was of higher rank than Aquila, a Roman lady, a proselyte of righteousness, who had married the well-to-do man of business. Certainly Priscilla was the leading spirit ; in four out of the six references to the pair, Priscilla's name comes first. She became a leading Christian lady and evidently did much evangelistic work.

Aquila and Priscilla appear as living in so many different places that they have given critics an excuse for attacking the integrity of the text of the Epistle to the Romans. They had lived in Rome, now they were at Corinth, later on they were St. Paul's hosts at Ephesus, then they were at Rome again, and when one last hears of them in 2 Timothy they are once more at Ephesus. This is one of the reasons which has led some eminent scholars to deny that Romans xvi. really forms part of that Epistle and to maintain that it is the tail end of a lost Epistle to the Ephesians which has got tacked on to Romans by mistake. But it is becoming more and more recognised that the integrity of that portion of the Epistle to the Romans cannot really be shaken. The fact is that life under the Empire was extraordinarily migratory, and expecially so, owing to their close commercial freemasonry, among the Jews. Further, Corinth was the half-way-house between Italy and Ephesus on the straight route. Ephesus, Corinth, Brindisi, were like London, Edinburgh, Aberdeen. The reason why Aquila and Priscilla were now in Corinth was that Claudius had expelled the Jews, for the time being, from Rome. Pompey, in 61 B.C., had planted a settlement of Jewish prisoners in Rome, and they had multiplied so rapidly and become so turbulent an element in the population that the Romans had come to regard them with fear and dread. Tiberius deported 4,000 to Sardinia in the hope that the malaria, which is rife in that island, would destroy them, and now Claudius had banished the Jews altogether because, says Suetonius, they were in a constant state of tumult at the bidding of one Christus. ' One Christus ' is our Blessed Lord, and the secular historian is no doubt referring to the disturbance in the Jewry over the preaching of Christianity. It is this that make its probable that Aquila and Priscilla were Christians when St. Paul found them.

The Jews soon came back to Rome and the whole episode is very characteristic of the great Empire, its contemptuous way of dispersing a noisy crowd, and then leaving it to collect again gradually, with the lesson of its dispersion before it to keep it quiet.

It is very pleasant to think of the quiet Christian home which received St. Paul, of the care and nursing of Priscilla, and the happy days of work at the old trade. He now settled down and, as we know, spent eighteen months at Corinth. I think it not improbable that St. Paul at first decided he would change his

THE ADVENTURE OF PAUL OF TARSUS

tactics and would postpone a breach with the Synagogue as long as possible. It may be that it was merely
bodily weakness which prevented his preaching much,
and so postponed the crisis. Certainly there was
a change of attitude when Silas and Timothy came,
for the Acts says : ' But when Silas and Timothy
came down from Macedonia, Paul was constrained by
the Word, testifying to the Jews that Jesus was the
Christ.' He had reached Corinth in the winter, when
navigation down the coast from Macedonia had been
suspended. As soon as spring re-opened navigation,
Silas and Timothy came. Meanwhile St. Paul had
done some quiet work, he had appeared in the synagogue, as he says, with bodily weakness and fear and
much trembling.

The Bezan Text probably gives the clearest impression of this quiet time. ' And entering into the
synagogue he reasoned every Sabbath day, inserting
the name of the Lord Jesus ; and he was persuading
not only Jews but also Greeks.' He made a few
converts quietly, and as he had no assistants with him
he baptised them with his own hands. Gaius and the
household of Stephanas appear to have been baptised
at this time. But with the arrival of Timothy and
Silas came a great change in the situation. Their arrival cheered St. Paul very much : he was most
pathetically dependent upon the friends he loved.
The news from Thessalonica was good, although
there were naturally elements in the state of things
there which caused the Apostle anxiety. The travellers
also brought an offering of money from Philippi, the
greater part of which no doubt was supplied by Lydia.
This set St. Paul free for the moment from the need of

working for his livelihood, and he was able to give all
his time and strength to the campaign.

A Divine impulse moved the Apostle to make a great
and startling utterance. He had been reasoning and
interesting the Jews, now he testified. He proclaimed
his experience of and mission from the risen Jesus who
was Messiah. There was a great scene, the Jews
blasphemed and cried, " Anathema Jesus." It was
the most dramatic of all the scenes with the Jews.
St. Paul ultimately shook out his lap with a strong
gesture as if he were casting them out from their place
in the Kingdom of God ; for the first time he performed a kind of act of excommunication. I suppose
they had excommunicated him, and it suggests the
growing sense of the power of the Church that St. Paul
replied by excommunicating them. ' And the children of the Kingdom shall be cast into outer darkness.'

He then established the Church in the house next
door to the synagogue, the house of Titus Justus,
a God-fearing proselyte, and began a mission to the
Gentiles. It met with the usual success ; they came
in great numbers, and the tense of the Greek verb in
1 Cor. vi. 11 implies that baptism and confirmation
were being administered there in a steady stream day
after day. One of the most startling things that happened was that Crispus, the ruler of the synagogue,
was converted, and St. Paul marked the occasion by
doing what he very rarely did, by baptising him with
his own hand.

We do not know what the considerations were
which led St. Paul to plant the Church next door to
the synagogue. He must have had very good reason
for doing so and he never feared to do a strong,

disagreeable thing. It is difficult, when one studies this robust decisive action of the Apostle, not to feel that we moderns have grown squeamish in our proclamation and defence of the Faith, not to feel that in our desire always to speak and act with delicate taste we have lost the simple, hearty, straightforward power of long ago.

And now St. Paul began to experience some of the trials which attend the everyday routine of a growing Christian community. In all the places since the first days in the Syrian Antioch he had founded a Church and then gone on elsewhere, leaving the building-up to others. Here he stayed. There was of course a violent Jewish opposition and some personal danger, but after a little the Church itself became restless and difficult to manage. The more cultured people who had joined the Church wanted fine sermons and philosophical disquisitions ; they got neither and they grew discontented. And then our Lord intervened. Our Lord intervenes openly oftener than people imagine. I can recall several occasions on which persons whom I have known have had such vivid experiences of Him, and in every case the attitude of the person has been the same, very reserved and quiet, very unready to speak of the event, very thankful and very anxious to think of it as a privilege, rather than as something on which to lean.

I feel that this is a test of the reality of the experiences. Excitability, a tendency to rest upon a vision and argue from it, a tendency to be distracted by it from the sacramental system of the Church, would be signs of a lying wonder. We do not wonder that at a moment of so much trial and of such importance to the whole Church, our Lord gave to the Apostle this peep behind the scenes. It was followed by a great outburst of the signs and wonders of the Holy Spirit. Read 1 Corinthians again, see the extraordinary vigour and complexity of the Church life in Corinth, note from the references to the Resurrection and the Eucharist, in allusions which it is clear all readers were expected to understand, how full, deep and minute the teaching was ; note the extraordinary gifts which were exercised, miracles, prophecy, tongues ; note the varied functions of the greatly diversified ministries, and then remember that this was only about twenty years after the Ascension, and so realise that Catholic Christianity, as we now know it, is the Christianity of the first days. It was 1 Corinthians which made me a Catholic. When I first read it carefully at Oxford, I realised that the Church at Corinth was Catholic, not Protestant. We must not anticipate the analysis of that letter which St. Paul afterwards wrote from Ephesus, but we may see from it something of the varied and motley gathering which surrounded St. Paul. He got hold of some of the lowest and most depraved people. Fortunatus, Achaicus, Quartus, and Tertius (to whom afterwards St. Paul dictated the Epistle to the Romans) were probably of the substantial Latin middle class. Stephanas and Gaius could be hospitable on a big scale, Chloe was a widow lady with a retinue of servants, Crispus was the ruler of the synagogue, and Erastus was no less a person than the treasurer of the city.

In the next chapter I shall say a little about the two letters to Thessalonica, which St. Paul wrote, one directly after Silas and Timothy arrived, and the other just before he left Corinth. I shall also say some general things about St. Paul's letters. I must end this chapter by sketching the circumstance which ultimately led St. Paul to conclude his first visit to Corinth.

In A.D. 15, Achaia, which had been a province with a Proconsul under the Senate, was united by Tiberius to Macedonia, a province governed by a Propraetor. In 44, five years before St. Paul came to Corinth, Claudius gave Achaia back to the jurisdiction of the Senate, and a Proconsul once more came to govern it.

In the year 49, the year of St. Paul's arrival at Corinth, the great Seneca, the noble Stoic philosopher whose teaching had many points of detail in common with the Gospel, regained the favour of the Imperial Court which for some time had been estranged from him. A little while after, the Proconsulate of Achaia became vacant, and an exceedingly interesting appointment was made, an appointment which was paralleled in modern times when America out of compliment to England sent us as her ambassador James Russell Lowell. The Senate appointed to the vacant post Lucius Junius Gallio. The appointment was received with enthusiasm, and well it might be. Gallio was the dearest and most fascinating man imaginable. Seneca, like all the world, adored his brother, ' sweet Gallio,' as everyone called him. Seneca once wrote of him, ' No mortal man is so sweet to his dearest love as Gallio is to all mankind,' and again, ' Not even those who love my brother Gallio with a love reaching the furthest limit of all possible human love, love him enough.'

Mt

Gallio was a very distinguished man of letters ; his friends were amused at the appointment, and Seneca playfully speaks of ' my Lord Gallio.' Soon after the arrival of Gallio the Jewish opponents of St. Paul were prompt to take advantage of his inexperience. They had heard of his sweet and gentle character, and they tried to shake his nerve by the violence of their pleading. They consequently waylaid St. Paul, and with a great uproar dragged him into the Proconsular court. He was teaching, they shrieked, an unlicensed religion under cover of their own. " Let not Gallio be deceived," cried Sosthenes, who had succeeded Crispus as ruler of the synagogue. Paul's religion was not theirs, it was a new and dangerous cultus. But Gallio was equal to the occasion. " I am not one of your ecclesiastical judges," he said ; " I am here to judge civil and moral questions. I know nothing of the intricacies of your religion." Ah ! how eagerly Paul waited for an opportunity to speak, how earnestly he looked into the face of this fine flower of Rome, this beautiful soul whom Jesus loved. But Gallio scarcely noticed the poor little Oriental who was the object of all the clamour. " Lictors," he cried, " clear the court " — so the opportunity never came.

The Corinthians were deeply incensed by the conduct of the Jews. They were disgusted that the great and honoured Gallio should receive a bad impression so soon after his arrival. So they seized Sosthenes, the ruler of the synagogue who had brought the charge against Paul and gave him a good beating. Gallio thought this a healthy proceeding, and pretended not to notice it. No doubt the affair gave him scarcely a moment of serious thought.

From a practical point of view the result was satis-
factory. St. Paul was not driven from Corinth, although
he took the episode as a signal to move away presently
for a time. The protection of Rome was for the
moment practically extended to the Corinthian Church

But what a terrifying scene this is !

It is nothing short of terrifying that one so sweet
and fair as Gallio should lose his opportunity of hearing
the Christian message merely through the inherited
patrician attitude. Gallio died a truly heathen death ;
he died by his own hand.

CHAPTER XIV

Gallio's toleration of the Christians had been a matter for profound thankfulness. St. Paul remained long enough after the scene in the law court to demonstrate that he had liberty to stay in Corinth, and then he concluded his visit, leaving the Church sufficiently organised to consolidate and develop her life. In a less degree it was true of St. Paul as of his Divine Master that it was expedient for his disciples that he should go away. As long as his tremendous personality continued to dominate a Church, any real initiative in its members was impossible. St. Paul now felt himself free to visit Ephesus. He had twice been turned back, as he believed by the Holy Spirit, from Ephesus, but he recognised that the task set for him had been fulfilled ; he had founded the Galatian, Macedonian and Achaian Churches, and now at last he was free to attack the capital of the province of Asia.

Apparently he mapped out all the first part of the third missionary journey at Corinth. Priscilla and Aquila had determined to share his fortunes at Ephesus, and they decided to leave Corinth with St. Paul, and go straight to Ephesus, and arrange a lodging for him there. Meanwhile St. Paul was to pay a visit to Jerusalem and hold conference with what Apostles were there, and afterwards he was to go to Syrian Antioch and take some rest in what I suppose

he regarded as his Christian home. Then he was to
work up by the land route to Ephesus, going home to
Tarsus, crossing the Taurus by the Cilician Gates
once more, and making an Apostolic visitation of the
Galatian Churches at Lystra, Derbe, Iconium and
Pisidian Antioch. Then from Pisidian Antioch he
was to do what the Holy Ghost had twice stopped his
doing, he was to go straight to Ephesus.

His plan made out, St. Paul prepared to start, and
we are told that at Cenchrea he had his hair cut because he had been under a vow for thirty days. It
is a valuable bit of evidence as to St. Paul's exact
religious position at the moment. Here was a
widespread religious practice which he did not feel
in the least incompatible with the Catholic Faith, by
means of which indeed it was natural to him to ex-
press his thankfulness to Almighty God. The treatment of the hair has in many religions been a means
of religious expression. In those days mourners would
shave after a death, sailors in thanksgiving for deliverance from peril ; and pilgrims would allow their
hair to grow till the accomplishment of their pilgrimage. Very especially was the cutting of the hair
associated with the taking of vows, either as a form
of intercession to avert an evil or in thanksgiving for
deliverance from evil. Among the Jews the Nazarite
vow fulfilled such an office and was especially legislated
for. In thanksgiving, as we suppose, for Gallio's
decision, and the protection it had brought to the
Churches, St. Paul took the temporary Nazarite vow.
He had abstained from wine and had allowed his hair
to grow for thirty days. Had he been in Palestine he
should, properly speaking, have appeared in the

Temple on the thirtieth day, offered the concluding
sacrifice, shaved his head and burned the hair with the
sacrifice. Being in a foreign land he availed himself
of the permission accorded to the foreign Jews, to cut
his hair in the usual way at the end of the month, and
put the hair into a box to be offered at the next visit
to Jerusalem when the concluding portion of the vow
must be carried out.

He did this just before going on board his boat at
the Port of Corinth, and so, with the hair safely
treasured up to be burned with the rest of his hair,
when his head was shaved in the Temple, he started
for Jerusalem.

It was near the feast of Pentecost and this was
probably a Jewish pilgrim ship. It crossed the
Ægean first to Ephesus, and stopped there long
enough for the pilgrims to go to synagogue on the
Sabbath.

By this time the Jews of Ephesus must have heard
of Christianity. The Jewish body there was an important one. It had obtained decrees from the Roman
Governors, and the Ephesian people allowed it the
free use of its religious customs. All the contributions
of the Jews of Asia to the Temple were sent up by sea
from Ephesus, and they were very large indeed. The
Jews of Ephesus evidently questioned St. Paul. He
did not, I imagine, open the subject of Christianity
to them. They had some apparently courteous argument, and St. Paul, explaining his plans, promised to
return, and proceeded on his journey, leaving Priscilla
and Aquila behind. He landed at Cæsarea, paid his
official visit to the leaders in Jerusalem, fulfilled his
Nazarite vow and went down to Antioch.

About this visit to Jerusalem only one detail survives. The Apostles spoke to him of his promise to
' remember the poor.' At a previous meeting at Jerusalem, the Heads of the Church there had proposed to
St. Paul that he should start collections in the Gentile
Churches for the poor Christians of Jerusalem ; it
was agreed that such an exhibition of charity would
be powerful to preserve the unity of the Church.
But up to this time St. Paul had not begun to make
the collection ; he had been so afraid in Macedonia
and Achaia of being regarded as a money-making
orator that he had refused maintenance and kept himself by his trade, and had not asked for a penny for
any purpose at all. He must have explained his action
to the other Apostles, and he undertook to make the
collection during his next round of visits. Throughout
the third missionary journey, the collection for the
Jerusalem poor was an important incident.

And now we approach the greatest tragedy in the
life and work of St. Paul, the opposition to him within
the Church. That it should have arisen is perfectly
natural, quite in accord with what we should expect
under all the circumstances.

The Church had emerged from Judaism ; the
Incarnate Son had made His entrance into human life
as Messiah of the Jews. He and His message, that is
to say, fitted in with certain human expectations, but
His closest followers came to realise that these expectations fell very far short of an adequate conception
of His Person, Nature, and work. So there arose two
groups among " Christians " – people who had left their
human expectations behind like some childish gar-
ment, too small for the full-grown youth, and had

accepted the full Catholic Gospel, and those others
who clung to the human expectations, who continued
to see our Lord through Jewish spectacles, who refused to see that there could be anything better than
the fulfilment of the old Jewish hope as the best Jews
had held it, and who thought the Catholic Gospel a re-
volt against the noblest tradition the world had ever
known.   The Council of Jerusalem had been called
together to deal with the situation, and the Council
of Jerusalem had affirmed the Catholic Gospel and
had framed some rules devised to make religious and
social communion throughout the whole body possible.

This had brought peace for a time – but only for
a time.   In the two years preceding this visit of
St. Paul to Jerusalem the disaffected Christians had
become a vigorous proselytising body, and now it was
that they began a systematic campaign against St. Paul
through all his Churches, a campaign which continued
up to his death.   The martyrdom of St. Peter and
St. Paul at Rome silenced the Judaic opposition in the
Church, and henceforth the Judaisers ranked as
heretics.

After his rest at Antioch, St. Paul, as I have said,
travelled to Ephesus by the land route through the
Cilician Gates and the Galatian Churches ; as St. Luke
says, *stablishing* all the disciples, and it is an interesting
question what relation these visits bear to the Epistle
to the Galatians in which St. Paul replies to the
Judaisers.

Did St. Paul find at Jerusalem that the Judaisers
had gone through the Galatian Churches ?   Did he
write the fiery Epistle to the Galatians from Antioch,
and did he follow it up by these visits in which he

regained the adherence of those who had been led astray ?

That he did is a widely held modern view, and one would like to think that it was so ; but I am afraid I feel that the older view is the more probable, and that the bad news about the Judaisers reached St. Paul at Ephesus – that they had followed him through the Galatian Churches, upsetting the work he had so lately confirmed there, and that the Epistle to the Galatians was written just before the Epistle to the Romans, which it so much resembles, and at a time when anxieties from many quarters, external persecution, and ill-health combined to make St. Paul's life almost unendurable.

St. Paul is now approaching a centre of imperial activity second only to Rome, and a centre of religious influence second to none. For the headquarters of the world's spiritualism lay round the shrine of Artemis, where amid surroundings of extraordinary splendour lay the image which had fallen down from heaven. Timothy and Titus are with him, and probably three European disciples, Erastus of Corinth, the Treasurer of the city, a very noble gentleman, and Gaius and Aristarchus who had attached themselves to him in Macedonia.

CHAPTER XV

THE Roman Province of Asia, the coast line of which stretched from the Sea of Marmora to a point opposite the island of Rhodes, was so called because it was the first land of that continent which the Roman conquerors touched. Early in history the Greeks had colonised it. Then the Persians conquered it. Later the coast towns had freed themselves with the help of Athens, and the whole was re-conquered by Alexander the Great. It became a Roman Province in 133 B.C., and Ephesus was its capital. A desolate and malarious marsh now covers the ground on which Ephesus once stood, that great Vanity Fair, the Marseilles of the East. It lay a mile from the sea on lovely and luxuriant water meadows, which were alive at sunset with flights of swans and other water fowl. The buildings of the city clustered beneath and ran up into the heights of Mount Coressus and Mount Prion. It was no walled Eastern town, but spread itself at luxuriant ease into delightful suburbs, where the wooden chalet-like villas with their deep verandahs were hidden amid luxuriant foliage.

The third metropolis of Christendom, Ephesus was in later years a centre of that vigorous movement for an organised unity which resulted in the creation of diocesan Episcopacy. In one of the streets which lay beneath the shadow of Coressus or of Prion the Gospel according to St. John was compiled.

Ephesus is the Babylon of the Apocalypse, with her

costly merchandise of gold and gems, her cinnamon, odours and ointments, her beasts and sheep, her chariots and slaves, and souls of men. Her climate was equable and delicious, and hence she was a sociable city. The matrons spun their flax upon the doorsteps of their houses, the lovely children played before them on the marble pavements, and at night-time the city where Anacreon sang was gay with wine and mirth and serenade. If I am to show you the Ephesus which St. Paul was now approaching, I must insist upon the romantic charm of the place.

High above the city and gleaming, so they tell us, like a star across the sea, stood the Temple of Artemis. It stood on the site of a primitive sanctuary.   Its worship was a survival of the primitive worship of God in Nature. The Greeks had adopted the aboriginal goddess and identified her with Artemis, the Romans with Diana. The builders of the Temple had feared for the safety of its foundations, and they had reared it upon a vast artificial substructure of skins and wood and earth.   It was built in the Ionic style, 418 feet long by 239 feet broad.   It was adorned by the noblest statuary, the work of Pheidias, Polycletus and others. Its paintings were equally famous, though perhaps not equally beautiful.   The roofs of the Temple were of cedar enriched with vermilion and gold, its columns were of jasper upon bases of Parian marble.   Many of these survive to-day, and are among the greatest glories of St. Sophia at Constantinople.   One hundred and twenty gigantic columns of Parian marble enclosed the shrine itself.   The shrine was dark and mysterious. At the east end stood an altar before a purple curtain, and behind that curtain stood the image which fell down from heaven, the most sacred image of the classical world, no beautiful statue from a master's hand, but a hideous log of wood black with the touch of unmeasured centuries. The upper part of the log was cut into the rude representation of a woman holding in either hand a bar of metal. Cut upon the crown, girdle and feet of the image were certain symbols known as the Ephesian letters. These letters were held to have a magical virtue when pronounced or when worn as an amulet. Their study was a science, and many treatises dealing with their value were in existence. Behind the image and secure under its protection lay the strong room of the Province of Asia, for all the riches of the Province were deposited here for safety. Imagine an institution which combined the varied importance of the Grotto at Lourdes, the Bank of England and Westminster Abbey, and you will have an inadequate notion of the importance and sanctity of the Temple of Artemis. It was a fountain of evil. Not only was organised evil part of its routine, but since, like the cathedrals of the Middle Ages, it formed sanctuary for criminals, it had attracted to its precincts all kinds of evil characters who had fled from justice and whose presence in the city was adverse to its morality. The Temple had an immense staff of priests and priestesses, templewardens, theologians, choristers, vergers, tirewomen, eunuchs and acrobats. The priests, who were an evil crew, had a custom of scouring the city for votaries from time to time, and St. Paul must have been sometimes interrupted while teaching by the yells of these frenzied processions of devotees mingled with the sound of jangling timbrels and piercing flutes.

When Aquila and Priscilla had settled into their new home and made themselves ready to receive St. Paul, they began to study the religious situation. They found a Synagogue prepared to be unusually friendly to the Gospel owing to the presence in Ephesus of some undeveloped Christians. Before anything else could be done in Ephesus these immature Christians had to be attended to and brought up to the level of full Catholic faith and practice. Aquila and Priscilla dealt with the distinguished Apollos before St. Paul came, and St. Paul on his arrival at once dealt with the little group of devout but unbaptised converts who had had no opportunity of intercourse with the chief Apostles. Perhaps we have never remembered that there must have been a good many such people scattered about the world in the first years of the Church's life. The movement of the Baptist had been very widespread ; he had had many followers among the Jews of the dispersion. Some must have returned to distant countries before his death, and others who had accepted our Lord as Messiah, but had never placed themselves under the authority of the Apostles, were still without the Gift of the Spirit and the grace of the Sacraments. And now out of this immature Christian faith and life there comes into the Catholic Unity the great teacher, Apollos. Apollos was a Jew of Alexandria, the first of the many important contributions of that philosophical centre to the ranks of the Defenders of the Faith. Alexandria was the headquarters of that liberal Jewish theology of which the great Philo, now an old man, was the chief exponent. These liberal theologians aimed at making the Greek language an accurate vehicle for Hebrew ideas, and in doing so they greatly helped the work of the Christian Church, for they helped to fit Greek to be the classical Christian language. They also aimed at commending Judaism to the Pagan world, and in doing this had gone to lengths which horrified the more conservative Jews of Palestine. They had even built a Jewish Temple at Leontopolis, near Alexandria, as a kind of Hellenistic counterpart to the Temple at Jerusalem.

Apollos was an eloquent and learned Jew of Alexandria, a disciple of Philo. His position as a Christian at the time of his arrival in Ephesus is clearly described. He had received the Baptism of John, he had been instructed in the way of the Lord, and he knew the things concerning Jesus. Perhaps he possessed the volume of sayings of our Lord which contained the Sermon on the Mount, and possibly he possessed an earlier edition of St. Mark's Gospel ; at any rate he knew the facts of our Lord's ministry, crucifixion and resurrection. It is felt that this is implied in the assertion that he taught ' accurately ' or ' exactly.' Evidently, then, he was the leader of a group of Alexandrian Christians who possessed the essence of the Bible but not the fellowship of the Church. No Apostle had as yet planted the Church there. We are told that when he came to Ephesus he was ' boiling in his spirit.' He was all afire with love of our Lord, but he knew nothing of the Holy Spirit and of the Church. So Priscilla and Aquila took Apollos to their cottage and put before him more exactly the way of God, showed him, that is to say, the new life of the Spirit in the Church, in other words, made him a Catholic. The simple old couple with the great Apollos at their feet is one of the beautiful early

Christian pictures. Although Apollos must have
been received into the Church by Baptism and Confirmation like the twelve disciples St. Paul afterwards
dealt with, there is no mention of it. He had gone to
Corinth before St. Paul got to Ephesus. The probability is that Apollos was very quietly received by an
Apostolic delegate, someone like Silas or Timothy,
deputed by St. Paul to confirm, but that no mention is
made of it lest a stigma might attach to Apollos because
an Apostle had not confirmed him. The idea of the
delegation of the Apostolic authority would still be a
difficult one for the rank and file of the Church to
accept. At once a sphere of work offered itself to
Apollos. The Bezan text tells us that certain Corinthians were staying at Ephesus at the time. They felt
that Apollos was the very man for Corinth, and they
begged him to go there. He consented and arrived
in due time at Corinth armed with a commendatory
letter from the Church of Ephesus. When St. Luke
says he utterly confuted the Jews at Corinth, a much
stronger word is used than the words applied to St.
Paul's success. Unfortunately he had not met St.
Paul, his powers and his methods were of another
order, and unintentionally he created a school within
the Corinthian Church which waxed so combative after
a while that Apollos decided to return to Ephesus
rather than endanger Christian unity.

Let us now rejoin St. Paul as he ends the series of
visits to his Churches in the Province of Galatia and
crosses the border into the Province of Asia at a point
only about 20 miles distant from Pisidian Antioch.
There were two ways down from Pisidian Antioch to
the coast at Ephesus. The usual road went through

Apamea, the biggest city of Phrygia, 60 miles south-
west of Antioch, and then joined the great highway
down the valley of the Lycus past Colosse and Laodicea
into the Mæander valley, and so down to the sea-
board. But there was a shorter though rougher track
which left the first route at Metropolis between Antioch
and Apamea, and made for Ephesus, 190 miles away,
in an almost straight line along the higher ground.
Metropolis was the spot at which St. Paul had felt
himself to be forbidden by the Holy Spirit to proceed to
Ephesus during his second missionary journey, but
now he was bidden to go forward, and it is characteristic of him that he took the quicker rougher route
through what the narrative calls 'the upper country.'
It is an interesting confirmation of the truth of this bit
of the Acts that St. Paul reminds the Colossians in his
Epistle to their Church that up to the time of writing,
some years after this, he had never been to Colosse.

As soon as he was settled in at Ephesus, St. Paul
began his work by dealing with the Christians who were
not yet Catholics. He found twelve men there
confessing our Lord but ignorant of the existence of
the Holy Catholic Church. It may be that they had
formed themselves into a little Jewish ascetic community in imitation of the Baptist's ascetic life, or St.
Paul may have discovered them by finding them
unable to understand his teaching. They puzzled
him, and he put the plain question to them, "Did you
receive the Holy Spirit when you believed ? " Their
reply was pathetic. " No, we did not even hear that
the Holy Spirit is being given." " Into what then
were you baptised ? " said St. Paul. " Into John's
Baptism," they answered simply. " John's Baptism,"

said St. Paul, " was only an expression of sorrow for
sin and of belief in the coming of the Christ Who is
Jesus." There was no hesitation or difficulty in the
minds of the twelve men as soon as they understood
their position ; they desired and received Catholic
Baptism. They were baptised into the name of the
Lord Jesus, the narrative says, the Bezan text adding
' for the forgiveness of sins.' ' And Paul laid on his
hands and the Holy Spirit came upon them.' Spiritual
phenomena accompanied the reception into the Church
of these devout believers in our Blessed Lord.

For three months St. Paul preached and argued in
the Ephesian synagogue. The Jews were not indis-
posed to listen to a non-Catholic Gospel, and it was
once more St. Paul's painful task to produce the violent
division which always arose when the full Catholic
message was proclaimed, and the universality and
finality of the Church asserted. ' He reasoned and
persuaded,' we are told, ' of the Kingdom of God,'
in other words, of that ' Church of God which He had
purchased with His own Blood.' The Epistle to the
Ephesians which he afterwards sent to the Churches of
the Province of Asia from Rome gives us the gist of his
teaching at this time.

When the separation from the Synagogue came St.
Paul organised the Church. He had Timothy and
Titus with him, and several other travelling companions, but he also ordained a body of presbyters to
whom he gave the Greek title of episcopoi, to be the
permanent settled pastors of the Church under the
supervision of the wandering Apostolate. The situation at Ephesus was for some time sufficiently peaceful
to permit St. Paul to teach publicly, and for this
Nt

purpose he hired a lecture-room well known in the city
as having been the scene of the lectures of Tyrannus,
a teacher whose fame survives only in this allusion.
This lecture-room was probably in a gymnasium ;
this was no longer a place of severe athletic exercise,
for the name had come to be applied to places of
organised amusement.   Ephesus had five of these
big pleasure gardens, and no doubt the school of
Tyrannus was in one of them.   The lectures of poets
and philosophers played an important part among
the entertainments of these places, and many halls were
built for their accommodation ; they were often alcoves
opening into colonnades.   Such halls were called
schools, and the derivation of the word is amusing.
To listen to lectures was a favourite form of recreation,
and so the word for leisure, *schole*, came to be applied
to the lecture itself, and then to the lecture-room, and
to the class who attended.   The word school, then,
originally meant leisure !

CHAPTER XVI

THE Bezan Text tells us that St. Paul's daily instructions went on from half-past eleven in the morning until half-past four in the afternoon. These were, of course, the hours of leisure and recreation during which it would be easy to gather audiences. It was for St. Paul a very busy time ; there was a good deal of house-to-house visiting among the inquirers, and much individual instruction was going on. In the earlier morning St. Paul worked at his trade. He did this, not so much from necessity, but rather as an example to others. Wherever the Church made a great impression it was very necessary to teach the converts that they must continue to be ordinary good citizens, doing their every-day work quietly and well. Speaking roughly, St. Paul worked at Ephesus for the inside of three years. He had learnt some lessons during his ministry, and he was careful not to be disrespectful to Artemis. He met with a great response. ' Great ' was the adjective invariably applied to Ephesus and all that concerned it, and St. Luke is able to apply it now to the demonstration there of the power of God in His Church. It is possible that St. Paul paid a short visit to Corinth during this time, and he evidently went to some of the other cities in the Province of Asia. The ' Seven Churches of Asia ' were all now developing. To Colosse St. Paul did not go ; Philemon, the wealthy Colossian who was one of his

converts at this period, must have come under his
influence during a visit to Ephesus. St. Paul made an
impression even on people of political importance, for
we learn that some of the members of the Legislative
Council, which consisted of the Governors of the chief
cities of the Province of Asia under a Governor-
General, were affected and became favourably disposed
to the teaching of the Church. Ephesus was a place
where religion was taken seriously and theosophy
had many students. Various theosophical and spirit-
ualistic teachers were struck by the psychic force Paul
and his converts displayed ; and no doubt it was they
who brought the Church before the notice of the
wealthier classes of society.

For a brief time, then, St. Paul tasted worldly success,
and the converts lavished upon him an immense
personal devotion. But the Second Epistle to the
Corinthians, which was written towards the end of this
time, or perhaps after the popular explosion, shows us
another side to the picture. It was a time of many
tears and many trials. He dies daily, he fights with
wild beasts, and both the Book of the Acts and the
Epistle he afterwards wrote from Rome to the Churches
of the province of Asia – the Epistle inscribed ' to the
Ephesians ' – give us a clue to this suffering. St. Paul
was wrestling ' not with flesh and blood.' He was
conscious of a great spiritual opposition behind the
scenes. Evil personalities of the many grades of evil
spirits were organised against him. Such a situation
draws out corresponding powers in spiritual men, and
St. Paul's miracles at this time were remarkable ; in
other words he was adequate to the occasion. It is
particularly recorded that, as in the case of the relics

of the later saints, handkerchiefs and aprons carried from his person to the sick wrought cures. Then there arose a set of counterfeit miracles in the power of the Holy Name.

That concentrated mental effort can have curative effects upon certain morbid conditions of the body is well known, but some strong incentive in the form of a powerful suggestion is needed to produce the required state of mental concentration. St. Paul had made such an impression upon Ephesus that it had become possible to conjure in this way with the Holy Name. The Holy Name could be employed with success to dominate the minds and change the bodily conditions of persons who were in no saving sense Christians.

The seven sons of Sceva were evidently an effective troupe of Jewish spiritualists. The father was a priest and also the ruler of a synagogue. Two of the sons of Sceva, at a moment when the whole matter was arousing intense public curiosity, gave a test exhibition of this power of using the Holy Name. The result as described in the Book of the Acts was a dramatic and extraordinary triumph for St. Paul and the Catholics and brought over to the Church many who believed.

The triumph of St. Paul at Ephesus was not only the triumph of Christian over Jew and Pagan that occurred in varying degrees wherever the Gospel was preached ; it was the triumph of Catholic Christianity over all other forms of belief in Christ. The non-Catholic Christians who now entered the Church made their confessions in public, and the form their amendment took was remarkable. They brought all their treatises on occultism, to the value of 50,000 drachmas,

corresponding, if we remember the change in the pur-
chasing value of money, to about £5,000, and made a
public bonfire of the rolls and parchments. We seem
to have jumped 1,400 years to the renaissance of such
rolls and parchments and their destruction again by
Savonarola in the Piazza at Florence. ' Thus,' says
St. Luke, ' the Word of the Lord, manifested in power,
continued to grow and prevail.'

And then all of a sudden the whole Catholic
movement in Ephesus came to grief with a great
crash.

It was the month of May in the year 54 – May,
which was still the month of Artemis, not yet the
month of Mary. The Ephesian Fair was in progress,
and all the world had come to do honour to Artemis
and enjoy itself. All the lodgings had been taken
months beforehand, there were masked carnival processions by day, and dances and serenades under the
stars all through the night. A committee of ten wealthy
and influential men directed the revels and bore the
expenses. It seems amazing that ten such people could
be found every year, but so it was ; the Ephesian
merchants were enormously wealthy, and the distinction of being one of the ten Lord Mayors was more
than a recompense.

But in this year 54 the Ephesian Fair showed a
distinct falling off, owing to the impression which St.
Paul's power and teaching had made on the place, and
the trade of the place was affected. It is easy to imagine
how the natural man woke up in the Catholics at this
their first popular success. It is easy to imagine the
eager reports to St. Paul. " Yes, it is quite true, there
are nothing like as many people in the Temple."

" Yes, I have been round the booths this morning and hardly any business is being done in religious emblems; the sellers don't know what to make of it."

St. Paul had written to Corinth at the Passover that he must stay in Ephesus through the month of Artemis and until Pentecost, because a great door and effectual was opened unto him. The Church held its breath and stood on tip-toe ; the conversion of vast multitudes to the faith hung in the balance, and then one single city man scattered the whole Catholic movement to the winds, Demetrius, the master of the Worshipful Company of Silversmiths.

In those days the City Companies still controlled the trades they represented. Of all the trades in Ephesus the silversmiths had been most sharply hit by the Church. People carried back to their families little souvenirs of the shrine modelled in clay or in silver : the tradesmen depended on the fair and now their stocks were hanging on their hands.

Demetrius did what anybody in his position would have done. He called a general meeting of the Company and said, " Gentlemen, things are critical, immediate action is necessary; this man has actually so upset the people that the trade which brings us bread and butter is in imminent danger of coming to a disreputable end, and more than that, our very religion is in danger of destruction."

The appeal to religious enthusiasm through self-interest and patriotism never fails. It did not fail now. ' Great is Artemis of the Ephesians.' It was a moving cry under the shadow of that gorgeous shrine, and soon a mob was aflame. It gathered strength as it charged through the narrow streets of the poor quarter

and made for the shop of Aquila. By a merciful providence, Paul was not at home, and I suppose in order to
gain time and to appease the fury of the mob, Priscilla
and Aquila gave themselves up and offered their lives
in sacrifice to God. God accepted their sacrifice, but
somehow, we know not how, He preserved them from
death. 'Greet Priscilla and Aquila, my helpers in
Christ Jesus,' writes St. Paul in after years, ' who for
my life laid down their own necks.' The mob failed
to catch St. Paul, but they caught Gaius and Aristarchus and dragged them to their trial in the theatre.

The theatre, cut out of the solid rock of the side of
Mount Coressus and faced with a gigantic portico, held
50,000 people. The mob broke in through the semi-
circle of great doors at the top of the building, and
inundated it down to the pit. You can see them – can't
you? – pouring down like swarms of bees over the stone
benches ; you can hear the babel of inquiry. The
majority of the crowd were pilgrims. Who were these
two pale, closely-pinioned Greek prisoners, and how
had they challenged the supremacy of Artemis ?

The din was terrific ; it echoed across the city, it
quickened the pace of a breathless man who dashed
into the great portico and was caught and held by some
friends – St. Paul. St. Paul had flung every consideration of prudence to the winds ; he only remembered that Gaius and Aristarchus stood in his stead in
the presence of death. But his friends overpowered
him and held him back, and now his mind was relieved,
for the committee of the games had reached the
theatre, and some of these gentlemen courteously
begged Paul not to show himself. " Your friends,"
they said, " are in no danger ; the mob have realised

that they have caught the wrong people ; they will soon have spent their energies in shouting, if you will keep quiet."

Meanwhile the scene in the theatre had become a comedy. The Gentile rioters could not find a Gentile who knew enough about the Church to explain what all this meant to the mob, so they were obliged to put up a Jew. But as soon as the mob saw a Jew get up they thought this must be not an accuser but a defendant, and they refused to give him a hearing. In vain the unfortunate Alexander gesticulated and begged for silence, nothing could stop the endless roar, " Great is Artemis of the Ephesians." At last the Recorder arrived on the scene and read an improvised Riot Act with triumphant success. " Nothing," he said, " can shake the position of Ephesus – these men are really unimportant, and at any rate there is a whole equipment of law for dealing with them. On the other hand, if this kind of thing happens in Ephesus, the authorities will take away the privileges of the city and stop the Ephesian games." With a perfectly uttered word of contempt he dismissed both the mob and the Catholic Church. But St. Paul's work was in the dust, and, once more a fugitive, he fled along the coast to Troas.

CHAPTER XVII

THE riot at Ephesus filled St. Paul with despair ; he was easily cast down and suffered very much under circumstances such as these. He says he was weighed down and overwhelmed by it ; life seemed over for him, and the sentence of death had been passed upon him and his work. He summoned the disciples to his lodging and bade them farewell ; it was the first of the long series of farewells of the great martyr during his progress to Jerusalem and Rome. Then he went up to Troas, the port on the Asiatic coast for Macedonia. He had been there before, and on that occasion had felt himself forbidden to preach by the Holy Spirit ; now he found a door was opened to him, but he could not preach, he failed to avail himself of the opportunity.

This glimpse into the mental state of the Apostle is interesting and consoling ; a great part, it seems to me, of the confessions of good people consists of the be-wailing of failure under such circumstances as these, through nervous or physical breakdown. St. Paul longed for Titus to come. He had enormous devotion to his friends, and in times of weakness he yearned to have them round him. He also longed for news from Corinth.

Here a word must be said about the state of things at this moment in the Church of Corinth. The Corin-thian converts had received the Gospel with great enthusiasm, but also with a great deal of intellectual curiosity. They eagerly debated its relation to the Jewish Church and to Gentile manners. They quickly realised that their Apostle was in conflict with a Jewish party in the Church, and they soon took sides on this and on other questions. Most of the difficulties with which the existing epistles to the Corinthians deal rose out of a restless interest in everything connected with Christianity. Apollos had gone to Corinth to take command before St. Paul arrived at Ephesus ; he greatly strengthened the Church on the intellectual side, but his preaching brought party feeling to a head. During his stay at Ephesus, St. Paul wrote a letter to Corinth which has been lost ; it was a very stern letter. Did St. Paul destroy it at Corinth when he had finally made peace there ? We cannot tell, but it is not unlikely. In this letter he sketched his future plans. He was to sail to Corinth, make a circular tour through Macedonia, return to Corinth, and then sail for Jerusalem, taking with him the alms which he had asked from the Christians of Macedonia and Greece, in aid of the poor Christians of Jerusalem. At the same time he sent Timothy and Erastus into Macedonia to begin the great collection. But in the last year of his stay in Ephesus he changed his plans, owing to news from Corinth.

A deputation of elders, headed probably by the Sosthenes who is associated with St. Paul in the title of the First Epistle to the Corinthians, arrived at Ephesus with a list of questions for the Apostle. About the same time, a Corinthian Christian lady and her household also arrived. This lady was a friend of St. Paul's, and she and her family felt it their duty to speak plainly to him about the sad state of the Corinthian Church – this is an office which good ladies often discharge with great effect – and Chloe and her family succeeded in terrifying St. Paul. And so at the Passover of 54 St. Paul wrote the letter we call the First Epistle to the Corinthians, and dispatched Titus with disciplinary authority ; at the same time he determined to postpone his own visit to Corinth until he had watched the effect of his letter and the mission of Titus. He recast his plans in this way. Titus was to go to Corinth, do his work, and then travel to Philippi through Macedonia. St. Paul was to go up the coast of Asia Minor to Troas, where Titus was to meet him. They were to cross to Macedonia together, and Timothy was to join them at one of the Christian centres there. Then they were to go together to Corinth. It was this nicely adjusted plan which got disarranged by St. Paul's sudden flight from Ephesus. He was before his time at Troas, and in an acute state of nervous anxiety he crossed over to Macedonia and met Titus, probably at Philippi.

On the whole, the news Titus brought him from Corinth was good. There had been a grave moral scandal in the Church there, and the authorities had been reluctant to deal with it. Now St. Paul learned that they had obeyed his directions and punished the offender. He experienced an enormous sense of relief, and under the inspiration of it he wrote the first seven chapters of the Second Epistle to the Corinthians. But there were still certain difficulties and anxieties. Owing to the efforts of the Judaising party, the collection for the Church at Jerusalem had not got on well, and so he was obliged to write the 8th and 9th chapters. He felt he must send a fresh mission with fresh directions about the collection, and he decided to send St. Luke. Fresh news again came from Corinth before the Second Epistle was finished ; the great Judaiser, the man who had made shipwreck of St. Paul's work in the Churches of Galatia, whose name, owing to St. Luke's conciliatory attitude, we do not know, had apparently arrived in Corinth with a complete case against St. Paul and his Gospel, and for the moment he carried all before him. If you think it out, you will see how much easier it was to present the case for the Judaisers than the case for the Catholics ; there was so much to be got out of the letter of the Old Testament, and even from our Lord's own words. On the one side a religious system rounded off and complete, the fulfilment of the prophecies. On the other hand, the great, ragged, unfinished conception of the Catholic Church which seemed to go so much further than the prophecies, something not contemplated by the best minds of the past.

These were the circumstances under which St. Paul wrote the last chapters of the Second Epistle, those fiery chapters, which have been called ' The Confessions of St. Paul.'

The difficulty about the collection for the poor at Jerusalem is a pathetic one. You will remember that it was absolutely necessary : the poor Christians were cut off from the alms of the synagogues of the Dispersion, and they were starving ; and it was also felt, both by the Church at Jerusalem and by St. Paul, that such a collection would be a means of binding the Churches together. To poor St. Paul the effort brought a little alleviation to his never-ending sorrow for his treatment of the Christians in Jerusalem in his pre-Christian days. But now the Judaisers, wherever they appeared, claimed to represent the Church for which collections were being made, and not only repudiated St. Paul and all his works, but even hinted that he was not to be trusted with the handling of money. What a pathetic sentence that is in the Epistle to the Romans, when St. Paul calls upon his readers to pray that the saints at Jerusalem may be graciously pleased to accept his offerings !

The Epistle to the Galatians was also written about this time. We do not know where, but it must have been written between St. Paul's departure from Ephesus at Pentecost, and his arrival at Corinth for the winter. It was probably sent from some small town where the Christian Church was not yet organised, for it was St. Paul's custom to associate with himself in his salutation the Church of the place from which he was writing, and in the salutation in this Epistle he only speaks of ' the brethren who are with me,' that is to say, the members of the missionary band. It is impossible to fix the spot ; it was either on the Asiatic coast or the Macedonian, probably the latter.

I want you to realise the terrible position of the Galatian Churches at the moment. They had not merely repudiated St. Paul's authority, they had accepted the Judaissers position in its fullness, and our Lord had ceased to be their Redeemer and King ; He had sunk in their eyes to the level of the national Messiah of the Jews. They were beginning to base their hopes of salvation, not on the Atonement and on faith in Christ, but on the performance of Jewish works of righteousness. So this stern Epistle was

written, Renan thinks, at a single sitting, in letters of
fire. In temper, tone, and phraseology it bears a close
resemblance to the Second Epistle to the Corinthians;
in its arrangement and doctrine it is a rough sketch of
the Epistle to the Romans, which was written later.
Under God we owe the Epistle to the Romans, that
great exposition of the fundamentals of the faith, to the
Galatian apostasy. St. Paul saw that a treatise must be
written working out the new relation of man to God
through Christ, and contrasting it with the Jewish and
Pagan systems. He did this in the Epistle to the
Romans, which he wrote at Corinth in the following
winter. I want you to think earnestly and long of the
tragic gloom that rested on this part of St. Paul's life.
Now we see that he has conquered all along the line.
The Catholic Gospel has conquered Judaism utterly,
but it seemed likely to be far otherwise at this time.

From Philippi St. Paul made a great tour through
Macedonia, which lasted till the beginning of the
winter, when he arrived in Corinth and took up his
abode with Gaius. He spent the winter months at
Corinth. We know next to nothing about these
months, and from this I argue that it was a stormy time.
St. Luke's temper is so thoroughly conciliatory that
he would avoid dilating on the overthrow of the
Judaising party, but that this overthrow was complete
I feel sure. There were no further lapses on the part of
the Church of Corinth, and the two Epistles of St. Paul
were carefully treasured. St. Paul's friends rallied
round him, and I like to picture that inner circle
gathered to hear a fresh bit of the Epistle to the Romans
on which the Apostle was labouring ; Timotheus and
Lucius and Jason and Sosipater were of the circle.

Above all I like to think of the moment when the great letter was signed and sealed and ready for its bearer, Phebe, who, having made her communion, bore away the priceless charge in the brave hands which had lately held the Body of Christ, and guarded it sleeping and waking till she rendered it up to the elders at Rome.

When Easter approached St. Paul prepared to spend it in Jerusalem, for he knew that the road to Rome lay through Jerusalem. His star was once more in the ascendant, but this made things very dangerous for him ; the Jews were now more furious than ever against him, and the chances of assassination were very great. It was quite understood by everyone that he was going into great peril, and all the prophets in the Christian assembly foretold bonds and afflictions for him at Jerusalem. There was to be a thoroughly business-like side to the journey ; the collection for the poor at Jerusalem was to be taken up, and delegates were chosen to represent the various Churches – Sopater, Aristarchus, Secundus, Gaius, Timotheus, Tychicus and Trophimus. Passages were taken at the port of Corinth, no doubt in a pilgrim ship which was going to Cæsarea, but the whole plan was changed by the discovery of a plot to murder St. Paul, probably on board the boat. I suspect there is a thrilling story here. Perhaps the plot was overheard by a Christian slave forced to work in the low haunts of Cenchrea. It was easy to buy assassins at the port of Corinth. So St. Paul took Sopater of Berea and went to Macedonia, but to put the enemy off the scent all the others went on to Ephesus. Instead, however, of going south to Jerusalem they went north along the Asiatic side to meet St. Paul at Troas.

So St. Paul lost his Easter in Jerusalem, and he now aimed at getting there for Pentecost, which would give him fifty days more. He spent Easter at Philippi. The Christians there were sad, for they were to lose their beloved St. Luke, who was now to accompany St. Paul. St. Luke appears to have taken the place of Sopater as one of the seven delegates, and as he kept a diary and put the diary into the Acts, we know a good deal about this journey.

On Easter Tuesday, St. Paul and St. Luke sailed from Philippi, and took five days to get to Troas, so they just missed Low Sunday there, and had to spend it on board. Renan suggests that for a large part of the way a boat was privately chartered, as it is improbable that any coasting vessel could have spent so much time on the way and stopped at so many places. He thinks that St. Paul and St. Luke crossed to Troas in one of the trading vessels, and then took a boat on their own account and went all the way down the Asiatic coast in it. If this was so it would be a simple half-decked boat making about forty to forty-five miles a day. At night the travellers would sleep on shore or on an island, in some fisherman's hut perhaps, drawing up the boat on the sand, or anchoring it safely. During the greater part of the way they would be upon sparkling blue sea, among beautiful islands.

At Troas, where they met the other delegates, the travellers stayed over the second Sunday after Easter and we get a little incidental picture from an eye-witness of the usages of the early Church. We find first, that they observed Sunday and not the Sabbath. We know from the 20th chapter of St. John that this was done from the beginning. Secondly, we find the
Ot

duty observed of gathering together for worship, but
the Sunday was in no sense a Christian reproduction of
the Sabbath.   Thirdly, we find that Sunday began at
six o'clock on Saturday evening with a long service
which lasted many hours.   The Jews always had a festal
supper after the close of the Sabbath in the evening.
These were the big dinner parties our Lord was bidden
to from time to time.   The Christian Agape was a meal
of the same kind and at the same hour.   Apparently the
order was – first the sacred meal, or Agape, then a
long pause with much prayer and instruction, and
after midnight the Breaking of Bread, the Eucharist,
the service concluding in the early dawn.   We find,
also, that there were many lights in the chamber, ceremonial lights, lit for the purpose of adorning the
function.   The Jews always lit ceremonial lights, and
the Christians were carrying on the Jewish custom.

Then we get the story of the miracle of Eutychus,
which is told with extraordinary fullness.   He was
sitting in the window, we are told, and he struggled
long in the great heat against sleep ; then came the
accident, and he crashed down into the courtyard
below.   There was great lamentation, for the boy was
beloved by all.   This was an occasion when St. Paul
put forth his spiritual power ; he stretched himself on
Eutychus, imitating the action of Elijah and Elisha,
saying, " He is alive, and not dead."   Eutychus re-
vived amid general rejoicings, and St. Paul went back
to the chamber and celebrated the Eucharist.   The
Bezan Text says : ' As they were taking farewell they
brought Eutychus back alive and well.'   He was
entirely recovered.   The whole Church recognised the
miracle as a sign of St. Paul's victory over death.   Next

came his beautiful and triumphant departure towards martyrdom. He bade farewell last of all to Eutychus, whom he had restored from the gates of death by his spiritual power.

So they went on their way, as Renan says, the first band of Christian pilgrims going up to the Holy Places together. St. Paul sent the ship on without him to Assos, as he wished to go across the mainland alone on foot, a distance of twenty miles. At Assos he joined them again, and then day by day they went on among the islands till the Temple of Artemis hove in sight, like a star rising from the sea. But they passed across the harbour of Ephesus without putting in. St. Paul longed to stop there, but he feared it would not be wise so soon after the riot. Next day from Miletus, he sent to the leading elders of Ephesus to come and bid him farewell. St. Luke describes the scene minutely, and we get an example of St. Paul's many touching partings. He made a long and solemn speech to the elders and offered up prayer, broken by the bursting sobs of the Ephesian Christians, who quite understood that he was going to his martyrdom, and the group stood on the beach watching the little ship till it disappeared from view.

Wherever the ship touched and the travellers joined themselves to the local assembly, all seemed possessed by the same solemn foreboding. At Tyre the disciples warned him that he was going to his death and went with him to the shore, and the little children knelt on the rocks and watched the great martyr sail away. At last they arrived at Cæsarea, and were received by Philip the Evangelist, one of the original seven deacons, who was president of the local church. Philip

had four daughters who were Christian virgins under
vows ; it was in fact, a religious house, a convent.
St. Luke was evidently greatly impressed by these four
religious women. Apparently they were afterwards
able to attend to St. Paul's wants when he was a
prisoner there. They all had the gift of prophecy, and
at Cæsarea came the greatest scene of all.

Agabus, a prophet of Jerusalem, came down
purposely to stop St. Paul going any farther ; in the
middle of the service he went up to St. Paul, took his
girdle from him, and bound his own hands and feet,
signifying the treatment that St. Paul would receive.
And now the fortitude of St. Paul's companions gave
way ; so far they had been a calm, determined band
of men, who had been self-controlled when the
Christians at the various places on the road had given
way to grief, but now the whole band broke down and
entreated St. Paul not to go any farther. But St. Paul
said : " What mean ye to weep and break mine
heart ? For I am ready not to be bound only, but also
to die at Jerusalem for the name of the Lord Jesus."

They spent a week at Cæsarea, and then began the
last stage of their journey on the Wednesday or
Thursday before Pentecost. They loaded their baggage
on their animals ; they had a great deal of treasure
with them, and it was a large caravan that went up and
a great company ; for sixty miles they went through
the hills, and spent the night with Mnason of Cyprus,
one of our Lord's own original disciples. It is very
interesting and delightful to think out the position of
this old disciple of our Lord, quite apart from the great
Christian movements, and yet doing his bit of work,
receiving the caravan fraught with such tremendous

powers, doing what our Lord wished him to do, fulfilling his simple part.

Next day the great caravan started early and went on to the Holy City. On Friday, the day before the Sabbath, they arrived and were received in various houses. To St. Paul's immense relief they had a kind welcome ; they were ' received as brothers.'

CHAPTER XIX

ONCE more St. Paul is at Jerusalem. It is his fifth visit since he became a Christian, and the last visit recorded in the Acts. He feels that it is the beginning of the end and that he is facing his passion and his death. The opposition to his teaching had largely increased since his last visit, and the friends he might expect to find in Jerusalem he could count upon his fingers. To the Jews he was a renegade and an apostate of the worst type, and it was scarcely possible that he could escape death at their hands. His friends gave him a loving welcome, but he did not see the heads of the Church till the second day. He arrived on the Friday and on the Sabbath a formal assembly of the Church was called. His appearance before that assembly must have been one of the most painful moments in St. Paul's life.

The Church at Jerusalem had grown greatly, and St. James the presiding Apostle was now firmly installed as Diocesan with his presbyters. The Apostles were all absent. The Church had grown large. St. James speaks of tens of thousands as belonging to it, but he was probably counting in the other Christians who had come up to Jerusalem to keep Pentecost ; nevertheless, the local Church had now become quite large. The effect of St. Paul's mission to the Gentiles had been to confirm the Jewish Christians in their devotion to the Law, and the Church at Jerusalem was now

definitely and enthusiastically Jewish. This propiti-
ated the unbelieving Jews and there was no persecution of the Christians. St. James had an enormous
reputation for sanctity among the Jews, who had now
come to regard belief in our Lord as Messiah as merely
a foolish craze which had not proved destructive to the
orthodoxy of those who held it. All the heads of the
Church were prepared to accept St. Paul and his work,
and were quite loyal to their promise to him, but, as we
know, a group of his bitter enemies had made the tour
of his Churches and had borne false witness against
him to the Christians at Jerusalem, telling them that
St. Paul was teaching the Jewish Christians not to
circumcise their children or to keep the Law. This
was untrue : St. Paul did not attack the customs of
his Jewish converts. It is quite probable that the
heads of the Church at Jerusalem had read the Epistle
to the Romans ; soon after this St. James wrote his
Epistle which is directed against a faith which looses
people from obedience to the moral law. It was not
written in opposition to the Epistle to the Romans,
but it was probably written to quiet the excitement
which the latter had made among the Jewish Christians,
and to point out to them that there is no necessary
antithesis between faith and works.

Picture this assembly of the Church. In the chair of
dignity sat the ascetic, white-robed, stern-faced St.
James, round about whom were grouped his presbyters.
It had not been thought wise to summon the whole
Church ; the tension was too great ; only the presby-
ters were present. St. Peter was probably at Rome ;
St. John probably in Asia Minor ; none of the great
Apostles was there ; all the Catholic influences were

removed. Only the sternly Jewish element was represented. How the Gentile converts must have trembled
as they entered the presence of one who had walked and
talked with the Lord ! Each of the converts held the
contribution which his Church had sent to the poor
of the Church at Jerusalem and waited his turn to
present it. They looked at their great master in
surprise. Was this indeed he – grave and humble,
gazing with a pathetic wistfulness at the President and
the clergy ? St. Paul and St. James exchanged the kiss of
peace and the presbyters also greeted St. Paul ; the
Gentile converts watched eagerly, and then their faces
fell ; the mark of brotherhood was not exchanged with
them ; all was formality and constraint. The converts
advanced and laid their contributions before the
Bishop. St. Luke is silent as to the way in which the
gifts were received, but we seem to gather that it must
have been a crushing disappointment. Then St. Paul
rendered up an account of his years of work since his
last visit seven years ago, and as he told the marvellous
story the coldness of his hearers melted ; their
indifference became interest, and interest grew into
enthusiasm, until from lip after lip broke forth the cry,
" Glory be to God." We must remember that these
people had always remained loyal to the compact with
St. Paul ; they must not be credited with any share in
the hatred of the bitter party at Jerusalem, although
they had not found it possible to sympathise with all
St. Paul said and did. Now they were filled with fears
for his safety ; he was the hated of almost all men in
Jerusalem, and his life was not worth a moment's
purchase. He would be safe in only one place – in
the Temple – in the inner part of the Temple. Thus an

idea struck them and they said to him, " We have a plan to propose which will keep you in safety until the crowds begin to disperse. We have four poor Christians here who are Nazarites and have a vow. Will you undertake to discharge the payment of their sacrifice for them and spend a week with them in the Temple in the room set apart for those who are under a vow ? This plan will secure your safety and will also partly clear your character ; it will be recognised that you are still a Jew and keep the Jewish customs."

It will be remembered that on a previous visit St. Paul had come up to Jerusalem with a vow and had made the usual offerings. The offerings for a Nazarite vow were very expensive and included two lambs and a ram, as well as unleavened bread and other things, and poor people found much difficulty in providing them , so it was a popular work of charity for rich Jews to pay the expenses of their poorer brothers. St. Paul agreed to the proposal and put himself next day under a vow.

Just at this time all the Jews in Jerusalem were in an irritable state ; the air was electric ; there were many premonitions of the doom that was hanging over the city and the Temple. Some of the Ephesian Jews had seen St. Paul passing by in the company of Trophimus, their Gentile fellow-townsman, and they had marked him down. They had not forgotten the scene in the theatre at Ephesus. Towards the end of his retreat it was necessary for St. Paul to leave his room in order to make arrangements with the priests. He was standing in the Court of the Women, so called not because it was reserved for women, but because it was the nearest point of approach to the sanctuary permitted to them. It was a large space capable of

holding 15,000 people, surrounded by high colonnades ; in it were the thirteen trumpet-shaped alms-
boxes into one of which our Lord saw the widow drop
her mite. St. Paul, doubtless, hoped to escape notice,
but mean and insignificant though his stature might
be, there was that about Paul which marked him out
for a person of importance. The lynx-eyed Ephesian
Jews who had been scanning every face in the crowds
pounced on him now with the shout " Here is the
apostate Saul. Help ! help ! he has polluted the
Temple ; he has been bringing heathen into the inner
court." Of course this was not true.

To understand what follows it must be remembered
that the Court of the Women was surrounded by an
immense outer court with four cloistered walls, the
Court of the Gentiles. The Roman barracks which
overlooked the Temple communicated with this court
by two flights of steps, one from the Castle of Antonia
itself down to the cloister roof, the second from the
roof to the ground. A flight of fourteen steps led up
from the Court of the Gentiles to the Court of the
Women, which was encircled by a high wall through
which entrance was gained by a massive gateway with
magnificent gates of brass which it took twenty
men to move. Some yards from the walls of the Court
of the Women stood a low barrier which went all round
it, and on this partition there were pillars at intervals
with notices on them in Greek and Latin to the effect
that any Gentile trespassing within the barrier would
be punished with death.

No words can paint the dæmoniacal fury of an
enraged crowd of Eastern people. We must try to
imagine the position of a Mohammedan who had been

caught introducing a Christian into the sacred enclosure at Mecca. The yelling and seething mob forced their victim through the great brass gates down the steps to the outer court. The moment they had got through the gates a company of Levites pushed them to and barred the mob outside the Court of the Women, and the Temple was shut against St. Paul. He must have felt it to be symbolic. The moment foretold by Agabus had come. St. Paul's heart must have leapt with strange gladness ; after a few fierce moments he would see the Lord. The crowd dared not slay him within the low wall, and as they dragged him towards it, it must have been a curious thought for him that this low white wall in the brilliant sunshine would be for him the gate of death. He never forgot that middle wall of partition, and he employed it as an illustration afterwards in his Epistle to the Ephesians, an illustration of what his Gospel had broken down. They had nearly reached it when a stream of burnished metal rushed along the cloister roof and precipitated itself into the court, and in a moment St. Paul stood in safety within the ranks of Roman soldiery.

Claudius Lysias, the military governor, thought he had made a great capture. During the earlier months of the year an Egyptian had appeared at Jerusalem, had attracted to him 4,000 people of the scum of the city, and had led them into camp in the hill country. Having succeeded in imposing upon many of the foolish country people he had returned to Jerusalem at the head of 30,000 men. His force was dispersed by Felix, but he himself had escaped capture, and was supposed to be hidden in the hill country.

Lysias now thought St. Paul was he, and questioned

the mob about him, but could get no clear information out of them. Seeing this he commanded the soldiers to take Paul into the barracks. To gain the staircase the soldiers had to get him across the court. It took all their strength and discipline to do it. When the mob saw they were losing their victim they made a rush, and it was necessary for the soldiers to take St. Paul off his feet and to pass him up the stairs over the heads of the soldiers, a most undignified position for an Eastern, and a sight St. Luke never forgot.

On the roof they set St. Paul on his feet again, and then he asked to be allowed to speak to the people. He addressed the military governor in Greek. Claudius Lysias was much disgusted, for he knew now he had not caught the Egyptian ; he showed his contempt by the way he answered St. Paul, who replied with dignity that he was a Jew of Tarsus, a citizen of no mean city. Claudius Lysias gave him leave to speak ; he thought it the best way of getting information about the prisoner. Then St. Paul began to shout down to the crowd in Aramaic, standing on the steps with guards below him and on either hand, and chained to a Roman soldier on either side. It was a strange pulpit for the Gospel, and a strange congregation. The mob heard him until he came to the words : – " Depart, for I will send thee far hence unto the Gentiles." Then there burst out a fresh uproar ; throwing off their clothes, they made movements with their hands in the air as though they were stoning the prisoner. Claudius Lysias turned away in disgust ; he did not understand a word that had passed, but he ordered the prisoner to be taken to the torture-room that information might be extracted from him by torture, and he told them to examine him by scourging. St. Paul allowed them to strip him and to string him up to a post and to bring out the scourge. Then he said, with, I feel sure, a twitch of amusement : " May an uncondemned Roman citizen be scourged ? " The centurion hurried away to Claudius Lysias, who came at once and asked : " Are you a Roman ? "   " I am," said St. Paul. To have given that as a false excuse meant death, so it was never said untruly. Lysias looked at the poor prisoner with torn clothes and said : " It cost me a great deal of money to become a Roman citizen." " I was born a Roman citizen," rejoined St. Paul. Claudius Lysias was in a difficulty. He had incurred a serious risk in thus maltreating a Roman citizen. He ordered St. Paul to be partially loosed, though his right wrist was still bound to the wrist of one of the soldiers, and that night the prisoner slept the sleep of the innocent.

As soon as Claudius Lysias had recognised that this was one of the Jewish religious squabbles so utterly incomprehensible to the Romans, he requested the Sanhedrin to try Paul, and on the following day Paul stood before the great semi-circular tribunal of his nation, the tribunal which had condemned his Master. He had not the pleasure of feeling that he stood upon the same square of pavement, because the Sanhedrin had moved from the Hall Gazith to the Booths of Annas, but he had the pleasure of feeling that he stood in the position in which he had placed St. Stephen, that this was exact retribution for the past.

St. Paul was now for the first time brought into collision with the Sadducæan aristocracy. As a group they were men of a very slight, if any, religious

experience ; expediency governed their ecclesiastical
policy. Their principal aim was to put down enthusiasm,
lest it should lead to disturbance and to the disestablish-
ment and disendowment of the Jewish Church. Dean
Farrar compares them with the Avignon Cardinals and
the Bishops of the Church of England in the earlier
Georgian period.

The High Priest Ananias was president of the
Council. He was a disgusting creature, equally
greedy of money and of food, who was finally murdered in a drain where he had hidden from vengeance
just before the fall of Jerusalem. After Paul had
uttered but a single sentence Ananias told the attendants to smite him on the mouth. Now to strike a Jew
on the mouth was to place the deepest insult upon him.
The implication was that the man struck had ceased
to be a Jew, for there was a dictum of the Rabbis
which forbade a Jew to strike a Jew. ' He who
strikes a Jew strikes the Holy One.' St. Paul's anger
blazed out in fierce and scathing protest.   It has been
suggested that defective eyesight prevented his recognising the speaker, or that he had been given to understand that the High Priest would not sit that day, but
more probably his apology should be read, ' I had not
reflected, brethren, that he was High Priest.' Or with
a touch of satire he is suggesting how unlike a High
Priest such conduct was.

St. Luke is very reticent about this trial. We gather
most that we know of its procedure from the letter of
Claudius Lysias. Claudius Lysias seems to have
asked the authorities to formulate their charge at once.
Ananias evidently made it heresy — teaching the
existence of a crucified and risen Messiah. St. Paul

then appears to have made his defence in the usual way, describing his interview with our Lord, and producing his proofs of our Lord's resurrection. This would arouse the ridicule of the Sadducees who appear to have scoffed openly in the Council, not merely at the particular narrative, but at the whole doctrine of spirits and of resurrection. They turned the story in fact into a weapon of ridicule against the Pharisees, so that the end of the story found the two parties in the Council at open loggerheads. In this particular dispute the Pharisees stood for faith and hope against Sadducæan cynicism and scepticism, and St. Paul did not hesitate to appeal to them. " It is clear, then," he cried, " that I am not a heretical Jew. I am a Pharisee, a son of Pharisees, I have renounced nothing of the Jewish creed. From my old orthodoxy I deduce my present position. The cardinal fact of my message turns upon those two test questions of Pharisaic orthodoxy, the Messianic expectation and the resurrection of the dead."

The scene got noisier and noisier, and at last the Council broke into a free fight. Claudius Lysias had to send up to Antonia and bring down the full force of the soldiery, and even so they got St. Paul out only with great difficulty – ' And I scarcely brought him out by force,' says the Bezan text of the letter to Felix.

That night our Lord entered into communion with His great follower, and Paul gained a conviction that he had years of work before him. It is sad that St. Luke seems to have no act of affectionate sympathy on the part of the Church of Jerusalem to chronicle. But the position was very difficult. James was living at peace with the Temple authorities, and it was best for the

Christian cause to make this as far as possible a personal affair between Paul and his former employers. It is a boy of fifteen, a nervous frightened boy, who brings the news of the plot. The relatives were probably people of condition, and the boy was made the messenger as less likely to arouse suspicion. Claudius Lysias, who throughout the affair is the courteous Roman gentleman, got the information out of the boy kindly and privately. The danger was imminent : forty fanatics of the physical force party had sworn to kill Paul immediately.

At nine o'clock that night two hundred legionaries, two hundred lancers and seventy horse stood before the fort of Antonia under order to convey the prisoner to Cæsarea. That strange night ride through the hills — how often must St. Paul in captivity have remembered wistfully the shadows and scents of the hollows, the wind and the starlight of the slopes! On the following afternoon he entered Cæsarea, and the Christians there who had prophesied his martyrdom and who saw him ride through the city chained to his guards bowed their heads and said, " God's will be done."

CHAPTER XXI

S T. PAUL'S escort took him at once to the court of the Procurator, who proceeded to read the memorandum Claudius Lysias had sent. Having discovered to what province the prisoner belonged, and that he had jurisdiction over him, having no doubt also verified his Roman citizenship, Felix ordered him to be detained in what was called free custody in the Prætorium, the Governor's own residence, formerly the palace of Herod Agrippa I, until the plaintiffs in the case should come down from Jerusalem. In order to understand who and what were Felix and King Agrippa, who will presently appear upon the scene, I must again remind you of the tiresome, involved story of the government at this time. Judæa was a Roman province under a Roman Governor. Pontius Pilate had been Governor in our Lord's time, but he was removed in 36 and two short-lived Procurators succeeded him — Marcellus and Marullus. Then in 41 the Emperor Claudius added Judæa to the kingdom of Herod Agrippa I and he held it for three years. Just at the end of the time he beheaded St. James and imprisoned St. Peter. Then it again became a Roman province under a Procurator.

Herod Agrippa I was a grandson of Herod the Great. He had been brought up in Rome in close relations with the Imperial family, and became a great friend of Caligula. When Caligula succeeded Tiberius as Emperor he gave Agrippa first Trachonitis, with the title of King, and then the territory of Herod Antipas, Galilee and Peræa. Later, when Caligula was murdered, Agrippa persuaded the Senate to make Claudius Emperor, and so Claudius in gratitude added Samaria and Judæa to his dominions. St. Luke describes his death. Herod Agrippa had had a quarrel with Tyre and Sidon and had stopped their corn supplies, for which they were dependent on Galilee. At last they sent an embassy to him at Cæsarea to sue for peace. Herod Agrippa was engaged in celebrating a splendid festival in thanksgiving for the safe return of the Emperor Claudius from his expedition against Britain. Herod gave the embassy a public audience, and in order to make a public impression on them he had himself veiled from head to foot in cloth of silver and sat in this garb on the high throne in the theatre and made a gracious speech to the ambassadors. The crowd politely shouted, " It is God's voice, not man's," they were so fascinated by the cloth of silver in the sunlight. While he was seated on the throne, Herod Agrippa was seized with the pains of his last terrible illness and had to be carried to the palace, where he died in five days. Josephus gives an elaborate account of it all. Cuspius Fadus became Procurator of the reconstituted province of Judæa when Herod Agrippa I died; he was succeeded by Tiberius Alexander and Ventidius Cumanus ; then, in 52, Antonius Felix was made Procurator. Felix and his mother Pallas were Greeks and had been slaves of Antonia, the mother of the Emperor Claudius. They were freed by Antonia, and Pallas obtained great influence over the Emperor Claudius. Claudius made him his Prime Minister and

he amassed enormous wealth. Pallas gave Felix his
opening and Felix got a military command in Palestine.
When Ventidius Cumanus the Procurator was banished for his great cruelties to the Jews, Felix stepped
into his shoes.

Having become Procurator he managed by the aid
of a Jewish magician, Simon, whom some suppose to
be Simon Magus, to induce Drusilla, the wife of the
King of Emesa, to leave her husband and live with him.
She is said to have left her husband in a fury of jealousy
of her sister Berenice, who was a rival beauty. Drusilla
was the daughter of Herod Agrippa I and the sister of
Herod Agrippa II and Berenice. Felix ultimately
married her, and it was this edifying and charming
couple who now gained possession of St. Paul.

Herod Agrippa II, who presently arrived and
brought Berenice his sister with him, was the son of
Herod Agrippa I, and was being brought up at the
court of Claudius when his father died so horribly.
Claudius did not give him his father's kingdom because he was too young – he was only seventeen. A year
after, when Herod, King of Chalcis, died – he was
Agrippa II's uncle and had married Agrippa's sister
Berenice – Claudius made Agrippa II King of Chalcis.
This he exchanged in 53 for some principalities in
North Palestine. Claudius gave Agrippa II the nom-
ination of the Jewish High Priests and the supervision
of the Temple.   When Berenice's first husband and
uncle, Herod of Chalcis, died she joined her brother
Agrippa II at Rome. After a time she left him and
married Polemo, a Cicilian prince, but soon abandoned
him and returned to live with Agrippa. Berenice
had the reputation of a Lucrezia Borgia . she was

beautiful, magnificent and clever, and after the fall of Jerusalem she formed a relation with Titus, but when Vespasian died and Titus became Emperor, the scandal of his relationship with Berenice was considered too great and he dismissed her into obscurity.

St. Paul had not to wait long for his first trial. The feeling against him was acute. All the Zealots and the whole multitude were against him, and after the scene in the Sanhedrin he had roused the bitter hostility of the Sadducees also. The High Priest came down in person to Cæsarea and brought a professional advocate with him. Next morning the embassy opened their case against Paul in the law courts – the crier publicly cited his name ; then the counsel for the plaintiffs opened the prosecution. The counts were three :

1. Paul was a public nuisance and hence guilty of treason against the Cæsar.

2. He was ringleader of a sect which had no legal authorisation.

3. He had actually attempted to profane the Temple by taking a Gentile inside the barrier.

Notice that they no longer affirmed that he had done this. They knew they could not prove it. Had he done so it would have been fatal in the eyes of Roman law. Even Romans were put to death for going inside the barrier.

We have only a short summary of St. Paul's reply, but he appears to have traversed the whole of Tertullus' statements very ably, and he wound up with a great characteristic burst of indignation. Felix, who had been a Prefect in Samaria before he was Governor of Judæa, had a very clear notion of the controversy between the Jews and the Christians, and saw that St.

Paul's one crime was that he was a strong and consistent Christian, and therefore that the Jews, who
were living at peace with the bulk of the Jerusalem
Christians, had no real case against him. But he was
afraid to offend the Jews by releasing Paul ; he had
already had difficulties with them. So he uttered the
technical word ' Amplius,' and adjourned the case
under pretext of waiting for the evidence of Claudius
Lysias.

He gave orders that Paul should be made as comfortable as possible under the circumstances and let the
matter rest. Lysias did not come, the Jews saw they
were unlikely to get a conviction, and it became ever-
body's policy to do nothing further in the matter.
Meanwhile St. Paul suffered the injustice of being
kept in custody though uncondemned. He was an
object of much curiosity. It seems clear from what
St. Luke tells us that Christianity became a subject of
much discussion in aristocratic circles. A smatter-
ing of letters, a little philosophy, a little religion sometimes becomes a short-lived fashion with the smart set,
and Drusilla headed a band of gay folk who were
curious about Paul.

Some of the MSS. tell us that Felix's conversations
with Paul began at his wife's instigation. She had run
away from one husband and married another, but she
was still only a girl of seventeen, and she persuaded the
Governor to let Paul give some account of his faith,
probably at a sort of party. St. Paul knew his company
and he gave them a very unexpected oration on righteousness, continence and the judgment to come. We
know from Romans i. that he was able to be exceedingly
plain-spoken when it was necessary. Felix grew

alarmed – the speech had become very personal – and he broke off the audience, saying he would give St. Paul another public opportunity of saying what he wanted to say when it was convenient. It was never convenient, but Felix had many private talks with his prisoner. St. Luke says that he hoped he might get a bribe from him, but probably he was also genuinely interested in St. Paul, whose immense knowledge of the condition of Greek cities would impress him. As an exceedingly shrewd bad man he must have been conscious that St. Paul embodied a spiritual force which had after all to be reckoned with.

St. Paul was two years in this semi-captivity at Cæsarea, and they were years of the greatest value to the Church. In the first place, his health probably improved ; he was obliged to rest ; his life too was safe for the time being. Then the prolonged imprisonment by the Romans must have softened the hearts of the Jewish Christian communities towards him. Much reconciliation and explanation were possible and were doubtless accomplished in those two years.

But the supreme treasure which those two years almost undoubtedly gave to the Church is the basis of the Gospel according to St. Luke. This was St. Luke's opportunity of consulting the eye-witnesses and examining the documents already written. Possibly at that time he made his researches into the early history of our Lord and was entrusted with that very early and Jewish document which forms his first two chapters and which is no doubt in the main due to our Lady herself. By this date the general Apostolic account of our Lord's ministry had been fixed on the lines of the Gospel according to St. Mark, and it was this early document which St. Luke incorporated into his Gospel. He enriched it with much first-hand detail and addition, often grouping these according to their subject and sometimes probably in the order in which he had received them, when he is uncertain as to their proper chronological place. It seems probable also that a great deal of the material for the history of the Acts was collected there. Philip the Evangelist and the Cæsaeran Christians would be a mine of information as to the early history of the Church. St. Paul would have leisure to give his reminiscences, and there were St. Luke's own notes to be set in order.

Meanwhile affairs in Cæsarea were growing disturbed. It was a city in which Jews and Gentiles enjoyed equal civic rights, over which they frequently wrangled. At last there was an open brawl on a larger scale than usual, and Felix ordered the Jews to their houses. They refused to go, and the Roman soldiery attacked and killed a great many and looted many Jewish houses. There was a fierce outcry ; Jewish influence was strong at Rome at the time, and Felix was recalled, tried and deposed. In these circumstances he thought it best not to liberate Paul when he left, and the Bezan Text says that Drusilla begged him to leave Paul in prison. No doubt, like Herodias, she would have liked his head on a charger.

Porcius Festus, who seems to have been a strong, sound Roman of the good old school, was sent to Palestine in place of Antonius Felix. He landed at Cæsarea probably in the early summer of 57, and after two nights' rest went up to Jerusalem so as to get in touch as soon as possible with those at the centre of Jewish affairs. There was a new High Priest, Ishmael

Ben Phabi, but this made no difference. At once the Sanhedrin lodged their indictment against Paul. They knew that Festus was totally ignorant of Jewish and Christian affairs. He was very much in the position of a newly arrived Englishman in India who was being requested to arbitrate between two conflicting sects of Hindus. A popular and very disorderly demonstration was also organised, and Festus found himself confronting a yelling mob which demanded the blood of St. Paul. The special request of the Sanhedrin was that he might be brought to Jerusalem and tried there ; of course they meant to have him assassinated on the way up. Festus replied that he could not stay long in Jerusalem itself, that he had to return to Cæsarea for the reception of the surrounding magnates, and that they had better send down a strong body to represent them at the trial of Paul, which he certainly meant to hold soon.

In about ten days' time Festus returned to Cæsarea and he had St. Paul tried almost immediately. It was Festus' first experience of the fanatical Jew and he was entirely bewildered. It was a little like a French criminal trial, for the accusers encircled the accused and insulted him in the wildest and most violent manner. Two things became clear to Festus. The whole matter concerned the inexplicable Jewish religion, their precious Temple and their precious laws. And it circled round a certain Jesus, whom the Jews said was dead but whose claims were inimical to Cæsar, while Paul on the other hand insisted that Jesus was alive and that His claims were not inimical to Cæsar.

In these circumstances Festus felt he must do what

the Jews asked, he must refer the whole matter to the Sanhedrin. He would be present at the meeting of the Sanhedrin and see that justice was done, but he could not hope to arrive at any just estimate of the facts of the case himself. So he proposed to St. Paul that he should be taken to Jerusalem and tried there. He could not remit St. Paul from an Imperial court to a provincial court without his consent, because he was a Roman citizen, and a Roman citizen could always claim the right to be tried only in an Imperial court, just as an English peer to-day can claim the right to be tried by his peers.

This was one of the supreme moments in the life of St. Paul, but he was in no doubt whatever as to his course. He had an interior certainty that our Lord had a mission for him to fulfil in Rome, that the time of his departure was not yet at hand. To consent to go to Jerusalem would mean to consent to be assassinated sooner or later. Festus might think that the arms of Rome could protect the prisoner, but St. Paul knew his own countrymen better.

" I am standing before Cæsar's judgment seat, and at Cæsar's judgment seat judgment ought to be pronounced on me. I am guilty of no crime against the Jews, as you know very well. If I am a criminal and have committed a capital crime I do not refuse to die, but if none of these accusations of the Jews is true, no man has a right to make them a present of my life. *Cæsarem appello !* " *Cæsarem appello !* Two magical words. They asserted the supreme privilege of the Roman citizen. His privilege, no matter to what part of the Empire he belonged, to be taken to Rome and tried in the Emperor's court. There is no doubt that the justice of the Emperor's court was of the most careful kind. Of course it was wise Roman policy to keep it so, to keep this right of appeal a really valuable privilege.

The two words took St. Paul out of the grip of the Jewish courts for ever. There was the usual consultation between Festus and the accusers, as to the legality of the appeal, but in this case there was no doubt that the prisoner was a Roman citizen, and so Festus pronounced the usual formula – Thou hast appealed to Cæsar, to Cæsar thou shalt go – and nothing remained but to find a convenient ship and dispatch Paul under a military guard to Rome. The Procurator was, however, in a considerable difficulty ; it was highly important to him to be able to send an accurate précis of his first legal difficulty to Rome, and he had been quite incapable of getting a clear understanding of this case.

His difficulty was solved by the arrival of Agrippa II, King of Ituræa and Trachonitis, with his sister Berenice, to pay a short complimentary visit to the new Procurator. Herod Agrippa II was ideally qualified to help Festus in the matter. As you remember, he had been brought up in Rome and had never seen Palestine until his accession. He was a friend of Cæsar's and devotedly Roman. On his coins he calls himself Philocæsar-philoromaios. At the same time he was, in a cultured dilettante sort of way, very Jewish. He had specialised in his own religion for the sake of the whole political situation, and he was something of an expert. He had the guardianship of the Temple, as I have said, and it was he who had deposed Ananias, the former High Priest, St. Paul's bitter enemy. He was building a tower to his palace in Jerusalem which should overlook the Temple. This made the priests very angry and they were building a party wall to shut out his view. So Agrippa was quite prepared to criticise any action of theirs at the moment. He was about the best of the Herods, and St. Paul did not disdain to explain himself before him.

Festus was glad of the opportunity of paying Agrippa a compliment by asking him to help him with the case of Paul. Agrippa replied that he would be charmed, that he was feeling curious about Paul and very much wanted to hear him, and so one of the greatest scenes in the history of religion came about. Great, because St. Paul determined to use the occasion to the full, and delivered a most carefully prepared and elaborate speech, the speech which St. Luke makes the climax of the Book of the Acts. It was not of course a trial, and it was made a great social occasion. Festus arranged the audience hall of the palace to resemble a basilica, and gave the young King the semblance of authority. Everything was done to make the scene as magnificent as possible, and when all was in readiness St. Paul in chains stood before Agrippa. And Agrippa said unto Paul, " Thou art permitted to speak for thyself." Then Paul made the orator's opening gesture with his chained hand, and, says the Bezan Text, taking courage and inspired by the comfort of the Holy Ghost, made his defence.

The speech was listened to in profound silence, but it was never finished. As he passionately cried that his mission was to convert the whole world, small and great, to believe in the resurrection of Jesus, Festus, startled out of himself, broke in, " Paul, you are mad ;

your ingenious learning has turned your brain." And
St. Paul paused and, having replied with perfect sober
courtesy, burst into a passionate personal appeal to
Agrippa. The young King was not wholly bad, he
was more moved than he cared to show, and he
defended himself with a light sentence – " A little
more persuasion and you will make me too a Christian." At this exquisite joke the court, no doubt,
burst out laughing, and then, I think, were quite still
again when St. Paul replied, " I would to God that,
whether with little or with much, not you only, but all
that hear me this day, might become such as I am,
except," he raised his hands and there was a jingle of
steel, " except these bonds."

It was the kind of remark which makes polite people
uncomfortable, and it seemed merely delicate for the
King and the Princess Berenice to smile their thanks
to the Procurator and say that they now had a very
clear view of the case.

They retired with their assessors and discussed the
whole matter. Everybody felt a strange sympathy
with the prisoner and they all decided that he had done
nothing worthy of punishment. They returned to the
hall of audience. Festus put the question publicly
to the King, " What is Your Majesty's decision in this
matter ? " And the King replied, " The man might
have been released if he had not appealed to Cæsar."

St. Paul's life was twice saved by that decision.

He was kept in custody. He would have been
assassinated had he been released.

And the précis of the inquiry saved him when, two
years later, he stood in the Emperor's court.

CHAPTER XXII

A T once Festus handed Paul over to the proper authorities for conveyance to Rome. These were the Imperial police.

The commissariat of the legions was a great and splendidly organised work. The headquarters were at Rome on the Cœlian Hill, and the Army Service Corps were called the *frumentarii*, and because so many were foreigners, the *peregrini*. This corps became utilised for two or three other purposes, for secret service, as Imperial couriers, and as Imperial police for conveying prisoners to and from Rome. Julius, ' centurion of the Augustan cohort,' commanded a division of this corps – Augustan was probably a popular title for this division, not an official title.

Julius was collecting a sufficiently big batch of prisoners to send to Rome together. The other prisoners – who appear to have been in another class to St. Paul – were probably criminals who were being sent to Rome to be butchered in the gladiatorial games. With St. Paul went St. Luke, who was a Gentile ; and Aristarchus, who was a Jew ; and it is an interesting question in what capacity they went, since Julius would certainly not have taken them as ordinary passengers. Writing later on from Rome, St. Paul calls Aristarchus ' my fellow prisoner,' and probably he had got involved in the original scene in the Temple and had all the while been a companion

of St. Paul's captivity. But St. Paul does not call
St. Luke ' my fellow prisoner ' ; he calls him ' the
beloved physician,' and probably it was in that capacity
that he went with St. Paul. St. Paul's health was
almost certainly in a bad state. If so, St. Luke's legal
position on board was that of St. Paul's slave. There
would be nothing unusual in this ; prisoners of
consideration were often allowed to have slaves in
attendance on them. St. Paul was a Roman citizen,
and Agrippa, Festus and Julius were all thoroughly
well disposed to him and were prepared to treat him
with all possible consideration.

In order to understand what followed you must
remember certain things about the Mediterranean
and seamanship in those days, and the whole ancient
attitude towards the sea.

The Mediterranean, supposed by untravelled North-
erners to be ever smooth, can be very rough, so that
although travel by sea was in some respects safer than
land travel it was very uncertain. During the winter
months at the time St. Paul lived, the sea was practically
closed for navigation. Knowledge of navigation was
very imperfect, and there were few nautical instruments. Towards the end of summer and through the
autumn, incessant west winds blew in the Eastern
Mediterranean, and it was almost impossible for one
of the old, clumsy sailing ships to make any steady
way westward.

All this helped to maintain the ancient view of the
sea as the chaos out of which the order and beauty of
the land had been evolved. No nation held this more
strongly than the Jews : the coast-line of Palestine
seemed to justify it. There is no country in the world

with a more inhospitable coast-line. It has no har-
bours except the poor little indent under Carmel ;
from north to south, land and sea stand in frank and
relentless antagonism to one another.

So to the Jews the waves always typify disorder and
rebellion ; the passage on dry ground through the Red
Sea into the Promised Land is the type of salvation, and
in the ideal future, as pictured in the Revelation,
' there shall be no more sea.'

It was nearing the end of August before Julius was
ready to go. The sailing season was really over, and it
was impossible to find a ship, but Julius could not wait
the whole winter, and there was, of course, the chance
of a beautiful calm autumn. So he determined to take
passages in a ship going to Adramyttium on the coast
of Asia Minor, a place near Assos, only just south
of the Dardanelles. This ship would touch at Ephesus,
and there Julius would almost certainly find a ship
going to Corinth, late as it was, and with some connection on to Rome from the other side of the isthmus ;
or, if he failed in this, he could go on to Adramyttium
and get across from Troas to Philippi and there take
his prisoners by land across Macedonia, then over the
narrow strip of the Adriatic to Brindisi, and so up
Italy. Fifty years later St. Ignatius of Antioch was
taken by this route to Rome, to be thrown to wild
beasts in the amphitheatre. It was on this last journey
that he wrote the Seven Epistles, the most precious
writings we possess of the age immediately succeeding
that of the Apostles.

The day came and the voyage began in the most
favourable way possible : they ran seventy miles on
the first day. They put in at Sidon, and Julius, who

was a fine Roman gentleman, gave St. Paul's friends
leave to take him ashore and minister to him ; he had a
little rest amid comfortable surroundings at Sidon.
From Sidon the voyage proper began.   The straight
course now was across the open sea, leaving Cyprus
to the east, to Myra on the coast of Asia Minor.   That
would be a north-westerly course and so the beginning
of the voyage west.   But now their ill fortune began,
the great west winds of the autumn were already
blowing and they could make no headway north-west ;
they had to sail along under the lee of Cyprus and to the
east of it, and get under the Cilician coast as far westward as the wind allowed them.   Then began the dreary
work of beating up westward against a west wind and
using what currents and land breezes they found to
help them.   It took them fifteen days to get to Myra.
I suppose it would take about a day now in a steamer
from Sidon to Myra.

Myra was the great Syrian port for the Egyptian
traffic, and here they found an Egyptian ship bound for
Italy with wheat.   Rome was entirely supplied with
bread from foreign countries, mostly from Egypt, and
these corn-ships were of an unusually big build,
immense ships for those days.   The arrival of the
corn-fleet at Puteoli, the port of Rome, was always
an occasion of great rejoicing, and the corn-ships could
be at once recognised as they were the only ships which
were allowed to enter the Bay of Naples with their
topsails set.   The ship had been driven across the
Mediterranean from Alexandria, as the ship for
Adramyttium had been driven from Sidon, and Julius
was delighted to put his company on board ; it solved
all his difficulties.   Altogether there were now 276 on

the ship's list. But the weather was no better, and for
many days, probably almost a fortnight, the big corn-
ship continued to beat along the coast against the
north-west wind, working westward to Cnidus, which
is at the south-east point of Asia Minor. After Myra
you begin to get among the islands, and when once the
big island of Rhodes is passed the islands dot the sea
in all directions and the voyage is most beautiful and
attractive.

By the time poor St. Paul got to Cnidus they had
taken a month to do what one does now in two days in a
steamer ! At Cnidus the coast of Asia Minor turns
north, and the true route of the corn-ship was a straight
course westward to Cape Matapan, the southernmost
point of Greece ; but as soon as they got out of the
shelter of the land the strong north-west wind made it
impossible to steer a straight course. Their only hope
of getting westward was to make south-west for Crete
and run westward along the south coast which runs a
long distance from east to south, from Cape Salmone to
Cape Matala. They did this, but although the Cretan
mountains sheltered them from the north-west, still
there was enough west wind to make it very difficult,
and they were thankful to arrive at the roadstead, still
called Fair Havens, which is six miles east of Cape
Matala. On the west side of Cape Matala the coast of
Crete runs up north, so that when the corn-ship doubled
the cape it would find itself again in the teeth of this
ceaseless wind. Consequently they waited at Fair
Havens in the hope of a change. But no change came.
The winter drew on and it became a very grave
problem what to do. It was now October ; the day
of Atonement was past. This note of time by St. Luke

Qт

is interesting. It would have been more natural if
St. Luke had marked his time from the feast of
Tabernacles, which occurs five days after and which
was held by the Jews to close the sailing season. Of
course he did not keep the day of Atonement himself
because he was a Gentile, but his mention of it on the
voyage makes it clear that St. Paul and Aristarchus did.
St. Paul and Aristarchus could not keep the feast of
Tabernacles on board ship and consequently it is the
day of Atonement which forms a note of time in St.
Luke's memory. St. Paul, then, not only when he was
among the Jews, that he might gain the Jews, but also
when he was his own master in the matter, seems still
to have kept the great days of the Jewish year.

In the early days of October, Julius held a council
(as principal Roman officer on board he was the chief
person, not the captain, nor even the owner of the ship,
who was also on board). To this council Julius
summoned St. Paul ; his doing so shows the very high
place the great prisoner had come to hold in the estima-
tion of those who were travelling with him. It is also
remarkable that his great personality at once made itself
felt in the deliberation. Everyone felt that he was in
the presence of a great spiritual person. St. Paul
strongly dissuaded the officials from continuing the
voyage to Italy and advised them to winter in Crete.
This was agreed to. But a further proposal of St. Paul
that they should remain where they were, at Fair
Havens, was strongly resisted and pronounced im-
practicable for a score of reasons. It was an open
roadstead, there was no town there, and Lasea the
nearest town was evidently a small place and wanting
in supplies. After rounding Cape Matala the coast of

Crete, as I said, runs north for some way, and that was why it was so dangerous for the corn-ship to attempt to weather the cape, for at once she would face the north-west gale without shelter. But after a time the coast runs westward again for a long distance and halfway along this second section of the southern coast of Crete is the port of Phœnix, with a good town and harbour facing east in a deep bay. Everyone except St. Paul set his heart on trying to get on to Phœnix. It was certainly a tempting venture, as it would make all the difference to the winter's comfort, and when, a few days after, the wind veered round to the south and a light breeze blew inshore, they weighed anchor with speed, and keeping close inshore, proceeded to round Cape Matala, hoping to be blown across to Phœnix when they had weathered the cape.

But unfortunately St. Paul had been a true prophet. A tremendous hurricane gathered in the Cretan Mountains and burst on them. It was a well-known type of storm of those parts and appears to have been called 'Euraquilo' by the sailors, a barbarous word meaning 'north-easter.' The ship was caught, the sailors could only fling themselves into the rigging and reef the sails, and then she was hurled along before the tempest to the south-west. Some miles to the south-west lies the little island of Cauda. Under lee of this island the corn-ship was mercifully driven ; for the land afforded a certain amount of shelter, enough to enable them to make some preparations for what lay before them.

They began by getting the ship's boat on board – it had been towed behind and happily had not yet been stove in. St. Luke probably lent a hand, and this

accounts for his remembering the particular point.
Then the sailors proceeded to pass coils of cable round
the hull to help the timbers resist the strain of the
heavy seas and prevent their starting. The great
danger lay in the fact that Euraquilo was blowing
straight on to the Syrtis, the great stretch of sandbank
in the South Mediterranean, off the African coast.
Their one hope lay in their being able to retard the
progress of the ship, and so either, as our translation
has it, they lowered the mainsail so as to drift under as
little canvas as possible ; or, since they appear to have
already done that, they lowered a weight to drag
behind (*skeuos* can be so translated), a common practice
of the time.

Before long they had drifted beyond the shelter of
Cauda and felt the full force of the hurricane again.
The strength of the gale increased, and next day they
had to part with the greater part of the cargo, though
they kept some for their own provisioning. The day
after, things were no better and they had to throw
overboard all the furniture and fittings of the ship
which were not necessary to her structure. Their
plight was now wretched indeed. As they could not
see the stars they had no means of knowing where
they were, sleep was impossible, and even if they had
had the appetite to eat it was impossible to prepare
any food.

At the supreme moment of despair St. Paul inspired
new heart into everybody. With the rest he had been
profoundly depressed. He knew he had given a
Divine warning at Fair Havens, and he knew it had
been disregarded ; he could not tell what the justice
of God might demand in such a case. They had

originally listened to him because of his spiritual force, and they had ultimately preferred their own counsels. But his intense prayer had been rewarded by a vision. God had given him the lives of those for whom he prayed. He himself would yet stand before Cæsar. They must lose their ship and be cast on an island ; but they would keep their lives if they took heart and played the man. Their co-operation with God was necessary for their safety.

All this while the cornship was being driven, not south on to the Syrtis as they feared, but westward on to Malta. St. Luke says that she was driven to and fro, and some of his critics say that there speaks the landsman – that such a thing could not really have happened, but that it is just what a landsman would think was happening. Mr. Rackham, however, considers that the phrase translated, ' As we were driven to and fro in the sea of Adria ' (the old name for the centre of the Mediterranean between Crete, Malta and Sicily), really means, ' As we were being driven across the sea of Adria.'

However that may be, on the fourteenth night after the cornship had drifted helplessly from under the lee of Cauda the ear of the sailors detected over the din of wind and waves the awful sound of breakers – as one of the MSS. puts it, ' Some country was resounding.' They took soundings and found they were near land. So they did what ancient seamanship dictated : they first took up and lashed the two great paddles which served for rudders ; then they lowered four anchors, not from the prow as usual, but from the stern. This was to keep the ship facing shoreward and ready to be beached in the morning. It is interesting to note here

that Lord Nelson, in the battle of Copenhagen, found
that by anchoring from the stern he would be able to
get the ship into exactly the position he wanted.

'They longed for the day,' says St. Luke ; he
never forgot the tension of that night, and under its
tension the nerve of the crew gave way. They con-
cocted a plot for lowering the boat and getting away
in her. They represented that it would steady the ship
to lower anchors from the bow also and that this
involved lowering the boat. The boat was hanging
from the davits when St. Paul warned Julius what was
really going to happen, and reminded him that without
the expert help of the sailors it would be impossible to
beach the ship safely.

As soon as the soldiers realised what was happening
they over-mastered the sailors and cut the ropes of the
boat, letting her fall into the sea and be lost. This
secured the absolutely united effort necessary for the
safety of everybody, and gave the Church one of her
great texts on the need of unity – ' Except these abide
in the ship ye cannot be saved.'

As the day began to dawn, the whole ship's company
was mustered for the great effort. But it needed
stronger men than they were at the moment ; they
were utterly worn out with watching and fasting. And
now St. Paul came to the fore again. He promised
that every man should be saved if he did his duty, and
to prepare for that duty he bade them take food – and
set them an example. A loaf was brought to him and
he said a solemn grace over it and gave portions of it
to St. Luke and Aristarchus. The others were
encouraged and impressed, and took their food with
better heart. When they had eaten they prepared for

the supreme moment by throwing into the sea all the rest of the foodstuff, and so lightening the ship as much as possible.

By this time it was daylight. Nobody recognised the coast, for this was a part of the island which they would not have seen by touching at Valetta, as at some time no doubt some of them had done. Before them stretched a bay and a beach, and they decided to run the ship aground here. So they cast their anchors loose and unlashed the rudder paddles, hoisted a small foresail, and made straight for the beach.

Then came the catastrophe. The end of the northern promontory of St. Paul's Bay at Malta has been cut in two by tidal action and forms an islet separated from the promontory by a narrow channel, and the force of the tide through this channel has worked up hidden sandbanks in the middle of the bay. On one of these the ship was run by the gale, which was still blowing. She stuck fast, and at once the heavy seas began to break up her stern. It seemed likely that some, at any rate, would get ashore alive, and the soldiers, who were responsible for the prisoners with their lives, thought that their only safety lay in killing them all, as otherwise some would probably escape.

St. Paul was never in greater danger in his life, but happily Julius got his men in hand and stopped the massacre. He had all chains unfastened and told them all to save themselves as best they could. He commanded that those who could swim should cast themselves overboard and get first to the land, and the rest follow, some on planks and some on other things from the ship. And so it came to pass that they all escaped safe to the land.

Malta was then part of the Province of Sicily ; it was inhabited by a mixed race, as it is to-day, mainly Phœnician and Carthaginian. It was highly prosperous and civilised, and you must not think that the inhabitants wore skins and blue paint like ancient Britons, because St. Luke calls them barbarians. He is writing as a Greek and merely means that they did not talk Greek. There was a Procurator and a local self-government, a senate, deputies and a widely extended franchise. Local feeling was further respected by paying great honour to a personage who was called First of the Maltese. This gentleman, whose estates lay near St. Paul's Bay, was very kind to the castaways when he heard what had happened. Everyone was kind ; the country folk down by the shore had made a great fire and helped the poor things to dry their clothes and had been enormously impressed when St. Paul showed no bad effects from the viper bite he got in collecting sticks. They were struck by his personality and at once said ' he was a god.' Indeed, the atmosphere was so sympathetic that St. Paul's spiritual powers were able to manifest themselves. He performed a striking cure in the case of the father of Publius and gained such a reputation that he and St. Luke were obliged to open a kind of clinic, in which, by means of divine power, personal magnetism and medical knowledge, great good was done.

They spent three months in Malta. It was a thoroughly happy and restful winter, and when the party resumed their voyage, the grateful Maltese loaded them with things which they needed, for of course they had lost everything in the shipwreck.

CHAPTER XXIII

THE shipwrecked crew and the prisoners spent three months in Malta. In February the sea was open again for navigation and Julius made arrangements to get his party on to Rome. Another Alexandrian corn-ship had been prevented by the storms from completing its voyage and had been wintering in the port of Valetta. It was called *The Twin Brethren* and bore upon its prow the figures of Castor and Pollux, who were the patron deities of shipping. Julius secured places on *The Twin Brethren*, and they set forth. They ran on the first day to Syracuse in Sicily. Here adverse winds kept them for three days, and when they started again they had to tack in order to get to Rhegium in the Straits of Messina. There was another day's delay here, and then at last the perfectly favourable wind sprang up, and they had a splendid run of 140 miles to Puteoli, which they reached the next day. Puteoli – now Pozzuoli – is a port on the Bay of Naples and is 140 miles from Rome. It was nevertheless the port of Rome in those days, because Ostia, the harbour at the mouth of the Tiber, suffered too much from the silting up of the quantities of deposit the Tiber brings down to be in any way adequate to the enormous trade and traffic of the world's centre.

St. Paul's letters do not show the slightest appreciation of the scenes of nature. I imagine that to him the whole world seemed marked out for destruction and that he passed through it, certainly in his earlier Christian days, entirely dominated by a sense of the impending catastrophe.

To a modern the first sight of Etna, the snow-clad stretches of mountain above the Straits of Messina, the ever active volcano of Stromboli, and the run up the coast to the lovely bay of Pozzuoli, would be intensely interesting. I should question whether they would attract the attention of St. Paul in any way, unless indeed the signs of subterranean fires led him to speculate on their possible relation to the catastrophe which must one day engulf the world.

The entrance to Puteoli would be gay and animated ; the corn-ships were always received with enthusiasm, and the unusual storms of the last winter, which had so impeded navigation, would add to the enthusiasm over the earliest spring arrivals. We must imagine the beautiful bay crowded with shipping, the great quays with their cheering crowds, the demonstrative greetings of relations kept apart by the winter storms, the sensation of having come to the world's mart, the impression of power, magnificence, luxuriance, beauty, and then we must reflect on the pathetic and awful seriousness of St. Paul's point of view as he surveyed it all ; and contrast it with the terrified despair of his poor fellow prisoners to whom all this was the heartless prelude to the agonies of the amphitheatre. Among the crowds there stood a little knot of Christians, and St. Paul experienced the joy of finding the unchanging Christian scene and the unchanging Christian spirit already established amid the bewildering activities of the port where, as Juvenal says, 'the Syrian Orontes first disgorged its crowds on the way to the Roman Tiber.'

The Church made great efforts to keep St. Paul over a Sunday, and Julius consented, since it probably took some time to arrange for the transport of the prisoners over the 140 miles of land to Rome.

St. Paul's Sunday at Puteoli – think of its surroundings. Round the curve of the bay Vesuvius rose against the sky, not the modern active, but the old sleeping Vesuvius, with its immense shallow cupped crater all covered with gardens and smothered in vines and sprinkled round its sides with marble villas ; below lay Herculanæum and Pompeii in all their Greek brilliancy and wickedness : they had just twenty years more to live. Over the blue sea lay the islands then filled with exiles from Pandataria to Capræa, where twenty-three years before Tiberius had died, so hated by all that none will ever know the truth about his later life. Think of that Sunday Eucharist, in which St. Paul celebrated the Holy Mysteries within sight of Baiæ, where the marble palaces of the Roman nobles were built out into the sea and where Nero, the Cæsar to whose justice he was appealing, had murdered Agrippina, his mother, who had set him on the throne.

After seven happy days in the Church of Puteoli, St. Paul began the last stage of his journey to Rome. The great road went by Cumæ, with its mystical traditions of the Sybil, to Capua – then the greatest city on the road – and thence keeping close to the coast for seventy miles to Terracina, passing along the edge of the Falernian wine country, where the vines may still be seen trained over the elms on the hillsides. The road would become more animated the nearer the

convoy drew to Rome. Lecticæ, the classical sedan
chairs – but much more comfortable than the modern
ones – would be often met, with well-to-do people
comfortably disposed in them. Cicero was murdered
in a lectica, and St. Paul passed through Formiæ,
the place where Cicero was murdered on his way to
Terracina. Every now and then a rheda would go by,
the big family travelling carriage of the wealthy classes,
on its way from Rome to some country house, while the
dog-carts of the period would continually dash past the
convoy one way or the other ; and it is a sign that after all
we have not got so far beyond the people of those days
in our devices that Seneca says you could write your
letters in a cisium, an exercise which even Bishop
Wilberforce could hardly have attempted in its modern
parallel. At Terracina a range of mountains drops
towards the sea in limestone cliffs, and a few miles
beyond, the Pontine Marshes begin. Augustus had
dug a canal through the marshes to help drain them,
and for twenty miles this canal now ran along by the
roadside ; on the canal there was a service of barges,
drawn by mules, and travellers had the option of going
by road or by canal for this bit of the way as far as
Appii Forum, where the canal ended. We do not
know how Julius took his party, but we do know that it
was this choice of road and the uncertainty as to which
Julius would take, which prevented the affectionate
and grateful readers of the Epistle to the Romans from
coming more than forty miles out of the city to meet
the great author. They were waiting in a big party
among the bargees and the low tavern-keepers who,
the satirists tell us, thronged Appii Forum, the
present Treponti, and we wonder how many of those

mentioned in the sixteenth chapter of the Romans were
waiting there, how many of the Ephesians, how many
of the converts of the further East who had found their
way to Rome. Were Aquila and Priscilla waiting at the
end of the canal ? We do not know, but we know that
a group of devoted friends was there, and that St. Paul
was made very happy by this fact. Ten miles farther on,
at Tres Tabernæ, a second group was waiting, perhaps
the more official group, to give the more official welcome in the name of the Roman Church. In all the
interest and delight of this affectionate companionship
St. Paul must have found the next seventeen miles to
the Alban hills an easy stage. The road climbed and
descended the big southern slope amid wealthy
suburban villas, and then entered the Campagna ; on
a great viaduct it crossed a crater-like valley and
reached Aricia, the beginning of the last stage to
Rome. Aricia was the kingdom of beggars ; many of
the Roman satirists have described its squalid tor-
menting armies. There is a slope up beyond Aricia, and
on the brow of the slope St. Paul would pause a
moment amid an eager shout from his friends –
Ecce Roma !

Roma ! yes, there was the long blue line of the
Sabine hills, there was Soracte still snow-covered, far
and wide to the sea stretched the flat Campagna, but
for the rest how unlike the modern scene ! Now the
dome of St. Peter's, where then the circus of Nero stood,
the great blue dome ruling the clearly defined city
standing amid the beautiful ruin-strewn desolation ;
then a city which covered the whole Campagna with
houses, villas and gardens, and ran in great splashes of
township up the base of the distant hills ; in the centre,

no domes, no campaniles, nothing but a closely congested mass of flat or tent-roofed buildings, piled on the low hills and showing nothing of their white marble splendours from this distance. There were magnificently executed buildings in Rome, and it concentrated richness of building material in masses which are unexampled ; but the more recent architecture was bad, coarse, debased stuff, and in comparison with Athens the Rome of Nero's day was a nasty, coarse, bloated, vulgar place, the city of the *nouveaux riches*.

Six miles from Aricia the road descended into the Campagna, and made in a perfectly straight line for the gates. It was extraordinarily grand, with its great procession of noble tombs on either side, its broad flagged surface and the low stone seats for the accommodation of travellers at every forty feet, and the endless statues of the protecting deities.

As the travellers approached Rome the buildings stood closer and closer together, and long before they reached the ancient walls they had been tramping through a great continuous city. By the Porta Capena, now the Porta di San Sebastiano, ' the moist gate,' as Juvenal calls it, because it always dripped water from the Aqueduct which ran over it, St. Paul, St. Luke and Aristarchus entered Rome itself. The street stretched between the Aventine and the Coelian on to the Circus Maximus ; before they reached the Circus Maximus the procession turned off to the right under the Palatine, with its towering terraces of building, the Palace of the Cæsars, and then, turning again sharply to the right, it climbed the Coelian Hill to the Castra Peregrinorum, the Headquarters of the Imperial Police who had brought St. Paul to Rome ; and there

on that pleasant hill which you associate with delightful
mornings in Rome – with San Gregorio and Santi
Giovanni e Paolo and San Stefano Rotondo, that hill
which through St. Gregory is so imperishably associated with English Christianity – there St. Paul was
handed over to the Chief of the Imperial Police. At
the same time the elogium, the official report which was
always forwarded with a prisoner, would be handed in.
This, as we know, was highly favourable to St. Paul.

The Chief of Police would note the number of
friends who accompanied St. Paul to his court, and no
doubt he received a strikingly impressive account of his
prisoner from Julius.   Accordingly he treated him
very favourably, allowing him to live in a house of his
own, outside the police headquarters, in charge of the
soldier to whom he was chained. He was not allowed
about the city, but no restriction whatever was put on
his movements or actions within the house, save those
involved in the torturing restraint of being perma-
nently day and night chained by the wrist to the wrist
of another man.

Here a word must be said about the Jews and the
Christians St. Paul found in Rome when he got there
in the spring of the year 58. The Jews had multiplied
enormously in Rome, as I reminded you in an earlier
chapter, and had become a serious menace to the
financial welfare of its inhabitants. Claudius expelled
them all for a short time, and it was probably this,
as we saw, which brought Aquila and Priscilla into
relations with St. Paul at Corinth. Now they were all
back again, and the Trastevere was one enormous
ghetto. There were several synagogues. Through
Herod the Jews had ingratiated themselves with the

aristocracy and the wealthy classes, and by means of proselytising wealthy ladies had got a considerable hold on society. A good many of them held posts about the Emperor — Haliturus, his favourite actor, was a Jew, and Poppœa, his mistress, was a Jewish proselyte.

Christianity apparently reached Rome soon after the day of Pentecost ; indeed so completely was Rome the heart of the Empire that it could hardly fail to do so. It was creating disturbances there in the reign of Claudius, and tradition tells us that St. Peter visited it then. The importance and size of the Church four years before St. Paul reached Rome is proved by the Epistle which he addressed to it from Corinth in 54, and we learn three things about it from that letter.

The Roman Christians were in enjoyment of all Christian blessings. St. Paul almost apologises for writing a letter to them. The Church of Rome was not one of his Churches, the ground was already apostolically occupied, and although he is not mentioned, the Epistle to the Romans indirectly suggests that the great tradition is true and that St. Peter was the first Apostle of Rome. But on the other hand the Gentile element predominated in the Church. The Jewish section of the Church had evidently suffered a setback when, under Claudius, the Jewish Christians had to leave the city together with the rest of the Jews. There had been, you must remember, this period, when all the Jewish section of the Church of Rome was in banishment and St. Peter was also certainly not in the city. During this time the Gentile Church continued to increase, and the probability is that when the Jewish Christians came back they did not amalgamate well with the Gentiles, but were very much a separate

body, so that although the ground had been apostolically occupied by St. Peter it is probable that at this
moment the Roman Church was not an organic whole.
It was rather a series of congregations under Jewish
and Gentile presbyters. It is probable also that the
Jewish side of the Church was laying great stress on its
association with St. Peter, and that a visit from the
Apostle of the Gentiles was very desirable, perhaps
less to encourage than to discipline the Gentile section
of the Church. During the remainder of the lifetime of
the Apostles they had an apostolic partnership in the
Church of Rome, though it was always St. Peter's
Church, never St. Paul's. There were discussions
between their followers, that we know, and these dis-
sensions were buried for ever in the graves of the two
martyrs, for the Church of Rome did not become a
perfect unity until St. Peter and St. Paul had given
their life blood for her. What happened has been
summed up by a sentence of St. Irenæus – ' Peter and
Paul having founded and built up the Church of
Rome, transmitted the office of Bishop to Linus.'

We have each of us, I expect, got our own picture of
St. Paul's hired house in Rome. The poorer classes
lived in immense, lofty, barrack-like tenements. You
must remember that an ancient city looked much more
modern than we are disposed to imagine ; it was not all
composed of buildings like the few great public
buildings of which the remains have survived. I expect
that if we were put down in the quarter of Rome where
St. Paul lived and in his day, it would take us a little
time to realise that we had been transported out of our
own period. We should have probably found ourselves in a narrow, dirty street with that very black

RT

mud, which seems to be an Italian peculiarity, smearing the roadway, and on either side great workmen's flats shutting out the sun, detestable smells, clothes hung out to dry, and babies, very much like modern babies, playing in the gutter. Climbing a common staircase, littered with bits of cabbage stalk and general untidiness, we should have found the Apostle with his soldier in a little flat, surrounded by grave and eager people. This was the picture of the 'hired house' Dr. Bigg used to draw for his students at Oxford.

It is a very interesting fact that St. Paul conceived it to be his first duty on arriving at Rome to meet the unconverted Jews. One would have thought he would have plunged immediately into Christian affairs. Evidently he had a rule, which in conscience he could not break, of preaching first everywhere to the unconverted of his own kindred.

It must have taken a little time to secure the 'hired house,' but on the second day after his arrival St. Paul invited the presidents of the various synagogues to his lodgings. They came in a body, and the fact shows that Christianity had become a big and important matter in Rome.

St. Paul made a speech to them. He said that although his nation had delivered him to the Romans, he had been guilty of no disloyalty to it. The Romans had held an inquiry and had pronounced him innocent, but Jewish influence had been so strong that the Romans had not dared to liberate him. Consequently to save his life he had appealed to Cæsar; then, lifting his chained arm, he cried that it was the Hope of Israel that was in question and that it was for the Hope of Israel that he was ' an ambassador in chains.'

The Jews were very cautious ; they said that they had nothing against Paul personally ; on the other hand the Nazarenes were spoken against throughout the whole Jewish world. They were aware that Paul was a ringleader of the Nazarenes and they would be glad to hear him expound their doctrine.

So a day was fixed for a disputation.

The comparative vagueness of these Jews about Christianity is curious. It may be accounted for by the edict of Claudius expelling the Jews from Rome. When they all came back the Jewish Christians re-organised themselves altogether apart from the Synagogue. The exile had snapped all threads, and henceforth to the Roman Synagogue Christianity was not a fact under observation. What they knew they got from hearsay ; it could not have happened anywhere in those days but in Rome, for Rome alone was big enough for such complete dissociation, and to-day only one city is big enough – London.

CHAPTER XXIV

WE now reach the final scene in the Acts. St. Luke has worked the book up to a dramatic conclusion. St. Paul has offered the Gospel to the Jews at Antioch in Pisidia, at Corinth and at Ephesus. Now he finally offers it in the capital of the world. In each case they reject it, and he hands on the offer to the Gentiles.

The last sentence of the Acts exactly sums up the extent of the Church's victory at that point. St. Paul is tied to a soldier, an ambassador in chains ; the persecutions are not over, they are only beginning. But he is in his own hired house ; evidently he paid the rent himself, and at one point was short of money until fresh supplies came from Lydia and those at Philippi. He receives all who come to him. He preaches the Kingdom. He teaches the things concerning our Lord Jesus Christ with all boldness, none forbidding him. The occasion itself shows the advance of the Church. Instead of St. Paul interrupting a synagogue service, the Jews come in great numbers to his lodgings. He delivers a great exposition of the Faith from early morning right on into the afternoon. The exposition causes a great division of opinion, and in the end St. Paul is left as arbitrator or judge in the controversy which arises between his hearers. He delivers the Divine judgment, Acts xxviii., 25–28. The last sentence, " Be it known therefore unto you that the salvation

of God is sent unto the Gentiles, and that they will
hear it,' St. Luke regards as finally dethroning the
chosen people.

As they went down the unswept staircase that
afternoon those men were beginning the most extraordinary of all national histories, the history of
the Wandering Jew.   St. Luke quotes Isaiah vi.
9–10.   Why is Divine Grace given to one man
and not to another ?   That is the question the
passage raises.   The believing Jew found satisfaction
to his intellect and peace of mind in the thought that
it did not mean that anything had escaped the eye of
God, but that it was all foreknown to Him and in His
hand.   The way in which this thought is clothed in
the original is very difficult to modern people.   The
expression, ' Make the heart of this people fat, and
make their ears heavy, and shut their eyes ; lest they
see with their eyes, and hear with their ears, and understand with their heart, and turn again and be healed,'
appears to us to be a statement that men's hearts were
deliberately hardened by Divine Will ; but that would
be a misunderstanding of the Hebrew idiom.   The
' make ' is the poetical description, in the Hebrew form
of expression, of the results of disobedience.   The
Hebrew does not hesitate to say that, in creating a free-
will, and so creating a possibility of disobedience, God
creates the disobedience ; and this, at least, must be
clear to us all, that where there is free-will the presentation of light and truth becomes, if rejected, the judgment of God.   This is quite plain ; for example,
St. Paul's preaching was either for life or for death,
and wherever he went, he divided the Jews into two
sections ; they either believed or disbelieved ; and so

the Gospel of St. Paul always hardened some hearts, but this hardening was not a fate predestined for some individual ; it must be thought of as the judgment of Divine Law on disordered wills.

To the Jew the thought left by all this is not the severity, it is the mercy of God.

Notwithstanding Jewish disobedience, God is determined that man should be saved, and so He turns to the Gentiles.

The detention at Rome lasted two years. At the end of the two years St. Paul was tried, acquitted, and liberated. We do not know the meaning of the delay : it may have been mere pressure of legal business, it may have been Jewish influence, or it may have been merely Nero's slackness. These two years, like the previous two years at Cæsarea, were the greatest blessing to the Church ; to this enforced leisure we owe four epistles.

You will remember that St. Paul had written the two letters to the Thessalonians during his first stay at Corinth. The two letters to the Corinthians were written at the close of his stay at Ephesus, the letter to the Galatians during his subsequent journeyings in Macedonia, and the letter to the Romans was carefully written, and dispatched by the hand of Phœbe, during the second important stay at Corinth. We know also that St. Paul wrote epistles that have not survived ; for instance, there were the lost letters to the Corinthians ; and he probably wrote letters from Cæsarea, most likely short practical directions, and none of these survive.

But now we get four more letters – Colossians, Philemon, the so-called letter to Ephesus, and Philippians.

It is not easy to be sure in what order these letters were written during the two years. Philippians, Colossians, Philemon, and the encyclical to the Churches of Asia Minor — the so-called Epistle to the Ephesians — were all written about the same time, and dispatched by Tychicus, who was accompanied by Onesimus, the dishonest runaway slave-boy whom St. Paul had converted in his hired house.

St. Paul received his information about the Colossians from Epaphras, the Christian who had evangelised the cities of the valley of Lycus in Asia Minor, not far from Ephesus — Colosse, Hierapolis and Laodicea.

It is plain from the Epistles to the Colossians and to Philemon that St. Paul had not visited Colosse up to this time, but that he hoped to go there when he was liberated. On the other hand, some of the Colossians had probably been converted by him at Ephesus, and probably Philemon — the wealthy Colossian gentleman to whom the slave Onesimus belonged — was one of these.

Epaphras had apparently gone from Rome as St. Paul's messenger to the East, and had returned with the alms of the Philippians, had had a terrible illness in Rome, from which he nearly died, and had recovered from it, and was the bearer back to Philippi of St. Paul's letter of thanks, which is our Epistle to the Philippians.

Since it was Epaphras who had furnished the information about Colosse, these facts make us think it probable that the Epistle to the Philippians was written last of the four, and in speaking of the four Epistles we will take them in this order — Colossians, Philemon, Ephesians, Philippians.

The letter to Philemon is a purely private note about Onesimus, but the Epistle to the Colossians, with which it was sent, is a very delicately-worded letter about a heresy which was developing in the Colossian Church. St. Paul does not know the Colossians personally, so all through the letter he is rather feeling his way; he is saying things indirectly rather than directly, and consequently it takes him a long time to get to his point – this curious development of angel-worship about which it was necessary he should write. At the end he asks that the letter should be sent on to Laodicea to be read there, and he tells the Colossians to get and read the letter from Laodicea. This letter which they are to get from Laodicea is supposed to be the letter to the Ephesians. In many ancient manuscripts the words in chapter i., 6, are omitted, and a blank is left, as if several copies had been made and blanks left to insert the names of various Churches. The absence from this Epistle of personal salutations to the Christians of any particular locality adds to the likelihood of its having been a letter intended for circulation in the Churches of Asia Minor. It would ultimately get associated with Ephesus, because Ephesus was the chief city of that province. Tertullian tells us that the Gnostic heretic Marcion possessed copies of this letter with the words, 'To the Laodiceans,' in them, and some people therefore think that Laodicea was the first point from which the circular was to be generally distributed.

Laodicea was the leading bishopric of Phrygia during the period when the whole of that district was Christian. It was eleven miles from Colosse, in the Lycus Valley, and was in a central position on the great trade route from the East. It was a considerable banking centre, and was noted for its manufacture of fine garments of black wool, and of a powder called Phrygian powder, which was a remedy for weak eyes. Laodicea is now called Eski-Hissar, the old fortress, and is utterly deserted. In Revelations iii., 14–22 – the epistle to the Church of Laodicea – there is a reference to the three sources of her riches : ' I counsel thee to buy of me gold tried in the fire, that thou mayest be rich, and white raiment, that thou mayest be clothed, and anoint thine eyes with eye-salve, that thou mayest see.'

Let us now think a little more in detail of the three letters which Tychicus the Ephesian carried from Rome to Asia Minor.

Of the three cities of the Lycus, Hierapolis and Laodicea were big, important, and flourishing, but Colosse was falling into decay. It had been the big place, and in the time of Herodotus it had been very flourishing, but it had got cut out by the others. It produced a particular kind of dye, colóssinus, and this gave it comfortable prosperity, but it was the small, old-fashioned, aristocratic place of the three. The inhabitants of Colosse were partly Phrygian natives, and partly the families of Greek settlers. There was much intellectual activity among them, much speculative thought, and at this very time, thirteen miles off at Hierapolis, there was growing into maturity the slave Epictetus, who was to give to the world some of its noblest thought apart from Christ.

In the rich water meadows below Colosse cattle were bred in great numbers. The cliffs of the valley were strikingly marked by the white, shining deposits which

the waters of the Lycus left. The valley has always
been visited by frequent earthquakes, and it is a curious
fact that there has always been a tendency to angel-
worship in this region.

Angel-worship had to be condemned in the fourth
century by the Council of Laodicea, and yet in the
ninth and tenth centuries this district was the centre
of the worship of St. Michael, who was believed to
have saved the countryside from inundation by opening the chasm of the Lycus. The exact character of
the false teaching which St. Paul condemns in this
letter is not easily determined, but there was a wrong
tendency in practice and in doctrine ; I put practice
first, because I think that the celestial visions and
knowledge, to which the teachers seemed to have laid
claim, probably grew out of their treatment of their
bodies. They appear to have taught and practised ex-
cessive austerity, not from the right reason of getting
the body into proper subordination to the spirit and so
bringing the whole man into a condition of effective
service in the cause of Christ, but for the wrong
reason of wishing, as far as possible, to get rid of bodily
life as an evil in itself. This way of thinking, if pushed
to its logical conclusion, works back, not into a Divine
Unity, but into a dualism ; it puts God and matter
into opposite camps, and denies the desirability, and
also, therefore, of course, the possibility, of Divine Incarnation. Of this heresy, Christian Science is a striking modern example. There was a sect of Jews called
Essenes, who practised an asceticism very like that of
the Colossians, and although we do not know of any
Essenes in Asia Minor, it seems as though the innovators at Colosse, who together with this asceticism

were insisting very much on the observance of the Jewish ceremonial year, had the Essenes in mind. This sort of wrong abasement before God led these innovators to insist that a line of mediatorial spirits is needed for a connecting chain between man and the Supreme Being. To use modern terms, they were becoming like the spiritualists and the Christian Scientists, and just in so far as they were becoming both, they were ceasing to be Catholic Christians : our Lord was ceasing to be the Catholic Christ to them ; the Incarnation, and its extension in the Sacraments, was ceasing to be the pivot on which their lives turned.

But St. Paul introduces his subject very warily and tactfully.

All that he has to say about our Lord's nature and work (Colossians i. 14–20), he says in a sort of ecstatic digression :

Christ is Redeemer.

He is prior to all creation, even to that of the Angels.

All creation coheres through union in Him.

He is the Head of the Church, in virtue of His resurrection, and also as embodying all the Divine attributes.

He is the Lord of Angels and of men.

But at last St. Paul gets to his controversial bit. He warns the Colossians against false philosophy. Christ is the sole Incarnation of Deity (chapter ii. 9, 10). God has not divided His attributes amongst spirits ; all are to be found in Christ. Salvation is in that union with Christ which begins at fully-accepted Christian Initiation ; in Baptism we receive the forgiveness won on the Cross, when

Christ blotted out the law and triumphed over evil angels. Then St. Paul directly condemns the false teachers, and goes on to the practical exhortation which has been selected for the Epistle for Easter Day. St. Paul sends a greeting from the ' beloved physician,' and writes the end of the letter with his own hand ; let it be remembered that he is chained all the while to a Roman soldier.

With this letter goes the letter to Philemon, and the letter to Philemon takes us, more deeply than anything else he ever wrote, into the personal life of St. Paul.

CHAPTER XXV ·

THE Epistle to Philemon is a short private letter and did not obtain its place in the canon of Holy Scripture without a challenge. In the fourth century, when men were absorbed in theological controversy, it was pronounced by many to deal with a subject of no importance. St. Jerome and St. John Chrysostom felt obliged to defend it against fierce attack. In all ages there have probably been some readers who have asked what message from God to His Church this private note can have been inspired to convey. The answer is that it shows us how the Apostles dealt with an individual sinner.

Among the aristocracy of Colosse the well-to-do Philemon, his wife the lady Apphia, and their son Archippus evidently held an honourable place. They lived the lives of people of their station and were served by a numerous retinue of slaves. It is an illustration of the change which Christianity made in human society that at the end of eighteen centuries there should be a story to tell about one of the most disreputable of these slaves. Think a moment what the position of a slave was in those days. He had no rights of any kind. ' There is no such thing as an illegal action towards a slave,' so the hideous statute ran. A slave could hold no property, he could not make a legal marriage, his evidence in a court of law was legal evidence only when given under torture. Under this infernal system slave character had so deteriorated that at the moment it seemed unfit for any other. One great philosopher said that slaves had only partially developed souls, while another debates the point as to whether a slave had ever really shown virtue. And yet there were many attractive and accomplished slaves ; you remember how amusing and lovable those corrupt, criminal slaves of Latin comedy are. Now among the slaves of Philemon in the year 56, when St. Paul was staying at Ephesus, there was a bright and handy little boy. As he had no name of his own they nicknamed him Onesimus or Profitable, the Bargain as we might say. We know something of the Bargain's disposition – he was tractable and affectionate with a wholesome capacity for hero-worship. He was evidently a favourite and apparently Philemon's page. During St. Paul's stay at Ephesus a great change passed over the household of Philemon ; its master and mistress and their eldest son became Christians. Colosse was not far from Ephesus, and, at some visit to the great seaport, Philemon had come under the influence of St. Paul. We can imagine the excitement and discussions in the slave household, some sympathising with the new strict life the family were leading, others making fun of it. The page Onesimus seems to have taken the wrong side. His had been a slave birth and a slave education, he had learnt foul words and seen foul deeds ; there was little that the Devil knew that Onesimus did not know, so gradually the boy went to the bad and a gulf opened and widened between him and his master. The one descended as the other ascended ; the affection of Onesimus became changed to sullen discontent, and he determined

to escape. There was only one way of doing that. So
one day or night at a convenient moment, he filled his
sash with valuables and escaped into the marshes of
the Mæander. Warily he slipped down to Ephesus,
and there, either by selling a jewel or working his
passage, he got himself conveyed by ship to Rome.
And so one fine day he entered the capital of the
world, bent on tasting every evil pleasure it had to
offer. He found kindred souls ready to welcome him,
and the scum of the moral cesspool of the old world
closed over the slave boy's head. Months passed and
years, and there came a moment when Onesimus found
himself a starving outcast, ruined in mind and body,
upon the pavement of a city in which mercy and
loving-kindness were unknown. And here comes a gap
in the story. When we next see him it is at a moment
of crisis. He is standing in a small, meanly furnished
room. Before him at a table covered with untidy
materials three figures are seated, a Roman soldier
listless and unemployed, a secretary writing, and
a small, black-bearded, bright-eyed man who is looking
keenly at Onesimus – St. Paul. Who brought the
runaway slave to the prison of the Apostle ? We do
not know, but Epaphras, a well-known Colossian
Christian, was in Rome at the time, and it is pleasant
to think that it was he who met the poor broken-down
young scamp in the street and laid his hand on his
shoulder and brought him to St. Paul. No matter
how he came ; here he is now ; what will St. Paul do
with him ? St. Paul was desperately busy. Besides
his work as teacher and director, he was at this time
engaged on three great Epistles – Ephesians, Philippians and Colossians – but if St. Paul had had no time

to attend to Onesimus he would have been no Apostle
of Jesus Christ. What did he do ? He brought all
the power of his purified, Christ-controlled, colossal
manhood to bear upon this wretched boy. With
tender, searching questions he probed his moral
wounds. He put his arm about him and showed him
the vision of the Crucified with its outstretched arms
of mercy, and he brought him to Jesus Christ through
the means of grace, and he gave him the hope of glory.
He clothed and fed and healed him, body, mind and
spirit, and as he began to employ him about his person
the boy's old brightness returned and St. Paul felt
that God had sent him to lighten his captivity. Think
of these two, Paul crucified to the world, all his earthly
ties broken for Christ's sake, finding this spiritual son :
' My child whom I have begotten in my bonds.' And
Onesimus, who had never known pure earthly love
before, finding father, mother and elder brother in this
great-hearted, strong, loving man. And so time
passed and the Epistles to Ephesus and Colosse were
ready, and Tychicus their bearer made ready to depart, and then there came for St. Paul what was,
I suppose, the last great struggle of his life, and he
tore out his heart strings when he said to Onesimus,
" Now you must go back to Philemon and take your
punishment." " What, Master, away from you who
keep me straight ? " " Yes, away from me, but never
away from your Lord and mine." " Back to the
horrible old life with the slaves and all its temptations ? " " Yes, back to it all, but fear not, you are
taking our Lord to be your companion." " But my
punishment, do you know what it is ? It is the cross
or the fire." " Dear son, I know it, and if your master

exact it our Lord will be with you on the cross or in the fire." And then the slave boy swallowed down his horror like a man and said, " I will go back " ; and St. Paul wrote the Epistle to Philemon, in which he pleads so pathetically for his son's safety and welfare. He sees the end of his imprisonment, and in a passage full of tender charm he makes himself responsible for the value of what Onesimus had stolen and invites himself to stay with Philemon.

So there came a moment when St. Paul put the letter into the hands of the boy, and they looked one another in the face perhaps for the last time, and Onesimus followed the grave-faced Tychicus down to their ship and they sailed away. The end of the story is not known, but we cannot doubt that Philemon pardoned Onesimus. Tradition makes Onesimus a Bishop and a Martyr, and it is just possible that he was the Bishop Onesimus of Ephesus, who is mentioned by St. Ignatius.

The third letter St. Paul sent to Asia Minor at this time was the encyclical intended to be read in all the principal churches, which we call the Epistle to the Ephesians. His imprisonment must have caused him to reflect upon the approach of the time when the personal influence of the original Apostles would be withdrawn from the world, and in the Epistle to the Ephesians he develops his teaching as to the universal society predestined before all ages, visibly united by Baptism and the Apostolic ministry, which was to enshrine the gifts of the Apostolate throughout all ages and speak with its authority. The union between Jew and Gentile had been so recent that it is natural for St. Paul to fear their falling apart again when the

Sᴛ

personal influence of the men who had been the human
instruments of the union were withdrawn.   If such
a danger arose it would be at the instance of the Jews,
and so St. Paul thought it well to emphasise God's
eternal purpose for the Gentiles.   His own peculiar
vocation, he says, has been the stewardship of this
wonderful secret, the inclusion of the Gentiles in the
promise as a step towards the final unity and perfecting
of all things in God.

There remains the Epistle in which St. Paul thanks
the Philippians for their liberal offerings to him.   He
had always loved the Philippians greatly ; they had
kept their first love and simplicity, and they are still
his 'joy and crown.'   The passionate outburst of
warning against the teaching and schemes of the
Judaising Christians was evidently inspired by some
fresh illustration of their venom not at Philippi but in
Rome.   St. Paul is afraid they may invade his dear
Philippi and break up its Christian unity.   Only a com-
paratively trifling difficulty of a personal kind had
interrupted the peace of the Philippian Church.   Two
earnest churchworkers, Euodia and Syntyche, had
fallen into a disagreement sufficiently marked to be
a matter of comment in the community.   Each of these
ladies had no doubt been animated by the highest
conscientious motives in all she thought, said and did
as to the matters concerned.   St. Paul begs the ladies
to compose their differences and is so bold as to suggest
that two members of the male sex shall attempt to
arbitrate between them.

The Epistle to the Philippians throws considerable
light on St. Paul's position towards the end of his first
imprisonment.   He has produced a great impression

in Rome.   Not only has the Church increased and penetrated into the households of the nobles, but St. Paul has gained for the Christian message a certain amount of curious but respectful attention from persons of position.   He gives an illustration of this in a much disputed phrase — ' My bonds became manifest in Christ,' he says, ' in the whole Prætorium.' It is possible that this means that he had been able to get the judges of the supreme Imperial court to take an intelligent interest in his case, but it seems more probable that the phrase is equivalent to ' throughout the whole Imperial Guard.'   If so, it throws light on the impression St. Paul had made upon the various soldiers to whom he was chained.   In a passage full of the finest Christian feeling he speaks of the internal controversies of the Church as having assisted in spreading the great facts of the faith ; to this extent God had overruled the evil of faction for good, " And therein," he exclaims, " I rejoice, yea, and will rejoice." Further, the activities which radiated from the ' hired house ' had been a great stimulus to the missionary zeal of the faithful, and during the latter part of St. Paul's detention a vigorous campaign was being prosecuted in Rome.

At the end of two years St. Paul's appeal was heard. Tradition is unanimous that he was acquitted and spent some years of freedom and active work before he was again imprisoned at Rome, condemned and executed towards the end of the reign of Nero.   It seems almost certain that he visited Spain.   He was also, during this period, in Ephesus, Crete, Macedonia, Miletus and Nicopolis.   From the various allusions in the Epistles of the first captivity, the

Epistles to Timothy and Titus and ecclesiastical tradition, the probable outline of the last chapter of St. Paul's life is as follows :

When he was liberated he probably fulfilled his promise to Philemon, travelling to Asia Minor through Macedonia and taking Philippi on his way. Ephesus would again be his headquarters in Asia Minor, but from Ephesus he now made a tour through the Churches of the interior, which so far had not seen his face in the flesh. From Ephesus he went to Spain and spent some considerable time there, and from Spain he returned again to Ephesus. By this time the situation was developing in Ephesus, which is discussed in the First Epistle to Timothy. It has often been urged that this situation did not arise until the second century and that the Pastoral Epistles cannot therefore be really the work of St. Paul. But the fact is that the second century heresies did not spring up like mushrooms : in a vague, confused, tentative way, they existed in the first century, and here in the Pastoral letters we see the first mutterings of the teaching which, in its developed form, was denounced by St. Ignatius fifty years later. St. Paul could not remain in Ephesus to deal with the heretics himself, and he may have thought it well to establish Timothy in a local apostolic charge there, some little time before his own death, so that he might be able to tutor his successor.

It is this transference of the Apostolic charge at Ephesus from himself to Timothy which gives us the first Epistle to Timothy, sent from Macedonia. From Macedonia St. Paul was called to Crete to deal with the condition of the Christian Churches there. They had

apparently been invaded by Jewish speculative teachers
who were not above the level of the astrologers, palmists
and sand diviners who haunt West London to-day.
St. Paul placed Titus in Crete to organise, ordain and
remain there as local Apostolic delegate.   And he ultimately addressed a letter to him, probably from
Greece, in which he castigates the charlatans, with
whom Titus has to deal, in stinging phrases.   St. Paul
was intending to spend the winter in Nicopolis, the
city in Epirus which Augustus had founded as a
memorial of the victory of Actium.   He began the
winter there ; but, before it ended, his final summons
reached him.   The time of his departure was at hand.

CHAPTER XXVI

ST Paul's work was over. For him, as for St. Peter, our Lord's summons came through the great fire at Rome. The dates are uncertain here and we can only conjecture the order of events. The great fire of Rome broke out on July 19th of the year 64. It destroyed half the city, and Nero, whose unpopularity was increasing, was suspected of the crime. Nero put the blame upon the Christians, who, thanks to the labours of St. Peter and St. Paul, had now become a large and clearly recognised body, no longer confounded with the Jews. So began the first great persecution of the Church. Multitudes were put to death with a variety of tortures. Many were crucified, others were sewn up into the skins of wild animals and hunted to death by dogs, others again were wrapped in canvas smeared with inflammable material and fastened to posts in the Emperor's gardens. At night they were set on fire and served as torches to illuminate evening fêtes during which the Emperor, dressed as a charioteer, went about among the people in a jovial mood. Warrants were issued for the arrest of the Apostles. St. Peter apparently went into hiding like St. Cyprian long after, and continued to rule the Roman Church from a hidden place. St. Paul was taken. We do not know when the arrest was effected ; it is not possible to frame an itinerary at this point from the scattered allusions in the Second

Epistle to Timothy, his last letter written in his Roman dungeon.   It may have been that St. Paul went hurriedly by Berea, Thessalonica, Philippi and Neapolis to Troas and that he was arrested in the house of Carpus.   His involuntary removal from the house of Carpus may account for his having left valuable books and parchments and a much-needed cloak there. If so, he would probably have been taken first to Ephesus and forwarded from Ephesus to Rome. ' The prison of St. Paul ' is one of the traditional sites at Ephesus.

The horrors of the Neronian persecution had resounded through the Church, which was now feeling the first fierce blast of the hatred of the Imperial power. We must remember how the world had deified the Rule of Rome, and indeed the Rule of Rome had been one of the most beneficent forces the world had ever known. We are not surprised then that there was panic in the Church of Ephesus.   The Christians quailed, and St. Paul felt himself to be alone.   He speaks with sadness of the defection of Demas.   One by one his friends departed.   Crescens and Titus had missions to Churches.   Trophimus became ill and had to be left behind at Miletus as the diminished party started for Rome in the company of the again chained Apostle. Apparently they went by Corinth and Brindisi.   At Corinth, Erastus remained : it was his own city, he had been its treasurer in the old days.   Tychicus St. Paul had to send back with dispatches to Ephesus. Only Luke was with St. Paul when he entered Rome for the last time.   We know no details of his imprisonment.   Tradition places him in the horrible Mamertine at any rate during some part of the time before his death, and it is clear, not only from the charge under which he was arrested, but also from the allusions of his letter, that this was no easy arrangement in a hired house, that he was now undergoing the experiences of a supposed enemy of the State.

Leading Roman Christians gave him cautious greeting. He names Eubulus, Pudens, Linus (who was the second Bishop of Rome) and Claudia. It is by no means improbable that the caution of the Christians arose from the fact that they had St. Peter in hiding and that they feared that any rash movement might betray his whereabouts. But St. Paul felt his loneliness intensely – he was an acutely sensitive man – and he records with passionate gratitude the brave affection of his Ephesian friend Onesiphorus, who, undeterred by the danger and unembarrassed by local anxieties, sought St. Paul out in prison again and again. ' He often refreshed me,' says St. Paul, ' and was not ashamed of my chain.'

It is probable that the first hearing of the case was not long delayed. Such a case would fall to the court of the City Præfect, who sat with a council of assessors. It is easy to picture the scene. The trial must have taken place in one of the big Basilicas, the general effect of which is preserved in scores of the Roman Churches. The broad oblong nave, the rows of shining columns, the apse, the aisles with galleries over them, the raised tribune in the apse with the magistrate's chair of ivory and the seats for the assessors. Before the apse at the top of the nave the arrangements for the prisoner and the advocates on both sides. Behind them a strong rail, and behind the rail the general public, who also crowded the galleries at exciting trials. St. Paul's description of this first hearing of his case is deeply pathetic : ' At my first defence no one took my part but all forsook me : may it not be laid to their account. But the Lord stood by me and strengthened me ; that through me the message might be fully proclaimed, and that all the Gentiles might hear ; and I was delivered out of the mouth of the lion.' It is a question whether this is meant to be taken quite literally, whether he could not even obtain the usual advocates. Perhaps it is rather such a strong expression of loneliness as Newman was moved to write time after time in describing the disappointments of his life. The Church at Rome had not recovered its nerve, and St. Paul would know who might have given signs of love and courage and who failed. But he looked back with thankfulness at the trial. He had been able to make such a defence as brought the facts of his message before the great hostile assemblage. Moreover for the time he had proved his point. He had not been in Rome for a long time previous to the fire. The result was an adjournment of the case that fresh evidence might be obtained as to what St. Paul's complicity might be with the crimes of the Christians.

St. Paul had no doubt about the final result ; the end had come and he sent to Ephesus for Timothy. Timothy was his son in the Faith as no one else was. He goes back in thought to the days when he had found his dear boy in the house of his mother Eunice and his grandmother Lois. He had received the lad from them as a sacred trust and had stood to him as

father ever since. He now proposes to make Timothy
his spiritual executor ; he has a hundred counsels to
give to his beloved Churches and Timothy shall convey them from him. But we do not know St. Paul if
we fail to realise that he was longing for the comfort
and support of his beloved son's presence, and so he
sends for him in one of the most pathetic letters in all
literature :

' I am now ready to be offered and the time of my
departure is at hand. I have fought the good fight,
I have finished my course, I have kept the faith.
Henceforth is laid up for me the crown of righteousness which the Lord, the righteous judge, shall give
me in that day ; and not to me only but unto all them
that love His appearing.

' Do thy utmost to come to me speedily. Do thy
utmost,' he adds in a postscript. ' to come before
winter.'

Did St. Timothy get to Rome in time ? There is
no clear evidence. If the Epistle to the Hebrews was
written from Rome, then it would seem that he did.
' Know ye,' says the writer of that Epistle, ' that our
brother Timothy hath been set at liberty ? ' This
might well imply that Timothy had braved the danger
of standing by his spiritual father at the last, and had
been imprisoned, but in the end had not shared his
fate. There is no clear evidence ; but it was very
easy to get from Ephesus to Rome, and I have no
doubt in my own mind that St. Timothy came and
that they received Communion together in the presence of the Roman soldier who was chained to the
arm of Paul.

At the second hearing Paul was condemned to

death. He was a Roman citizen and he was condemned to the death of a gentleman, death by the sword. It would seem that in the search for evidence between the first and second trials of Paul, Peter was discovered. Tradition asserts that they were imprisoned at the last together and even marks the spot where they parted before their deaths. This at least is certain, it was the almost simultaneous martyrdoms of the two Apostles which healed the divisions among the Gentile and Jewish Christians at Rome, and knit up the Church into an unbreakable unity under Linus.

Peter was no Roman citizen. He died on a cross in the circus of Nero, hard by where his Church now stands. But Paul had a long walk to his death. The road to Ostia was a finer road then than it is now. Fine villas, rich orchards, fair gardens covered what is now malarious plain. There were no railways then, and all merchandise and produce came in through the city gates. The file of soldiery and the little bent old prisoner with his bald head and his grey beard must have wound patiently in and out of miles of noisy traffic before they left the Ostian way and turned sharply up a steep hill to the left. At the top of this mound St. Paul may have paused for a moment ; it was his last sight of the great world. There to the north lay Rome, and east and south the Campagna was disclosed to its furthest limits bordered by its beautiful blue and purple mountains. In this part the Campagna undulates like the mid-Atlantic in a great swell, and here at St. Paul's feet amid these great green billows of grassy land lay the pleasant meadows of the Salvian waters, his valley of the shadow of death.

The Trappist monks, by planting groves of eucalyptus and other trees and shrubs, and by cultivating a beautiful garden, have given the place something of the appearance of long ago. As St. Paul descended the steep path to the stream the great prospect vanished and the soft green billows rose and met the tender blue of the Roman sky. It was a pleasant place to die in. Tradition insists that the Emperor Nero came, and it is not impossible. Certainly it was a popular event, and there was a crowd, but the little old man about to die was a Roman citizen, and all would be conducted with perfect dignity and courtesy. The death of St. Cyprian was a parallel in later days, but there was no great Christian crowd around St. Paul.

A cell is shown in which we are told St. Paul was kept until the great folks came. At last all was ready, and the beloved Saint came into the square of grass kept by the Roman soldiery. I do not think he gave even one farewell glance to earth or sun or sky, but I think he remembered the faithful hearts hidden here and there amid the breathless crowd and that he knit himself to them all in the Communion of Saints. And so he was free at last to go to his Lord, and he bent his head to the sword which with one mighty stroke sent him into the presence of Jesus Christ.

They buried him two miles away in the cemetery of Lucina. There was no difficulty about this, for the law allowed it. A few years later they built a *memoria* over his grave. These *memoriæ* were held inviolate by Roman law even in the case of Christian bishops. The *memoria* was probably quite a simple sepulchral chamber with the sarcophagus in the centre. Above such

a chamber a room was often built in which the Holy
Mysteries were celebrated over the body of the Martyr.
Here the body of St. Paul lay until the Valerian Persecution at the end of the third century.   In this
persecution an effort was made to destroy all Christian
treasures, and the cemeteries were confiscated.   The
Christians in anticipation removed the bodies of
St. Peter and St. Paul from their tombs and hid them
in some catacombs on the Appian Way.   So thankful
was the Church that God's providence enabled her to
preserve her greatest treasures that she has ever since
commemorated the fact in the Festival of the 29th of
June.   For in its original intention the day which the
prayer book calls St. Peter's Day is a thanksgiving for
the safe deposition of the bodies of the Apostles in the
catacombs of the Appian Way.   When the Empire
became Christian the bodies were restored triumphantly to their original resting-places, and the
Emperor built magnificent churches over them.

Pope St. Sylvester consecrated the Basilica of St.
Paul, and Constantine endowed it with much land and
enriched it with many gifts.   He is said to have enclosed the body in a bronze sarcophagus, and to have
placed over it a cross of gold.

Fifty years after, the church was pronounced too
small, and Valentinian II., Arcadius and Honorius
submitted to the Senate a plan for its reconstruction.
This new Basilica, which was completed in 395, is
described by Prudentius, the Christian poet.   'It is
a place of royal grandeur,' he says ; 'the roof is
covered with golden plates so that it flashes like the
dawn.'   The church was 411 feet long, and the
transept measured 279 feet.   The nave was divided

into four aisles, and the building contained 138 pillars of various kinds of marble.

The Vandals, the Goths, and the Visigoths all respected the sanctity of St. Paul's and left it untouched. Later invaders were not so respectful. The Lombards pillaged it twice, and it was seized by the Saracens in the ninth century, but not before Pope Sergius III. had so cleverly masked the crypt that the infidels never found the tomb of the Apostle. Up to the time of the Reformation the English Kings had a special connection with the Church of St. Paul, and its abbot was a prelate of the Order of the Garter. The insignia of the Garter remain part of the arms of the church.

In 1823 the glorious Basilica was destroyed by fire. Only the great arch over the tomb of the Apostle, the mosaics of the apse and about forty of the columns remained. The rebuilding of the church was one of the greatest ecclesiastical works of the twentieth century. No one living now remembers the glories of the Theodosian basilica, but the church which has replaced it is wholly worthy of the spot on which it stands.

Under one of the most splendid churches in Christendom the body of St. Paul lies to-day. The words of St. John Chrysostom still hold good. ' Where is the tomb of Alexander ? Show it me. His tomb even his own people know not, but this man's tomb the very barbarians know. He was cast into prison at the command of Nero. Now the Emperor is cast out, and lies no one knows where, but the tent-maker occupies the midst of the city as if he were king and alive. And he that wears the purple himself goes to embrace these tombs, and laying aside his pride, stands begging the saints to be his advocates with God, and he that hath the diadem implores the tentmaker and the fisherman, though dead, to be his Patrons.'

Sancte Paule Apostole, prædicator veritatis et doctor gentium, intercede pro nobis. Alleluia.